T H E
WORKING
L I F E

THE
WORKING
LIFE

The Promise and Betrayal
of Modern Work

Joanne B. Ciulla

THREE RIVERS PRESS • NEW YORK

Grateful acknowledgment is made to the following for permission to
reprint previously published material:

*Henry Holt and Company, LLC, and Jonathan Cape, a division of The Random House
Group Ltd.:* Two lines from "The Death of the Hired Man" from *The Poetry of
Robert Frost,* edited by Edward Connery Lathem. Copyright © 1958 by Robert Frost.
Copyright © 1967 by Lesley Frost Ballantine. Copyright 1930, 1939, © 1969
by Henry Holt and Company, LLC. Rights in the British Commonwealth are controlled
by Jonathan Cape, a division of The Random House Group Ltd. Reprinted by
permission of Henry Holt and Company, LLC, and Jonathan Cape, a division of
The Random House Group Ltd.

Oxford University Press: Excerpts from *Theogeny, and Works and Days* by Hesiod,
translated by M. L. West (Oxford: Oxford University Press, 1988). Reprinted by
permission of Oxford University Press.

Published by Three Rivers Press, New York, New York.
Member of the Crown Publishing Group.

Random House, Inc. New York, Toronto, London, Sydney, Auckland
www.randomhouse.com

THREE RIVERS PRESS is a registered trademark and the Three Rivers Press colophon
is a trademark of Random House, Inc.

Originally published in hardcover by Times Books in 2000.

Printed in the United States of America

Design by Meryl Sussman Levavi/Digitext, Inc.

Library of Congress Cataloging-in-Publication Data
Ciulla, Joanne B.
The working life: the promise and betrayal of modern work / by Joanne Ciulla.
      p.   cm.
Includes bibliographical references and index.
  1. Work ethic.   2. Work—Psychological aspects.   I. Title.
HD4905.C58   2000   306.3'613—dc21   99-15768

ISBN 978-0-609-80737-8

10   9

First Paperback Edition

for René

Acknowledgments

This book has been a part of my life for a long time. It was both a labor of love and a monkey on my back. I would write parts of it and then put it down for years, but the subject of work and what it means to people was never far from my mind. I was privileged to have Samuel S. Vaughan as my editor. One of my greatest pleasures has been corresponding with Sam about the ideas in this book. His knowledge and experience as an editor and a human being were invaluable to me. As a token of my gratitude, I yield to him all of the credit for what is right about the book and none of the blame for its shortcomings. I also want to thank Ulf Buchholz for looking after the many details of publishing the book, Janet Fletcher for her careful and intelligent copyediting, and my agent, Doe Coover, for starting me on this saga.

So many of my friends and colleagues have discussed the ideas in this book with me, or given me clippings relevant to it, that I can't list them all. Among them, the most notable is Robert C. Solomon, who redefined the concept of friendship when he read the manuscript in one sitting and then sent me useful comments on it. I am grateful to the people I have worked with as a consultant for sharing their stories about work and helping me to understand how they experience work in the corporate world. I also thank my students, who have expressed their hopes and fears about work in the future to me. This book is for them, too, as they ponder how to live good lives in a chaotic and uncertain world.

Most important, I want to thank my husband and best friend, René. His love and support have kept my own work in the proper perspective.

Contents

Introduction

Suppose that every tool we had could perform its function, either at our bidding, or itself perceiving the need. . . . Suppose that shuttles in a loom could fly to and fro and a plucker play on a lyre all self-moved, then manufacturers would have no need of workers nor masters of slaves.

—ARISTOTLE

The tools and machines that Aristotle dreamed of are the technology of everyday life in industrialized countries today. Aristotle might have rejoiced at the "lights-out factory" where robots work unceasingly. Many of us don't. Instead of greeting this era with joy, we cling ever more tightly to our work. Ours is a work-oriented society, one where "all play and no work makes Jack a big jerk." We live in a paradoxical culture that both celebrates work and continually strives to eliminate it. While we treasure economic efficiency, we seek humanly interesting jobs that offer fulfillment and give meaning to our lives. Perhaps the demand for meaningful work grows because we see the supply shrinking.

This book is about the meaning of work and work's place in life. In it I argue that work often promises to contribute more to our lives than it can deliver. We have gone beyond the work ethic, which endowed work with moral value, and now dangerously depend on our jobs to be the primary source of our identity, the mainspring of individual self-esteem and happiness. Furthermore, work sometimes substitutes for the fulfillment we used to derive from family, friends, religion, and community. This substitution is risky because the economy is unpredictable and employers are sometimes feckless. Work can also ruin lives. When companies "downsize" they leave some with too much work and others with none. Both groups face a less certain future. Overwork and unemployment place enormous strains upon individuals and families.

Work determines our status and shapes our social interactions. Some people can hardly talk to a stranger without first knowing what he or she does for a living. One of the first things that Americans ask when they meet someone new is, "What do you do?" Europeans used to consider this a rude question, but they too are changing. To be retired or unemployed in a work-oriented society dooms one to the status of a nonentity. Many people fanatically pursue careers as if a good job were the sole key to happiness—whether that happiness is derived from the status of the job itself or the goods and status that wages buy. They are willing to study the right things in school, wear the right clothes, and belong to the right clubs, even do volunteer work, all in the name of obtaining a position that will eventually give them freedom to choose how to live their lives. But not everyone exercises this freedom upon reaching such a goal, and most people don't make it. On the one hand are those who argue that they'll work seventy-hour weeks, make their fortunes, and retire at forty—some do but most don't. This mind-set may take a social toll in terms of loneliness, divorce, and sometimes even white-collar crime. On the other hand are those who work long hours just to put food on the table or because they are afraid of losing their jobs.

A consequence of this loaded meaning of work is that we put our happiness in the hands of the market and our employers. Earning a decent living is not enough; we want something more. This "something more" has challenged employers to find ways of motivating people who want jobs that satisfy a variety of abstract desires and needs, such as self-development and self-fulfillment. So managers, consultants, and psychologists guess at employees' needs and develop programs and rhetoric that carry the implicit promise of fulfilling them. This results in a vicious circle: employees desire more, management promises more, and the expectation for finding meaning in work rises. Both sides grope in the dark, searching for a workplace El Dorado.

This is not a self-help book, nor is it a rigorous social scientific study. I borrow from the works of scholars and writers from many disciplines, and I do my best to stand on their shoulders—and not step on their toes. As a philosopher, I look at questions that fall between the cracks of the social sciences and the humanities. I turn accepted and treasured ideas about work upside down to see how they fare—an unexamined work ethic may not be worth having. While there are many extensive studies on workers' values and worker satisfaction, questions about the meaning of work are also part of the meaning-of-life question, or as Aristotle would put it, what constitutes "the good life." These questions fall on the turf of philosophers and theologians. That is why Aristotle, who thought quite a bit about work, leisure, and life, floats in and out of the discussion.

Academics who write about work often mistakenly assume that everyone wants a job like theirs. Interview a variety of workers and you soon discover that this simply isn't true—not everyone wants to do mental work indoors and behind a desk. Society and institutions provide general frameworks for meaning, but individuals interpret meanings in different ways. There is a wide variance in the kinds of work that people like to do and the things in which they find meaning. I discovered this for myself in 1978 when I began teaching a course on the philosophy of work to adults in evening school. My students—from all walks of life—came to class after their work. They included police officers, nurses, boilermakers, secretaries, telephone company employees, and salespeople. They took the class, often reluctantly, to fulfill their philosophy requirement. Many of the night students needed seven or eight years to finish their degrees. Few students had the luxury of taking the course for fun. For the most part they were the managed who wanted to be managers. Some were at the end of their day shift and came to class still wearing the uniform of their trade. Some showed up with cups of coffee or a snack, since there wasn't time for dinner.

I was pleased to find that philosophy, often dismissed as irrelevant, still had something to say to ordinary people. I remember the first time that I explained Marx's theory of alienation and surplus labor value. The class was not particularly enthusiastic about reading Marx. Most students were business majors, and politically conservative. Marx, after all, was a communist. The students were wage earners who dreamed of being capitalists. After I explained how the more you worked and made profit for the capitalist the less your labor was actually worth, a woman who sat in the back and usually dozed off during class raised her hand and passionately began explaining why Marx was right. It was easy to see why the logic of communism once seduced so many people all over the world. It wasn't that she had a desire for socialism, but she did have a desire for fairness. Surplus labor value just didn't seem fair. It devalued the student and her work.

When I first read Studs Terkel's popular book *Working,* I wondered whether the people that he interviewed had really said what he reported. I no longer doubt it. During the seven years of teaching the class, and almost twenty years of talking to people about their jobs, I learned how eloquent people can be when they discuss their work. For some, work is "a daily humiliation." Their humiliation doesn't come from the task at hand, but from the disrespect and injustice of coworkers and superiors. My students hated being watched, resented not being trusted, and fumed because they had little power to right wrongs and correct incompetence. I came to admire the profound struggle that people carry on to maintain their dignity, and the many ways they find meaning even under the most difficult working conditions.

When I taught the work course my own experiences were not that different from those of my students. Like many young scholars, I began my career teaching a few classes paid on a per course basis. I sometimes taught four to eight courses a year. It amounted to full-time work for about a quarter of a full-time wage, with no benefits. As unfair as these conditions sound, I wouldn't have traded this opportunity for any other work. I was still working on my Ph.D. at the time, and philosophy jobs were scarce. So, I subsidized the first nine years of my teaching career by waitressing, bartending, and cooking in restaurants.

I enjoyed restaurant work. It was a welcome change from academia, and I always got a good meal out of it. One semester I taught philosophy in the morning, went to graduate seminars in the afternoon, and worked in an upscale hamburger restaurant at night. I thought quite a bit about work and identity. I was treated very differently by others as I went from college professor to graduate student to waitress. At the end of the day, I would often wonder which role was really me. In one job I worked alongside a ballet dancer and a model. We all had great ambitions. The manager took sadistic delight in making fun of our aspirations and verbally abusing us. Nowadays we would probably slap a harassment lawsuit on him. I don't know what happened to the manager, but the dancer eventually went on to become a prima ballerina, the model ended up on the cover of Italian *Vogue,* and I landed a fellowship at the Harvard Business School. This experience helped me understand the relationship between hope and work. We can endure the worst of jobs, if it is reasonable to hope that the job will get us where we want to go or at least feed us along the way.

After nine years of teaching philosophy and thinking about work from the perspective of the worker, I had an opportunity to think about work from the perspective of management: first as a postdoctoral fellow in business and ethics at the Harvard Business School, where I did research on business ethics, and then at the Wharton School of the University of Pennsylvania, where I taught the required M.B.A. course on management and courses on business ethics. After Wharton I went on to help design the Jepson School of Leadership Studies at the University of Richmond in Virginia. There I teach courses on ethics, leadership, and critical thinking. The problems of work have never been far from my mind in any of my academic positions. Since the mid-1980s I have also worked as a consultant, providing seminars on business ethics to large corporations. This has given me an opportunity to hear many stories about how people think about their work and how it affects their lives.

Throughout the years of teaching management, I was struck increasingly by the loaded meaning of work that has been created over the last century of management theory and practice. The social engineer joined up with the time-study man and the mild-mannered therapist. Corporations, which had always *had* cultures, *became* "cultures" that sought to transform employees into one big happy family. Companies tackled the problem of employee alienation with "entertaining" that encroached on workers' leisure time in the guise of business dinners, corporate beer busts, sports outings, and "networking" events. Managers, charged with the task of "making meaning," tried new ways of persuading employees to invest more of themselves in their work than the job required. Banal work got dressed up to look meaningful. At the close of the century the manager's mantra is made up of "quality," "commitment," and "teamwork." All of these approaches to management attempted to change and control the meaning of work in an organization.

Under the old school of scientific management, the alienated worker did what he or she was told, got paid, and went home. The work may have been boring, the wages low, but at least everyone knew where he or she stood. Today the transaction is not as honest. While we still trade our labor, most modern work requires us to give away a slice of our private lives. Workers of the past were just overworked; today many workers are overworked and overmanaged. The exhaustion that paints the faces of workers at the end of the day may be not physical but emotional, because work demands more of the self than the accurate and efficient performance of the task at hand. I began to wonder if work has really improved since the beginning of the century or if it is just clothed in fancy terms and done in cleaner, better-lighted places.

Work entered an era of mean streets and broken promises in the 1990s, when loyal, longtime employees of some of the biggest and best corporations in America lost their jobs. Massive layoffs signaled the end of the social compact between employers and employees that said, If you do your job well, you can keep it. Employees woke up to the fact that despite all the rhetoric of the caring employer and the improved quality of work life, workers were still commodities that could be replaced with computers, cheap foreign labor, or coworkers willing to do twice as much work for the same pay. When the social compact was broken, so too was the urbane façade of management that had been carefully crafted by social scientists and consultants over the past century. The one good that came from the 1990s was that people began to see their jobs for what they were: first and foremost, economic transactions in a fickle global economy. People began to question the priority of work over other things in their lives. They began to wonder whether the time and energy that they had sacrificed for their jobs was really worth it.

This book is not a lament about some lost golden age of work. It is about choosing how we want to live and work. The first part of the book explores the history of the idea of work, our ambivalence toward work, the values associated with it, and the work ethic. Since the biggest problems with work come not from the work we do for ourselves but from the work we do for others, the second part of the book shows how working for others has always been a struggle for freedom and control. Employers struggle for control over employees, employees struggle for autonomy and control over their work and lives. This part of the book offers a critique of the past one hundred years of management theories and how they have shaped our expectations about work. After this look at where we have been and how we have gotten to where we are now, the third part of the book considers how work and consumption have come to dominate the way we live.

I invite the reader to explore the meaning of work with me. By examining the historical and cultural presuppositions behind the meaning of work, I hope to give readers a place to stand so that they can examine their own ideas and expectations about work and the choices they have made about work and life. For most people the greatest challenge is not work, but how to make their lives work. While the book is written from an American perspective, the questions it raises are of equal, if not greater, relevance to those in cultures that have in recent years become increasingly work oriented as the result of global competition, the internationalization of American management theories, and escalating consumerism. For Americans and non-Americans alike, meaning in work, leisure, and life is not something that is hand delivered. We must all go out and find it for ourselves. This book is a journey into the meaning of work and life, but the destination is ultimately up to the reader.

PART ONE

THE MEANINGS OF WORK

1.

Why Work?

What's so good about work? Throughout history some have praised it, others have cursed it, but few have escaped it or had the luxury of deciding whether they should work or not. At one time or another we all wish that we didn't have to work. We fantasize about catching up on chores or hobbies, spending more time with family, friends, or a loved one, reading great books, and traveling. Lotteries seduce with the vision of freedom from work and material need, yet a surprisingly large number of lottery winners and other independently wealthy individuals continue to work. It is easy to imagine not working for a short time; the task of imagining a whole life without work is more difficult. For some people the question "Why work?" is ridiculous because they don't have a choice in the matter: "We work because we have to make a living." That is why people have paid jobs, but it doesn't explain why they do other kinds of work. Nonetheless, the economic interpretation of work is so strong in our culture and a growing number of other cultures that we tend to equate work with "being on the job." That is why most of this book focuses on work as paid employment.

Is the Idle Mind the Devil's Workshop?

One long-held belief is that if people didn't work, they'd get into mischief—that "an idle mind is the devil's workshop." This is sometimes the case for those who are unemployed and have no other source of income. A thirty-three-year-old mother from a poor West Side neighborhood in Chicago puts the problem of living with people who don't have jobs this way: "When you live in an area of your neighborhood where you have people that don't work . . . you have to worry if somebody's breakin' into your house or not. So, you know, it's best to try to move in a decent area, to live in a community with people that works."[1] But what if these people had income, but didn't work? Would they still get into trouble?

In his book *When Work Disappears,* William Julius Wilson observes that when work is scarce people not only suffer from poverty, they "lose their feeling of connectedness to work in the formal economy; they no longer expect work to be a regular and regulating force in their lives."[2] Wilson says work in the informal economy and illegal economy differs from work in the formal economy because it is usually less regular and does not place a premium on discipline and regularity. He believes that when jobless people live in low-employment neighborhoods, they lose their perception of self-efficacy, or their belief that they can take the steps required to achieve goals in a particular situation.[3] So according to Wilson, having a job means more than just meeting material needs. It also satisfies various psychological and social needs such as discipline, connectedness, regularity, and self-efficacy. But is work the only way to fill these needs? Why can't the unemployed fill these needs from leisure?

A sociographic study from the 1930s sheds some light on this issue. Researchers observed a small industrial community in Austria called Marienthal at a time when the entire community was out of work. The sociologists noted that before the economic depression, people in the community were active in leisure as well as work. They participated in political organizations, frequented the public library, and enjoyed organizing various social events. After the town factory closed and everyone was out of work, the citizens became apathetic. The researchers note that the workers of Marienthal,

> cut off from their work and the outside world, lost the material and
> moral incentives to make use of their time. Now that they are no

longer under any pressure, they undertake nothing new and drift gradually out of ordered existence into one that is undisciplined and empty. Looking back over any period of this free time, they are unable to recall anything worth mentioning.[4]

Unemployment seemed to suck the energy out of people and the community. Marienthal's citizens not only lost their work, but they lost their ability to enjoy leisure. Clearly, the people in Marienthal were different from those in Wilson's study. They had work and lost it, whereas most of the people Wilson studied either cannot get work or have never really had steady jobs. Marienthal's citizens lost work and its social benefits such as self-efficacy, connectedness, and regularity. Many of the people in Wilson's study never had work and its social benefits. Perhaps the reason that the unemployed do not have leisure is because they have no work. They have no *free* time because they have no *constrained* time. A writer for a labor union publication summed up the problem this way: "The trouble with unemployment is that you never get a day off."[5]

Aristotle offered another insight into why the unemployed don't have leisure. According to him, you could not have leisure without peace, the proper virtues, and education. "Courage and endurance are required for business and philosophy for leisure, temperance and justice for both, and more especially in times of peace and leisure, for war compels men to be just and temperate, whereas the enjoyment of good fortune and the leisure which comes with peace makes them insolent."[6] Aristotle used the case of Sparta to illustrate this point. Sparta's culture was centered around war and preparation for war. The work of Sparta was done by hostile serfs called helots. Sparta thrived as long as it was at war, but collapsed in times of peace. Aristotle said Sparta was not governed in a way that was conducive to a life of leisure. Men were given a military education, which taught them discipline, and that carried over into peacetime, but women had no such education and lacked discipline and self-control. As a result of this, in times of peace the women fell into luxury, vice, and chaos far worse than any enemy the Spartans had faced in war.[7] Furthermore, the Spartans could never really have leisure because they were surrounded by unwilling serfs, who could, at any time, erupt into violence. He concluded that without a safe and secure society, and citizens who were taught the right virtues, people could not have leisure. This idea partly explains the Marienthal case. Its citizens were educated in the virtues of the Protestant work ethic. According to their social values, paid employment was the most important activity in life, leisure or amusement a mere accompaniment. Without work they were not capable of leisure. Without paid work the workers of Marienthal were failures. But perhaps most important, without work they had no security.

For Aristotle our real work in life is the work of being human. Freedom from fear, material needs, and commitments allows us the liberty to develop ourselves through leisure. War and education, not work, provide people with moral virtues such as the temperance and discipline needed for leisure. Aristotle believed that education for leisure would teach people how to engage in learning and activities that are good in themselves, because it is these activities that make humans unique in contrast to animals. He suggests that students study subjects such as reading, writing, drawing, physical training, and music.[8] This idea of education is the basis of the liberal arts, which are the arts needed to live in a free society. The Roman Cicero also believed in the liberal arts. He said education should separate the truths needed for life's necessary cares from knowledge that is pursued for its own sake. The liberal arts ideal is knowledge that we pursue for its own sake. It is ironic that most students today pursue a liberal arts education so that they can get a job, when ideally it was meant to teach them how to use their leisure, not how to work.

After looking at Aristotle's criteria for leisure, one can see why it is callous and cynical to think that the unemployed lead lives of leisure. Leisure is more than free time; it is freedom from need and the necessity of work, and an opportunity to do specific things.[9] People who have lost their jobs or cannot get jobs are not free *from* work. If anything, they are *not* free *to* work, since they have little choice in the matter. Leisure also requires safety and security, which do not characterize the urban areas of unemployment described by Wilson. Lastly, Aristotle tells us, leisure requires education, which imparts knowledge and moral virtues such as justice and self-discipline. Leisure also gave the ancient Athenian time to participate in civic affairs, which would certainly enhance a person's feeling of self-efficacy. In theory at least, if you set up a society for Aristotelian leisure, it might provide people with the same psychological and social needs as a society set up for work. In an Aristotelian utopia there would be no idle minds, hence no workshops for the devil.

What is most interesting and distinctive about being human are the things that we choose to do with ourselves *after* we meet our basic needs. If those in poor neighborhoods with high unemployment were magically given an income that met their basic needs, safe streets, and solid liberal arts educations, they would be just as likely to go out and get good jobs as to lead lives of leisure. For example, the way lottery winners respond when the necessity to work is removed depends on their material wants and desires, their ambition, and whether they liked their jobs. But what about those who don't need to work and choose not to work? Do we really believe that without a job they will become morally decadent?

Do We Need Work?

Elizabeth Perle McKenna had never realized how much of her identity and self-worth was tied up in her high-powered job as a publishing executive. She writes: "The first week without a paycheck I became worthless instantly. I was a three-legged stool and without a job to do every day, I toppled over."[10] In her book *When Work Doesn't Work Anymore,* McKenna explains that she quit her job because she realized that she wanted a more flexible life. Her job no longer fit with her values and aspirations. Yet once she left it, she discovered the difficulty of constructing an identity outside of the one on her business card and a life without work. It's not easy to feel sorry for McKenna. Her husband makes a good living, she is well educated, and she is not "unemployed." McKenna had the luxury of deciding whether to work or not. Nevertheless, what cases like hers demonstrate is that choosing not to work has its costs. Without work we face infinite options about what we should do and what we should be. Also, people who can work but choose not to have to explain themselves to those who suspect the only reason they gave up good jobs and now choose not to work is that they are lazy or in some way deficient.

It's easy to see why—aside from the income it provides—having a job is so desirable in our culture. Work works for us. It offers instant discipline, identity, and worth. It structures our time and imposes a rhythm on our lives. It gets us organized into various kinds of communities and social groups. And perhaps most important, work tells us what to do every day. Even with education, income, peace, and security, the free choice not to work is difficult in a culture where paid work is so central to life. Many of us would find it a challenge to fill every day with activities that give the feelings of satisfaction and well-being we get from work.

The satisfaction and well-being that some people get from having a job is undeniable. Work provides for our material needs, but is work itself a human need? Many scholars have said no. For example, Jean-Jacques Rousseau argued that indolence is the natural condition of humans and the need to be productive is an artificial one produced by society.[11] Georg Wilhelm Friedrich Hegel wrote that the "habit of being industrious" is a product of work itself and that the practical education we get through working creates the need to have something to do and the habit of being busy.[12] We *feel* the need to work because of our training and moral conditioning, not because of any inborn disposition. If this is the case, then there is nothing "natural" about work. It is an artificial need manufactured by our history and culture.

The idea that humans *need* to work is so embedded in modern Western economic and moral assumptions that it is difficult to understand cultures where people don't share this need. Karl Marx once cited a newspaper story in which a West Indian planter is indignant about the fact that the free Negroes of Jamaica, the Quashees, refuse to work beyond their own consumption and look upon "laziness itself ('indulgence' and 'idleness') as the real luxury article."[13] An anthropologist made a similar observation in 1961. He wrote that the Yamana Indians in South America "are not capable of continuous daily hard labour, much to the chagrin of the European farmers and employers for whom they often work. Their work is more a matter of fits and starts. . . ."[14] Modern companies have faced similar problems in developing countries where they cannot get employees to work overtime because workers prefer leisure over the extra cash. Lately a growing number of overworked Americans have expressed a preference for free time over money, preferring to get time off rather than receive overtime pay for extra work.

In his study of hunter-gatherer societies, anthropologist Marshall Sahlins found that hunter-gatherers worked far less than people in other cultures. For example, the Arnhem Land aborigines in Australia spent about four or five hours a day getting and preparing food. Moreover, they did not work continuously and they usually stopped working when they had enough for the time being. When not working, they spent their free time in rest and sleep, not in Aristotelian leisure. He concluded, with a tinge of disapproval, that the reason why primitive societies fail to "build culture" or develop "is not strictly from want of time. It is from idle hands."[15] We usually think of development for hunter-gatherers or whole countries as something that makes life easier, but the increase in the material quality of life usually entails an increase in the quantity of work. Sahlins observed that maybe aborigines don't want to build culture. As one bushman asked him, "Why should we plant when there are so many mongomongo nuts in the world?"[16]

To Work or Not to Work?

Most people who live in industrialized, democratic societies have more choices than their ancestors did about where they live, what they do for a living, how they live, and who (what kind of person) they want to be. No one questions the necessity of work. But to explore the meaning of work we have to question its merit. Besides keeping us alive and reproducing, why is work better than play? What is the value of a job? How should we live? Different people in different cultures will answer these questions in different ways. Yet when it comes to work, it's doubtful that human nature varies much. Some like to work and some don't. In any culture at any time, there are and have been industrious people and lazy people. Only the standards of judgment are relative to the place and time.

The ancient storyteller Aesop sums up some of the basic questions about work and life in his fables. We still find meanings in his tales about animals who remind us of people we know, and we appreciate his moral lessons on how to live. Aesop's musings on work are all the more interesting because he was said to be a slave from Asia Minor who later bought his freedom.[17] His fables were written around 620 B.C. but some of the stories attributed to him exist in various forms on Egyptian papyri that date back to 1000–800 B.C. In the well-known fable "The Grasshopper and the Ant," Aesop locks horns with the question, To work or not to work? Aesop also explores the complexity of this question in other stories about cicadas, ants, and bees. These insects crawl, buzz, and hop their way through history. Each insect represents a set of dispositions, values, and ways to think about life and work. Consider, for example, the "Grasshopper and the Ant."

The ants were employing a fine winter's day in drying grain collected in the summer time.

A grasshopper, perishing with famine, passed by and earnestly begged for a little food.

The ants inquired of him, "Why did you not treasure up food during the summer?"

He replied, "I had not leisure enough. I passed the days in singing."

They then said in derision: "If you were foolish enough to sing all the summer, you must dance supperless to bed in winter.[18]

This is a cautionary fable. It does not say that a life of work is better than a life of singing, but rather that if you want to sing, you should be willing to pay the price. The issue here is fairness and self-sufficiency: if you don't work, you don't eat and you shouldn't expect others to feed you. Aesop's story gives us a choice. We can lead the brief happy life of the grasshopper, or the long prudent life of the ant. Yet it's not wholly clear what the wise person should choose. The ant teaches a clearer lesson in the Bible. Proverbs 6:6–8 says, "Go to the ant, thou sluggard; consider her ways, and be wise: Which having no guide, overseer or ruler, Provideth her meat in the summer, and gathereth her food in the harvest."

Unlike the good Protestants who would come along later, Aesop is somewhat ambivalent about industriousness. Greed, miserliness, and covetousness sometimes accompany hard work. In "The Ant," he tells us that the ant was once a farmer who kept a jealous eye on his neighbor and stole some of his produce. Zeus, angry, changed the man into an ant, and Aesop says, "Although his form has changed, his character has not, for he still goes around the fields gathering up the wheat and barley of others and storing it up for himself."[19] Aesop worried that industriousness, when motivated by envy, can lead to theft or avarice and miserliness. As we'll see later, the early Christians shared this concern.

Cicadas and Bees

Aesop is kinder to the grasshopper's relative, the cicada. He says that once there were men who, when music was invented, were so happy that they just kept singing and forgot food and drink until they died. From these men come the cicadas, who don't require food and sing their lives away.[20] The muses smile upon the cicadas because their singing brings joy. While Aesop doesn't exactly endorse the life of the cicada, he does express a somewhat romantic admiration. The cicada's brief life is spent in pursuit of beauty. Not everyone is as kind to the grasshopper, who became a shorthand icon for the noisy and useless. In Ecclesiastes 12:5 we read that "the almond tree shall flourish and the grasshopper shall be a burden."

The aesthetic virtues of the cicadas and the moral virtues of the ant come together in Aesop's "The Ant and the Bee." In this fable the bee and the ant have a dispute over who is more prudent and industrious. They appeal to Apollo for a judgment. The god applauds the ant's care, foresight, and independence from the labors of others, but he says, "it is you alone that you benefit; no other creature shares any part of your hoarded riches. Whereas the bee produces, by its meritorious and ingenious exertions, that which becomes a blessing to the world."[21] Again we see chinks in the moral armor of hard work. It's good to provide for oneself. It is even better to contribute a pleasing and useful product for society. Poetry and literature portray bees as more cheerful workers than ants. After all, bees work in flowers and make tasty honey. Remember the famous Isaac Watts rhyme: "How doth the little busy bee, / Improve each shining hour, / And gather honey all the day / From every opening flower!"[22]

Successful businesspeople don't want the public to think they are ants. We admire hard work much more if people do it for some purpose that lies beyond pure self-interest. During the period of hostile takeovers in the mid-1980s, investors such as T. Boone Pickens and the late Sir James Goldsmith strenuously tried to portray themselves as bees. In a PBS debate, Sir James claimed that hostile takeovers "cleanse" society of inefficient businesses. Pickens asserted that he helped the economy by getting rid of wasteful managers and doing a better job of running companies.[23] Both men argued in the tradition of the Dutch doctor-turned-poet Bernard Mandeville, not Aesop. Mandeville crossed the ant with the bee and came up with an explanation for an economic system based on self-interest, not thrift. His work *The Fable of the Bees* presented the paradox of how personal vices and vicious motives could lead to the public good. The work, consisting of a poem with a commentary and essay, was considered so immoral that in 1723 a grand jury in Middlesex, England, declared it a nuisance.[24] Mandeville believed that desires for money, power, and fame are the only reasons why people work. There is no moral value to work, only the instrumental value of what it buys and produces.

The poem begins:

> A spacious Hive well stocked with Bees
> That lived in luxury and ease,
> . . . .
> Millions endeavoring to supply,
> Each other's lust and Vanity,
> Whilst other millions were employ'd,
> To see their Handy-works destroy'd.[25]

The social order of the hive, like a modern market system, depends on competition and self-interest to provide for the needs of society. In this system, some win and some lose. Nonetheless, Mandeville goes on to say, "every part was full of Vice, / Yet the whole Mass a Paradise," and "Envy itself and vanity, / Were ministers of industry."[26] The idea that serving personal interests can lead to public benefit is central to capitalism.[27] Mandeville argued that thrift is not a virtue for the rich, because if they ceased to spend their money, the poor would be unemployed. (The economist John Maynard Keynes approvingly cited Mandeville's poem in the 1930s when he argued that thrift was not a virtue in times of chronic unemployment.[28] Mandeville's bees worked like ants, consumed like grasshoppers, *and* brought about the greatest good.

Life Strategies

Aesop's ant, grasshopper, and bee give us three ways of approaching life. Frugal, acquisitive, and hard-working, the antlike worker values security above all else. He spends all of his time working at a moderately interesting job, makes cautious career choices, has little involvement in nonwork activities, takes few vacations and fewer chances. Like the ant, this sort of person saves for retirement, mortgaging certain enjoyments for forty-five to fifty years of his or her life, in hopes of making up for it in the last twenty.

In Thomas J. Stanley and William D. Danko's study of American millionaires, one interviewee expressed the ant's position: "My long-range goal was, of course, to accumulate enough wealth so I can get out of business and enjoy life."[29] This plan can fail for a variety of reasons.

A lifelong habit like frugality is hard to break. Stanley and Danko found that most of the self-made millionaires they studied were thrifty and did not change their spending habits much after they had made their fortunes. One interviewee described to them his wife's reaction when he gave her eight million dollars' worth of stock. She said, "I appreciate this, I really do." Then she went on clipping twenty-five-cent food coupons out of the newspaper. Her husband explained, "She just does today like she always has done, even when all we owned was a kitchen table."[30]

For some people, the art of enjoying life is difficult to learn at a late age. There are those who retire with generous pensions but still carry on their antlike habits, whether it's saving string or refusing to buy a new car or some other commodity that will make them more comfortable. Others suffer ill health, and a sad few die the day after they receive their gold watch. While the ant may not take pleasure in spending money and owning things, he or she may delight in the daily challenges of living frugally. Many people work so that they can enjoy buying more; the ant may work to enjoy spending less. Hence the retired ant may spend a whole morning driving from store to store, looking for the best price on a can of tuna fish (especially if he or she grew up during the Great Depression).

The ant lives for the future, but doesn't always know what to do when he reaches it. The merit of the ant's life plan is that his frugality saves him from want and prepares him for emergencies. But money also ensures freedom. One of the millionaires interviewed by Stanley and Danko called his stashed-away money "go to hell money." He could work at will, knowing that he could walk away anytime he wanted. Work feels very different when you can take it or leave it.

One way to overcome the shortcomings of the ant strategy is to work hard, make a fortune, and retire at forty, which is what many young people today hope to do. That way they can still enjoy life while they are young. Often this kind of ant is really a grasshopper in disguise, or an *anthopper*. Such characters work long hours and focus solely on making money—and a few succeed. This strategy faces four possible pitfalls. First, unlike Aesop's ant, the anthopper is impatient and has a difficult time with delayed gratification. Anthoppers want to make *fast* money. Second, they often cannot quit working because, instead of hoarding money, they create a style of life that requires more and more cash. The third problem is that anthoppers, by putting all their time and money into work, risk harming their relationships with friends, spouses, and children. The anthopper's spouse or partner may not wait around to enjoy his or her early retirement. Finally, anthoppers can become so addicted to moneymaking pursuits that they don't stop working even when they reach their financial goals. They never have enough money, or they become addicted to the work itself and the excitement of making money.

Both the ant and the anthopper work for a vision of the good life in the future. They often fail to enjoy life in the present. How do the ant and the anthopper experience work? Clearly, work has instrumental value to them. But do they seek meaning in their work? Do they find pleasure in it? Some people spend all their lives working and sacrificing for some prize of happiness and freedom from work that they believe exists at retirement. When they get to retirement, they realize that the real happiness was in the striving. They don't know what to do with freedom from work. For others who have just worked to make a living, work becomes such a habit that they have a hard time living without it. When Eric Hoffer retired from the waterfront he said he still kept dreaming of loading and unloading ships and sometimes woke up in the morning aching all over from a night's work. He wrote, "One might maintain that a pension is pay for the work we keep doing in our dreams after we retire.[31]

In contrast to the ant, the grasshopper lives for the present and sacrifices the future. His playing goes nowhere and leaves nothing behind. There is pleasure in a life of play—but is there meaning? The bee works like an ant, yet enjoys its pursuits like a grasshopper. It takes pleasure and finds meaning in producing a good and useful product that is appreciated by others. The bee symbolizes a life of useful and rewarding work. (Needless to say, the life of the symbolic bee bears no resemblance to that of real bees.) While the ant represents a life of work and security, the grasshopper depicts a frivolous life of play and uncertainty. But what is wrong with a life of play?

Working at Play, Playing at Work

In his book *The Grasshopper: Games, Life, and Utopia,* Bernard Suits creates a dialogue between a philosopher grasshopper and his disciples about work and play. He raises a fundamental question about life. If we did not need to work to provide for the things that we need, what would we do with ourselves? The grasshopper defines play as any intrinsically valuable activity. Unlike work, which ants see as an instrumental activity, play is an end in itself. The grasshopper then argues, in the spirit of Aristotle, that the ideal of existence is doing "only those things whose only justification is that they justify everything else."[32] In *The Grasshopper,* Suits speculates that if we lived in a utopia where no one had to work, we would eventually invent games that resembled work. The carpenter would invent house-building games, the scientist, discovery games, even though there was no need to build houses and all discoveries had been made. Suits believes that in his utopia work activities would become play because people would freely choose to perform them, for their own sake and not for some outside goal. Here people would be playing at their work instead of working at their play. People who love their jobs or work in organizations that try to make work fun say work *feels* like play, but they are not playing at their work. According to Suits's argument, you can play at your work only if two conditions are met: first, you don't have to work, and second, you can work anywhere, anytime, and any way you want.

In Suits's Aristotelian utopia the ant's life does not make sense. It isn't necessary to save for the winter. However, the bee's life is plausible in this utopia. Like the ant, Aesop's bee works hard, but unlike the ant, it still enjoys making honey for either the process itself or the pleasure its product brings. Today people grow their own vegetables and bake their own bread, even though they can buy them in a store. Despite claims to the contrary, the home-baked bread and homegrown vegetable may not be superior in quality to the ones that people buy, but the very process of making and growing makes eating them more enjoyable. Some types of productive activities give satisfaction even though they are not necessary—or especially because they are not necessary. The bee's work has the *promise* of meaning even if it is not necessary for survival.

Sometimes people try to make play sound like productive work. We legitimize play in a work-oriented society by *working* out, playing squash to unwind, tennis to stay fit, golf to woo clients; we box for security, jog for cardiovascular health, and so on. We talk about efficient use of body energy; we train; we read books and watch videos on how to play. Intense competitiveness in games and sports shifts the focus of playing to winning, which makes play instrumental and more like work. Apparently, even animals aren't exempt from nonproductive play. Note how the narrator of a Discovery Channel show on lions solemnly explains to the viewer that the frolicking lion cubs may *think* they are playing but they are *really* practicing skills that will make them good hunters.

This takes us very far from Plato's idea of play. He said that play evolved from the desire of children and small animals to leap. Think for a moment of the delight children and puppies get simply from jumping up and down. Play is often illogical or inefficient. Games are intentionally inefficient. The things that people do when they play them have no meaning outside the game. For example, if your job required you to put a little white ball into eighteen holes, you certainly wouldn't do it by hitting it with a thin stick over lakes, hills, and sand traps. The point of golf is to make it as difficult as possible to get the ball into eighteen holes. Getting the ball into the hole is important to the player, but *having* the golf balls in the holes serves no purpose whatsoever outside of the game.

Play, like the cicada's singing, is done for no reason but pleasure. While Aesop's grasshopper starves because he is irresponsible, the cicada is portrayed as the "starving artist." It starves for love of music. The two fables convey different messages. Dying because of one's love of art seems to have a point, whereas dying because one prefers singing to working is foolish. For most of us the more relevant questions are, Does life have a point if you live like an ant, working and accumulating things until you are aged and feeble? and Given the freedom to choose, what should we be doing with the time allotted to us in life?

How We Choose Our Jobs

Four values shape how we make choices about work.[33] They are meaningful work, or work that is interesting and/or important to you or to others in society; leisure, or free time to do the things you want; money; and security. These values carry different weights at different times in life. Ideally it would be best to have a fascinating job, plenty of vacation time, a salary that allows us to buy anything we want, and guaranteed lifetime employment. Since few of us have jobs that provide all of these things, we make tradeoffs, and these tradeoffs signify what we value most. Consider the following thought experiment. Imagine that you are single and have just graduated from college. You have four job offers. The first is a well-paying position in an accounting firm, the second is with the environmental group Greenpeace, the third is a civil service job, and the fourth is a place as a waiter at an Aspen ski resort hotel that operates only in winter. Which one would you choose?

The answer derives from another question: What are you willing to give up? People driven by the values of meaningful work and leisure are often more willing to give up security and money. If meaningful work is most important, you might choose Greenpeace. This job entails long hours without much pay or financial security in a sometimes dangerous environment. The resort job may not give you much meaning, money, or security, but it will give you plenty of opportunities to do what you love best, namely, ski. Meaningful work and leisure have a lot in common. People who subscribe to these values like the idea of doing something that they want to do. They value certain activities either for what they are or for what they mean.

Some people prefer leisure to meaningful work because they do not want to or cannot engage in the activity they love as paid work. They turn to other activities (hobbies, music, sports, and even crime) and other institutions (family, friends, church, and community organizations) for the psychological rewards that they can't get from work.[34] For example, not everyone who loves to cook would enjoy working as a chef. In fact, working as a chef in a restaurant day in and day out may diminish the pleasure that one gets from cooking. Meaningful work and leisure consist of activities that aren't just instrumental, but are rewarding or pleasurable in their own right.

If you value money and security above other things, then work is primarily an instrumental activity, a means to those ends. The accounting job may not be exciting and few people ever make it to partner, but as a new graduate you will make good money to pay off college loans and buy a condo, nice clothes, and a sports car. Those who value material goods above and beyond what they need to live comfortably trade leisure for overtime or a second job to buy extra cars and other things. Their pleasure in buying and owning things overrides their desire for free time. Money is also important to those who value security; however, they value saving it over spending it. If you want security, the government job may fill the bill. Even though it may not be fast-paced and exciting, and you'll make less money than you would if you were in industry, the benefits are excellent, you get all the standard holidays, and it's relatively stable employment.

At different points in one's life, different values dominate. The new graduate may choose the resort job, because he or she likes to spend the summer months surfing or traveling, but this might not be an option if the person has a family to support. Single parents sometimes have to choose between a challenging and time-consuming career and one that allows more time to spend with their children. Here free time is more important than money or their job. Those in midlife face harder choices. New opportunities force them to decide what is really important. For example, they might be offered a choice between a challenging new job with a risky start-up company or their current mundane but well-paying job and the comfortable life that it has created. For some people, the choice is easy, because they know that twenty years in their current lucrative and prestigious job did not make them happy, or that their work no longer gives them satisfaction because the job or the organization has changed. Others will stick it out at the old job because they cannot give up their financial or psychological security. Our choices aren't always this stark or this simple, but we usually have to settle for more or less of each of these values when we choose a job.

Odd Choices?

There are many variations on how the values of meaningful work, leisure, security, and money play out in our lives. When people make unique choices about how they work, live, and spend, we often read about them in the newspaper or hear about them on the news. Consider the case of Thomas Cannon. Cannon graduated from college with a degree in art education but opted for the secure job and steady salary of a postal worker. He and his family lived very modestly on his salary: "We had food, we had clothes, we had all of the basic necessities."[35] For Cannon, meaning didn't come from his job, or from building up a nest egg. Work was instrumental for caring for his family and for what it could buy for others. By the age of seventy-two, Cannon had given away more than ninety-six thousand dollars to people in need.

People like Cannon are exceptional and admirable, but also a bit peculiar. We don't expect people who make so little to give so much away. Similarly, we don't expect people who have power, prestige, and money to throw it all away. For example, James J. O'Donnell, the chief executive of HSBC James Capel in London and HSBC Markets in New

York, made news when he announced that he was leaving his job to join the priesthood. The thirty-six-year-old O'Donnell had a B.A. from Princeton in comparative religion. He had successfully held a string of high-powered jobs in the financial world. O'Donnell declined to discuss his decision with the press, maybe because he didn't feel the need to explain himself or because he didn't think people would understand.[36] Apparently, even O'Donnell was unsure of his choice. In just over a year after taking his vow of poverty, O'Donnell left the priesthood to become deputy head of equities at Salomon Smith Barney in London. His return to the financial world was greeted with glee by the cynical press.[37]

Some people leave their jobs because the work fails to give them or no longer gives them what they want from it, or because they have a burning desire to do something else. Just before Christmas 1996 Jeff Stambovsky placed an ad in a magazine that caters to Wall Street traders. It read: "Jeff Stambovsky Left the Business. If He Doesn't Sell Enough Records, He's Coming Back."[38] Stambovsky, the forty-three-year-old managing director of Schroder & Company, quit his job to become a jazz musician and children's record producer.

Some anthoppers do make it. They build up enough savings to take the plunge into their dream job. Christophe J. Richter left her job as a bond saleswoman to start a message therapy studio. Judd S. Levy left Merrill Lynch to manage an inn in Vermont. He said that many people told him that they wished they could do the same. Levy said, "The truth is that many of them could have."[39] But they don't. Many of us have an image of work that we'd really like to do, but few dare to give up the security, prestige, and buying power of our current jobs to do it. Taking the plunge into meaningful work is risky: the musician may not sell records, the massage business may flop, and the innkeeper may discover that staying at a Vermont inn is more fun that running it.

Since women have had to overcome barriers to get prestigious, high-paying jobs, they may be especially ambivalent about leaving such jobs to pursue other interests. They don't want to ruin the chances for other women to make it to the top. They don't want to appear unable to handle the job. They do not want to reinforce the idea that women shouldn't be put on the fast track because they will leave when they have children. Yet stories abound of women who have left high-powered jobs to spend more time with their children. Brenda Barnes made headlines when she quit her job as chief executive of Pepsi North

America to be with her three children. On the one hand, these stories send the message that there is more important work in life than one's paid employment. On the other hand, they suggest that home is where mothers belong in the first place. About 63 percent of married women with children under six work.[40] As a result, some women, especially the ones who love their jobs, feel guilty about working. For some, going to work is like sneaking off to have an illicit affair. A television commercial for cell phones highlights these guilt feelings. The scene opens with a mother telling her two little daughters that she can't play with them because she has a meeting with clients. The wide-eyed younger girl pouts and asks, "When can I be a client?" But for many women work is simply a necessity, caring for children a tricky balancing act, and they do not welcome "mommy books" and television commercials that tell them they should feel guilty.[41]

When someone holds a well-paid, prestigious job, people sometimes question why she or he quit a job that is short in supply and high in demand. For example, columnist Anna Quindlen quit her job to become a full-time novelist. She said some of her colleagues couldn't understand why she would do such a thing. Some journalists would do anything to be a respected columnist for *The New York Times*. It is their idea of meaningful work. They wondered if the reason she left was because she had been passed over for a top editor's job or if she "wanted to spend more time on the playground." They just couldn't believe Quindlen when she said, "*The New York Times* is a great institution, but some things about it don't meet my needs anymore."[42]

In a similar case, a vice president of a securities firm in New York lamented the fact that his firm had a hard time keeping good female investment bankers after they got married and had children. He said the company had done everything in its power to keep one woman from leaving. They let her work part-time from her home and provided fax lines, computers, and car service. Despite all this, the woman still left the firm. The vice president understood the needs of a working mother and why those needs could *force* her to leave the business. He had a harder time understanding why, after her needs as a mother had been provided for, a successful investment banker would still not want to be an investment banker.

Affluent, well-educated married women have the greatest choice about work. That is why their defections from prestigious, high-paying jobs are most interesting. They are not pushed by economic necessity and they are not shut out of interesting jobs due to lack of education. Feminists fought to give women the option of working outside the home and the opportunity to advance to powerful, high-paying positions. But women didn't just want to work, they wanted a *real* choice between staying at home and working. Because of the value and prestige that certain jobs give people, we often forget that the choice can go either way. There have been many interpretations of highly publicized defections of women from good jobs, from the sexist "Women can't hack it" to "Women's natural mothering instincts call them home" to "The workplace isn't friendly to women's needs." But maybe the most radical explanation is that some women, like McKenna and the successful women she interviewed for her book, have discovered that the "great job" that they worked so hard to get wasn't what it was trumped up to be. Work was cutting into life outside of work. Life outside of work had more to offer than life at work. Poor women have always worked outside the home and have had few illusions about what work is and what it means. However, because women are still relatively new to the ladder of success and high-powered positions, it may be easier for them to see when work is an emperor who isn't wearing any clothes. In recent years a growing number of men have also come to this conclusion.

What is so great about work? Some jobs are interesting and fulfilling and some are not. Some jobs are worth investing large amounts of time and energy in and others zap us of our energy and time to enjoy other things in life. But what about work itself? In our culture work is virtuous and time without work is potentially dangerous. Work gives people identity, self-worth, and the sense that they can shape and influence the world around them. Perhaps the most fundamental satisfaction that work offers is the satisfaction of earning a living, the satisfaction of getting what we need to stay alive.

But why does so much of our personal well-being and identity rest on our jobs, when there are so many other types of work and activities that we do in life? How did paid work get such a good reputation in our culture and why is its stature growing in other cultures? To answer these questions we need to start at the beginning. The word *work* itself carries a history of contradictory emotions and values. That is why we begin our exploration with the question "What is work?"

2.

What Is Work?

Bertrand Russell quickly disposed of the question "What is work?" He wrote, "Work is of two kinds: first, altering the position of matter at or near the earth's surface relatively to other such matter; second, telling other people to do so."[1] His first definition comes from physics: work is equal to the product of force times displacement. Physicists got their formula for work from watching people work. When they see work, they see energy in transit.[2] But, Russell says, not all work involves moving things about: "There are those who give orders and those who give advice on what orders should be given."[3] This kind of work is capable of indefinite extension. When we consider the variety of physical and mental tasks that we call work, and the many ways in which we use the word *work,* we see that Russell's characterization only scratches the surface.

Work means different things to different people, but as English speakers we all use the same language to talk about it. A good place to begin an exploration of the meaning of work is by looking at what words like *work, labor, toil,* and *job* mean. By examining the way we use and define the word *work,* we will see how our own use of the word is connected to the collective use of it over time. The fact that more people now work in front of computers than behind plows does not mean that the plowman and the computer programmer mean different things when they say they are working or going to work. Technology changes the way we do work and the kinds of work we do, but it doesn't radically alter what the word *work* means. We will also discover in the definitions of these words the roots of what people have liked and disliked about work.

Definitions and Meanings

Usually the first thing that comes to mind when we think about the meaning of a word is its definition. We might just look up *work* in the dictionary. But this isn't as easy as it sounds. *The Oxford English Dictionary* offers nine long pages on *work*, *The Random House Dictionary of the English Language* lists fifty-four definitions, while *Webster's New Unabridged Dictionary* weighs in at forty-five. These tallies don't even include compounds such as *work bag, workbook,* and *workday*. After looking through a few dictionaries, you may wonder how well you would understand the word if you didn't already know what it meant.

The meaning of a word comes from the way we use it and the ways others have used it in the past.[4] That is why dictionaries not only give instructions on how to use a term, but also tell us where the word came from and how it has been used. When we think about how we use certain words, we discover that there is some "family resemblance" between particular objects, ideas, and activities. There may be no one particular feature present in everything that we call work, but rather many characteristics that overlap and intersect.[5] Metaphors, similes, and analogies use words in novel ways. They don't really change the meanings of words; they stretch them in new directions. For example, I may call taking a nap "hard work." What we know about napping and working makes this particular usage peculiar. But if I go on to explain that because of a back injury it is difficult for me to find a comfortable sleeping position, then, as an activity requiring effort, my nap may resemble other activities called "work." This does not mean that napping is the same as hard work, but rather that it is difficult and requires effort like hard work.

What's in a Word?

Naming something or changing the term for something is a potentially powerful act. When you name something, you forge a connection with it. In her book *Adam's Task*, animal trainer Vicky Hearne says that when Adam named the animals in Genesis 2:20 he created a moral relationship between animals and humans. Hearne believes that we should give people and animals names that "give the soul room for expansion." When a dog owner names her dog Belle, and goes from saying "Belle, sit!" to "Belle, go find!" it signifies that the dog named Belle has moved into "more glorious contexts."[6] When we name something, we give it significance. We capture this idea in the common expression "Bill Gates has really made a name for himself," meaning that Gates's name went from being the name of someone who works with computer software to being the name of someone who has done extraordinary things with software. One of Studs Terkel's interviewees observes: "Most of us have jobs that are too small for our spirit. Jobs are not big enough for people."[7] Sometimes we rename things to give them greater significance. The possibilities in the title "secretary" are not as great as those in "executive assistant." Possibilities for the salesperson are not as great as for the sales associate, for the marketing director not as great as for the "marketing Sherpa," and so on. Some titles are just euphemisms, designed to make jobs sound better than they are. For example, two recent college graduates gave their job the title "professional blended petroleum transference engineer," because it sounded much better than "gas station attendant." Other titles really do imply greater responsibility, as in the difference between "assistant director of marketing" and "director of marketing."

The names of the things we work with and the terms we use to talk about work form a conceptual map of the workplace. Often when employers want to change the culture of an organization, they rename things. I once knew a CEO who wanted to promote greater participation in the organization. He told all of his employees that he wanted to be called Coach. By renaming himself, he hoped to change his relationship to his employees. Needless to say, you cannot change the meaning of a situation by changing its name. People have to see some family resemblance between the old meaning of the word and its new application. If the CEO acts like a tyrant, his new name will be a joke to employees. When the words for things do not match up to reality, people usually become cynical.

Our language is our world. Words designate the people and things in our experience and our ideas about them. There is a sense in which the world of a physicist who thinks about quarks and gluons all day at work is different from the world of a sales manager who thinks about product lines and market share. While the sales manager and the physicist have different conceptual worlds, they both call the activities that they are engaged in work. Some companies try to influence the conceptual world of people's work by renaming things in the workplace. For example, consider the world constructed by Rosenbluth Travel. The company's meeting rooms are called "thought centers," the head of technology is the "travel scientist," the employees' advisory group is the "happiness barometer," sick days are "family responsibility days," and the company library is "the gathering."[8] Clearly, Rosenbluth is trying to create a more "glorious context" for its employees.

Activities We Call Work

The word *work* is not only a kind of activity but a set of ideas and values related to that activity. Consider why we say the following are performing work: a construction worker digging a ditch, an executive at a meeting, a professional basketball player practicing his shots, a critic watching a movie she has to review, a student reading a novel for class, a volunteer bathing a patient in a hospital, an artist painting a picture, a secretary typing a letter for the boss, a monk meditating, and a man washing his kitchen floor. What do these activities have in common. Essentially nothing, except for the fact that, as we say, all of these people are working. We usually don't term shooting baskets, watching movies, and reading short stories *work*. Some might say that getting paid for these activities makes them work. If I pay a group of noisy children to get out of the house and go to a movie, are they working? Students don't get paid to read stories, nor do hospital volunteers or people who wash their own floors get paid to do their tasks. And what about the monk? He doesn't seem to be doing anything.

A common thread of necessity runs through all of these examples. There is a sense in which all the people *have* to do what they are doing or feel that they *must* do what they are doing. This is clear for the wage earners, including people who play games for a living. They have a particular agreement with their employers to be at a certain place at a certain time, and to perform a particular task. It's also true of the student who must read the book to pass the course, but the student has fewer restrictions on when and where she'll do her work. The floor washer also has few external restrictions. He can choose to let the floor remain dirty. However, if he finds the filth distasteful and doesn't want to live with it, he must wash the floor.

The painter seems to have the most amount of choice, particularly if he actually earns his living as a cabdriver. While external necessities such as bosses, agreements on time and uses of energy, and dirty floors are strong defining features of work, they do not account for the artist who paints from the internal necessity of his or her desire. It is tempting to say that he or she is not working, but as Karl Marx wrote, "Really free work, e.g., composing, is at the same time the most damned serious, the most intense exertion."[9] Most artists would agree. The drive and motivation to work that come from inside a person can be far more powerful than outside forces. This is certainly true for the monk, who is driven by his spirituality.

Work as an Attitude

Sometimes we call an activity work if it is difficult or unpleasant, or is one that we prefer not to do at a particular time. For example, the basketball player might prefer to go to the movies, the movie critic might want to play basketball. If you ask a friend out for a drink and she says, "No, I have to work tonight," a natural response might be sympathy— "What a shame you have to work!" (Even if, as a critic, she has to go to the movies.) This is not because drinking is preferable to working or, as Oscar Wilde once said, "Work is a curse of the drinking classes," but because we tacitly assume that activities called work are less desirable than other sorts of occupations, since they keep you from doing other things.

Our attitude toward a task or activity often determines whether we call it work. Work is serious and play is nonserious.[10] Playing Monopoly with someone who takes notes, and counts every move you make, and never cracks a smile might feel like work. Working with people who play practical jokes on one another and come to work wearing propeller beanies and toting squirt guns might feel like play. Author Barbara Sher notes that the distinction between work and play impoverishes both activities: "We think work is dreary stuff that pays the rent and play is something that relieves stress."[11]

Not all cultures have the same attitude toward work. For example, in the Thai language, the word for work and the word for party share the same root. Speakers of English use the word *party* to talk about a group of people gathered together for some purpose. However, work parties, search parties, and political parties are different from birthday parties. Unlike Westerners, Thais do not think that work has to be serious, nor do they share the view that work per se is a good thing. Yet Thais are not lazy. Their culture places a high value on *sanuk,* which means fun. Activities are divided into *sanuk* ("fun") and *mai sanuk* ("not fun"). *Sanuk* is carefree amusement that is spontaneous.[12] It is the quality that makes any activity, whether work or play, worth doing. If, for instance, a Thai villager were given a job that required sustained attention to a monotonous task, he or she might walk away because it wasn't *sanuk.* On the other hand, the same villager might work for days on end to build the village temple because he or she finds *sanuk* in it. The Japanese discovered the importance of *sanuk* when they first set up factories in Thailand. In the beginning the Thais didn't work very hard and they particularly disliked the ritual of standing at attention and singing the factory song in the morning. The Japanese abandoned this practice and started playing music in the factory and giving more breaks, and they introduced games to play at work. Productivity increased because work became *sanuk.*[13] The Thais' attitude toward work and play activities is the same, that is, a work party should not be much different from a birthday party.

Every culture has its own values and social perceptions that determine what activities are called work.[14] So how do we recognize work when we see it somewhere else? Imagine that you are a traveler in eighteenth-century Chile. You walk by an open doorway and see a room full of old women chatting with each other and chewing on corn that they then spit into a vat or barrel in the center of the room. Would you guess that they are working? And if you did, working at what? Then you learn that the Chileans discovered, by chance, that one good way to make liquor was by chewing up corn and spitting it into a barrel.[15] The chewing and spitting ladies of Chile resemble employees in a modern distillery in an important way. They may or may not get paid for their work, but their chewing and spitting is a purposeful activity. Might we then say that any activity is work if it has a purpose? If so, then that definition explains why we can "work" on our suntans and tennis games, but it also makes the word *work* very broad, if it describes everything that is done with a purpose.

Anything Can Be Work

The word *work* is a very general term for human activity. It is derived from the Old English noun *woerc* and the verb *wyrcan,* which date back to the tenth century. A now obsolete definition of work characterizes it as "action (of a person) in general; doings deeds; conduct." The first definition that *The Oxford English Dictionary* offers is only slightly more specific: "something that is or was done; what a person does or did; an act, deed, proceeding, business."[16] *The Random House Dictionary of the English Language* begins with a more physical definition, "exertion or effort directed to produce or accomplish something; labor; toil,"[17] while *Webster's New Unabridged Dictionary* gives the first definition of *work* a teleological twist: "bodily or mental effort exerted to do or make something; purposeful activity; labor; toil."[18] English isn't the only language in which *work* covers such a broad range of activities. For example, an English-Arabic dictionary offers two Arabic equivalents to work. The first is *'amal,* which means action in general as contrasted with knowledge. The second, *sun',* means making and producing something.[19]

Work is an extraordinary word because it does so many different things. We *do* work and we *go* to a place called work. Work is something we *have,* something we *own,* and something we *make.* There are works of art, architecture, music, and literature. One can admire the work of a surgeon, an accountant, an auto mechanic, or a carpet salesman. We can work a room, a piece of wood, bread dough, or a stuck lock. We can work it out, work out, do good works, work someone over, or get worked up, and if we're not careful, we can even become workaholics.

The word *work* is both a verb and a noun, an activity and a product that comes from that activity. Philosopher Hannah Arendt said work provides us with the artificial world of things that are distinct from our natural surroundings. These things outlast us all. Hence, according to Arendt, the human condition of work is worldliness.[20] John Locke distinguished between the "work of our hands and the labor of our bodies" to separate man the maker (*homo faber*) from man the laboring animal (*animal laborans*). The work of our hands produces some material object; in a sense the memory of our lives is in this object. Hegel called work the process of turning ideas into objects or acts, "externalization."[21] The noun and the verb *work* form a continuum between the doer and what is done. On the one hand work is necessary and restrictive of our freedom, while on the other hand it is purposeful and creative.

The Labor of Our Bodies

Unlike the work of our hands, the labor of our bodies, or labor, is often impermanent. Labor, toil, and drudgery are expenditures of energy that are consumed and often leave no product behind. The word *labor* (*labour*) first appeared in the English language in the fourteenth century. Its root is uncertain, but some believe that it used to mean slipping or staggering under a burden.[22] As a verb, the word usually referred to plowing or working the land, but later came to mean other forms of manual labor.

The verb *labor* describes only an activity and not an object. We do not say a "labor of art," but we do refer to the "fruits of our labor." This expression implies a kind of indirect relationship between the actual activity and the product or state of affairs that it brings about. A farmer tills the field and plants seeds, but we do not say that he "made" the strawberries, even though he is much closer to making the strawberries than the migrant worker who picks them. Unlike the artist whose activity of painting produces the painting, those who labor usually do physical work that contributes to making something, but don't directly make it. Sometimes we perform a "labor of love." This kind of labor is done for someone else or done because the agent cares about it, but it is often unnecessary, time-consuming, or devoid of material reward.

The ends or products of labor are related to the laborer in a more abstract way than are those of the worker, but this is not enough to deny that labor can also have a product. Physical work in the service industry is often labor without a product or a lasting product. Mabel the maid is not remembered by the dishes she washed. Every day there are more dirty dishes. However, there is a sense in which both work and labor produce something. Adam Smith considered labor to be like the work of a menial servant that "does not fix or realize itself in any particular subject or saleable commodity."[23] Two factors distinguish *labor* and *work* from each other. First, *labor* is associated with greater physical effort than *work;* second, the relationship of laborers to their work is different from the relationship of workers to theirs. This is clearly seen in the definitions of worker and laborer. The first definition of *laborer* in *The Oxford English Dictionary* is "one who performs physical labour as a service or for a livelihood,"[24] whereas the first definition of *worker* is "one who makes, creates, produces or contrives."[25]

Friedrich Engels believed that the word *labor* could not be reduced to *work.* He said that work is something done by and for the individual. The word *labor* is a social term because it implies that an individual contributes to the making or doing of something.[26] While *work* is a noun for the product of labor, *labor* is a noun for the people who work. *Labor* refers to a group of people who do physical work, while *work* refers to an object or a variety of activities. We form "labor unions," not "work unions." Despite the fact that work in most organizations is cooperative and involves interdependent groups of people, we refer to "workplaces," not "places of labor," thus emphasizing the individualist, nonphysical work over collective, physical work.

Work That Hurts

While *labor* implies physical exertion, *toil* denotes continuous and exhausting labor, and *drudgery* refers to work that we dislike because of its minuteness or dull uniformity.[27] *Toil* is often used as a synonym for *labor* and it has an more unpleasant heritage than *labor.* Derived from the Latin *tudiculase,* "to stir," and the Old French *toeiller,* "to crush," it first meant turmoil and trouble before coming to mean arduous labor in the fourteenth century. Even though *toil* and *drudgery* do not always describe harsh physical labor, these negative terms for work highlight what speakers of English have always disliked about some kinds of work—its capacity to be boring, exhausting, and of seemingly endless duration.

In certain languages, words for work actually denote pain. The origins of the French word *travail* can be traced to an older term, *tripalium.*[28] A tripalium consisted of three posts to which one tied a horse's

legs so that it could be shod. The word *tripalium* then came t
kind of torture and then evolved to mean work. In ancient Gree
(*ponos*) and trouble or punishment are synonymous, and the
the Latin word for sorrow, *poena,* comes from the Greek wor
work.[29] In Biblical Hebrew, the words for work and for slavery are i
tical.[30] The German word *arbeiten* originally meant pain and trouble.
English, *labor* has been used to describe the pains of birth since the si
teenth century.

If labor, toil, and drudgery can cause pain and misery, then some
kinds of work are ideal for torture and punishment. The poet Lucretius
once described the most hideous torture as that suffered by "those
young and lovely girls the Danaïdes, trying in vain to fill their leaky jars
with water."[31] The Danaïdes were sisters who killed their husbands. As
punishment for this they were doomed to spend the afterlife filling per-
forated jars with water. The gods punished Sisyphus in a similar way
for outsmarting them. In the *Odyssey,* Odysseus meets Sisyphus in the
netherworld, where he is condemned to perpetually push a great boul-
der to the top of a hill, "whereupon the rock rolls back down, and the
process begins anew."[32] Of this punishment Albert Camus comments
that the gods "had thought with some reason that there is no more
dreadful punishment than futile and hopeless labor."[33] Three things together punish Sisyphus and the Danaïdes: exhausting and boring tasks,
loss of freedom, and purposeless, futile work.

The Old Testament also portrays toil as punishment. In the beginning, Adam was charged with tilling and "keeping" the Garden of
Eden. After the fall, God says to Adam, "Cursed be the ground because
of you. In toil shall you eat of it all the days of your life."[34] So Adam
goes from tending or maintaining a garden to the hard labor of coaxing
life from a recalcitrant earth. Eve's punishment is painful childbirth.
But unlike Sisyphus's useless rock-pushing, Adam's work in the rocky
soil and Eve's painful labor bear fruit. Painful, boring, and physically
exhausting work is not punishment in itself, if it has a purpose for the
people who do it. The punishment of Adam and Eve establishes work
as a necessary condition of life, but the work itself is no longer punish-
ing. The Hebrews gave work more dignity because it wasn't just punishment, but a means of atonement for sin. Work can rehabilitate as
well as punish. We still "work off" our debts and "work out" our problems.

Would then the Danaïdes' task of filling leaky water jars cease to be unishment if we paid them? Would they then be like modern work-rs, going though the boring motions for a paycheck? They might still aate the work, but at least doing it would serve the purpose of earning a living. What if we gave Sisyphus his freedom and said, "You may push the rock up the hill whenever you want"? Sisyphus might choose to push the rock up the hill to keep in shape. (People work out on stair-steppers that go nowhere, why not push rocks up a hill?) He is not only free from pushing the rock, but he is free to create his own purpose for pushing the rock. Finally, what if we gave both the Danaïdes and Sisyphus a spiritual purpose? Would they then be like Buddhist monks who work for weeks to make those lovely mandalas with colored sand and then sweep their work away in the Kalackra ceremony? People don't mind toil or drudgery if it serves a purpose and they believe in the purpose it serves.

It's Only a Job

Compared to words like *labor* and *toil,* the word *job* sounds almost cheerful. *The Oxford English Dictionary* tells us that some believe that the noun *job* came from the word *gob;* in the fourteenth century, *job* meant a lump or piece, and a little later on it came to mean cartload. By the seventeenth century, the word *job* took on a number of meanings. The most general was a "piece of work done and in the way of one's oc-cupation or profession." *Job* referred to work that was hired or used, not permanent employment. It also meant anything done with an eye to profit.[35] According to one source, the word *job* is first recorded in American English in 1858 as "work done for pay, a paid position and employment."[36]

The word *job* is usually used as a noun, "a job," whereas *work* is al-most equally used as a verb, "to work," and a noun, as in "their work." Rarely do we use the verb *job,* which means to strike, stab, peck, or prod, often with a sharp, pointed instrument.[37] (Instead, we usually use *jab* or *stab.*) The other difference between *job* and *work* is that work is an activity done with or without pay, whereas the word *job* has a spe-cific connection to work for pay or profit. Unemployed people may work or have a job to do around the house, but they do not *have* a job.

The affiliation of *job* with personal gain or self-interest accounts for its more negative uses. In the seventeenth century, *job* was a slang term for "a theft or robbery; any criminal deed, especially one that is arranged beforehand." At that time it also meant "a transaction in which public interest is sacrificed for the sake of private or party advantage."[38] Stocks were "jobbed" from the seventeenth century on by brokers and dealers who didn't own them but made their money from them. A stock jobber acts as middleman between holders and buyers of stocks.[39]

A *jobber* is also a "hack," or someone who does odd pieces of work and is not continuously employed.[40] Organizations break work down into pieces. There are job categories and job descriptions, and employees are given job evaluations. All of these terms refer to the particular type or piece of work. In a recent article on management, William Bridges asserts that we have to "de-job" organizations. By "de-job" Bridges means that people in organizations have to get rid of the fragmented idea of work expressed by the word *job*.[41]

Today, *job* is the most general term for paid work.[42] From the plumber to the physician, everyone who works for pay has a job. Nonetheless, the different elements in the definition of *job* come out in how we use the term. For example, when we want to minimize the importance of our work or distance ourselves from our work, we say, "It's only a job." This means that it's nothing personal, because it's just a *piece* of work that we do to get paid. We think nothing of hiring a plumber who says, "I have a job across town," but we might think twice about going to a physician who says, "I have a job across town." While both the plumber and the doctor work for pay, we don't want or expect a doctor to regard us as a "lump" or "piece" of work, nor do we like to think that the doctor regards us primarily as a way to earn a living. As we will see later in this book, doctors, as professionals, are supposed to identify themselves with their work. Ideally, professionals *have* jobs, but they don't *do* jobs.

The word *job* portrays work as an instrumental activity done for pay. It stands in sharp contrast to *work, labor, toil,* and *drudgery*. The definition of *job* doesn't imply there is a relationship between workers and their product. It also doesn't say anything about the quality of work—whether the work is physical or mental, creative or dull, painful or purposeless—but it does say something about the quantity. What matters is that the work is a finite amount of things that a person gets paid to do. *Job* is the word that best refers to the activity of economic beings whose work consists of specific tasks done in order to buy the things they want and need to live. In contrast, the definitions of *work, labor, toil,* and *drudgery* refer to the positive and negative characteristics of these activities, regardless of whether they are paid or not paid. The meaning of the actual work we do every day and the meaning of work itself in our culture may be different, but they are intertwined. The first is about one's own experience of work and the second is about work's cultural meaning and value. In the next chapter we will trace how work evolved from a necessary activity for life to the moral center of life.

3.

From Curse to Calling

How did we get from the idea that we work to live to the idea that we live to work? From ancient times to the early middle ages, hard work didn't get you into heaven, demonstrate your moral goodness, endear you to your neighbors, or promise insight into the meaning of your life. Over time, work emerged from a morally neutral and somewhat negative idea to one that is rich with moral and social value, and fundamental to how we think of ourselves. It's not easy to pinpoint when work began its moral and personal ascent. By looking at some historical snapshots, we will see how religion and ideas about fate shaped the social, moral, and personal meanings of work that we carry with us today.

The Curse

For the ancient Greeks, work was a curse. Around the eighth or ninth century B.C., Homer wrote that the gods hated humans and made them toil out of spite.[1] In that same era the poet and farmer Hesiod wrote that the gods were displeased with humans, so they buried their food under the earth. His epic poem *Works and Days* deplores idleness and begging and sees no inherent dignity in work. Hesiod longs for the return of the Golden Age, when people lived without working.[2] But he observes that "envy and strife" motivate people to work and that strife is good for mortals, "So potter is piqued with potter, joiner, with joiner, beggar begrudges beggar, and singer, singer."[3] In the fourth century B.C. the historian Xenophon wrote that work was the price that people had to pay for the goods of life.[4] If work was a curse from the gods, it was best given to people who were cursed because they were either vanquished enemies or captured foreigners or children of slaves. Slaves freed the affluent ancient Greek from work. The Greeks considered slavish all occupations that served the maintenance of life.[5] As we will see in chapter 5, the institution of slavery not only degraded people, it degraded the social and moral value of work.

Aristotle not only thought that work was something that should, if possible, be foisted off on slaves, he believed that work done for profit could be its own curse. Property (land and slaves), not work, was the basis of a person's livelihood. Aristotle distinguished between work done to produce things for use in the household and work done for commercial gain. He said that household work, done to produce the things we need to stay alive, is natural and finite because human needs are finite. He called household production *oeconomia*. Retail trade or work done for financial gain is not natural to humans, because, according to Aristotle, it is carried out for human wants. Wants, unlike human needs, are unlimited.[6] And the most hated and unnatural way to make money is through usury and interest. Money should be used for exchange, not for the breeding of more money. Those who believe they should spend their lives working at getting or not losing money are, according to Aristotle, "intent on living only, and not upon living well."[7] People who are consumed with getting wealth use everything as a means to wealth. They are not able to enjoy anything for its own sake, which, as we saw earlier, was Aristotle's definition of a leisure activity. Furthermore, people who work for wealth are never satisfied, because the things that they want and the work that they do to get it are never-ending. Aristotle's concern about people who focus their lives on working to make money was shared by Aesop and, as we shall see, later by the Catholics and Protestants, albeit for different reasons.

Work and Permanence

The significance of work is influenced in part by a culture's assumptions about what is real, how the world works, and how much control people have over their lives. Work takes on greater importance in a society where people believe that they can master the material world and shape their own destinies, and less where they believe that they can't. For instance, the ancient Greek philosophers thought that the material world was an endless recurrence of things that are born and die, in a state of constant flux. The cryptic writings of Heraclitus from the fifth century B.C. capture this notion of constant change: "Upon those that step into the same rivers different and different waters flow. . . . They scatter and . . . gather . . . come together and flow away . . . approach and depart.[8] The only stability in the world was within one's mind or soul, where ideas were secure from the unending changes that took place in the material world.

In ancient Greece, philosophers believed that a person's thoughts and ideas were more important than that person's work. Work in the material world lacked permanence. For intellectuals, at least, contact with the material world through work was a humiliating necessity.[9] The historian Plutarch wrote that the scientist Archimedes did not leave behind any writings on his mechanical works or instruments because he regarded "as sordid and ignoble the construction of instruments and in general everyday art directed to use and profit, and he only strove after those things which, in their beauty and excellence, remain beyond all contact with the common needs of life."[10] To the modern reader, Archimedes sounds like an intellectual snob. It is difficult to believe that the ordinary "Greek on the street" would feel this way about turning ideas into useful products. This we'll never know, because ordinary people don't show up in history unless they make history.

In various Eastern cultures in the era before Christ, the material world was thought impermanent and inferior to the mental and spiritual world, but work was not disdained. For instance, the Buddha, in the sixth century B.C., taught that suffering is the human condition because the world is impermanent. He said that people suffer because they thirst for material things and physical pleasures, and that the only way to get rid of suffering is to extinguish this thirst through love, compassion, and mental discipline. Work was one way to develop mental discipline. The process of working was more important than the product. For a Buddhist, even the most humble tasks, such as sweeping, scrubbing, and gathering fuel, can be a path to enlightenment. In the Buddha's teachings, work itself wasn't a curse, but some types of work were undesirable. His Eightfold Path to enlightenment includes "right livelihood," which means one should earn one's living by doing something that does not cause others suffering or involve deceit or treachery.[11]

Clean and Dirty Work

Work may have a positive, negative, or neutral value for a religion or a culture, but within a culture different kinds of work will carry different spiritual, moral, and social values. Every society has its own prejudices against certain types of work. For the ancient Greeks, the status of particular occupations depended on the degree of freedom a person had, the perceived moral integrity of the occupation, and the amount of mental and physical work it required. (These criteria still characterize the pecking order of jobs today.)

Athenians preferred living on fees from attending the assembly, jury duty, and military service over living on income from other occupations.[12] These were the tasks of free citizens and were usually performed by men who were financially self-sufficient and had slaves to take care of their land and households. Athenians maligned service jobs, such as those of innkeepers, cooks, and public criers. (One wonders what they would have thought of the multi-million-dollar salaries of today's TV anchormen and anchorwomen.) The street-smart Athenian was also wary of all small traders, because they had a reputation for dishonesty. However, Athenian law required that respect be shown to the working person. It was illegal to use contemptuous language toward men or women trading in the market—this included the bread women of Athens, who were notorious for their vulgar and abusive tongues.[13]

The ancient Greeks had a strong bias against work done in service to others and physical labor in general. Aristotle thought that the only people who should be citizens were those who were freed from necessary services. In the *Politics,* he says that artisans and laborers should not be citizens, because they are "necessary" people who "are the servants of the community."[14] (The other reason why artisans could not be citizens was that many of them were slaves.) Even though Aristotle was writing in the golden age of Greek sculpture, he did not think that sculptors should be citizens, because sculpting involves strenuous physical labor. The Greeks considered sculpture to be a servile art. In ancient Greece, manual laborers could not become citizens; however, some of the best sculptors were granted citizenship. Painting, in contrast, was considered a liberal art, done by a free person, because it was less physically strenuous. The liberal arts implied not only clean and cerebral work, but the work of a free person.

Plutarch, born in the first century A.D., wrote that although sculptors make admirable things, because of the physical labor involved "no well-born youth would have chosen to be a Phidias or Polyclitus" (two famous sculptors).[15] The bias against physical labor lasted through the Renaissance, when people considered painting to be somewhere between the liberal and the servile arts, whereas sculpting was still a servile art. This is understandable, given that large sculptures were usually produced by teams of skilled masons and their work was thought to require "more from the arms than from the mind."[16]

The Greek preference for pure over applied science provides an extreme example of the preference for mental over physical work, clean over dirty work. For doctors this bias lasted until the mid–eighteenth century. Doctors were considered "gentlemen" who did not work with their hands.[17] They did not examine patients and they left surgery to barbers. Even today such distinctions persist. For example, some medical doctors still consider themselves superior to dentists. (But surgeons feel superior to internists.) Today we tend to feel that working in an office is better than working in a coal mine, regardless of which worker makes more money. Even our language suggests that it is a privilege to work sitting down. We respect our chairman, honor the throne, seek a professor's chair, and run for a seat in Congress.[18]

The long-standing reign of theory over practice remains alive and well in universities, where some faculty still believe the experimental and applied fields hold a lower status than abstract and theoretical ones. The theoretical physicist might look up to the pure mathematician, but down on the chemist, who in turn might look down on the biologist. Theoretical economists in economics departments might feel superior to their brethren who do applied work in the business school, even though business schools usually pay their faculty more.

Good Works

Like the ancient Greeks, the early Christians emphasized the importance of contemplation compared to work, but for ascetic rather than
aesthetic reasons. Although a carpenter by trade, Christ had preached
that work was irrelevant. Counseling absolute trust in God, he said we
shouldn't worry about food: "Look at the birds of the air: for they sow
not, neither do they reap or gather into barns, and yet your heavenly
Father feeds them. Are you not worth much more than they?"[19] Nor
should we care about clothing: "Observe how the lilies of the field
grow; they do not toil nor do they spin."[20] As noted earlier, the problem
with work was that people sometimes used it to accumulate wealth and
glory. In the Bible Christ cautions his disciples: "It is easier for a camel
to go through the eye of a needle than for a rich man to enter into the
Kingdom of God."[21] The pursuit of wealth offered all sorts of tempta-
tions and distractions that interfered with the journey to paradise. In
the first few centuries after Christ, people believed that since they were
just passing through life on earth on their way to heaven, it made sense
to invest in eternity, through contemplation and prayer. While a few
people, such as the early monks, took Christ's asceticism literally, for
the most part the Christian attitude toward work was to trust in divine
providence and do only what was necessary to get by.

In the New Testament, St. Paul recognizes the importance of work
for order, just rewards, and discipline. He counsels the Thessalonians
to live regularly, "For we have heard that some among you are living ir-
regularly, doing no work but busy at meddling." Do not burden others
by eating their bread, he says, for "if any would not work, neither
should he eat."[22] There are two messages here. First, work is a part of
the rhythm of life and it keeps people out of trouble. Second, as in
Aesop's fable about the ant, it's not fair to eat food that you didn't earn.

In the third century, the missionary and theologian Clement of
Alexandria criticized the classical philosophers who said that manual
labor was disgraceful and worthy of reproach. According to Clement,
both work and learning are important. However, he did not say that
work itself is morally good. Clement only ascribed dignity to work
done for the sake of charity, and to spiritual work.[23] He called these
"good works." This notion of "good works" is still alive and well in a
Catholic tradition that emphasizes compassion and kindness to the

needy and service to the Church. A recent recruiting ad for priests read: "The work is hard, but the rewards are infinite."

The Church distinguished between work done to supply the basics of life or work done for others, on the one hand, and work done for personal or material gain, on the other. The seven deadly sins—pride, covetousness (greed), lust, anger, envy, gluttony, and sloth—reflect the potential dangers of work done for material gain. Most of the sins designate evils that lurk in the material world. Pride, envy, greed, and even anger may either motivate people to work hard or emerge from a dogged focus on work and its rewards. Pride and envy may be the result of how our work makes us think about ourselves and how we compare to others. The wealth that comes from hard work can also inspire passions and desires like lust and anger, greed and gluttony.

One wonders what the early Church fathers would have thought about the exploitation of these sins by advertisers in consumer cultures. Lust sells everything from toothpaste to tractors. Luxury cars play on people's desire to show off their wealth and make their neighbors envious. Restaurants bring out the gluttony in us with half-pound burgers and all the shrimp you can eat. And the whole system works by cultivating in people the desire to want more than they need, which the Church fathers called greed.

The Noonday Demon

The seventh deadly sin, sloth, seems almost out of place with the first six. What we call "sloth" is a loose translation of the Latin *acedia*. Today we understand sloth as laziness or disinclination to work. But that was not the original meaning of *acedia*. It was neither a condemnation of laziness as we understand it, nor an affirmation of the value of work. Sloth wasn't about not working, it was about not caring.

Acedia is a temptation first described in the writings of Evagrius, a fourth-century monk who lived in Egypt and wrote about the "wisdom of the desert." Evagrius called acedia the "noonday demon." It was the most oppressive demon because it attacked monks in the afternoon and made the day seem as if it lasted fifty hours. Evagrius writes of the demon:

> Then he causes the monk continually to look out the windows and forces him to step out of his cell and to gaze at the sun to see how far

it is from the ninth hour and to look around, here and there, whether any of his brethren is near.[24]

According to St. Thomas Aquinas, acedia is a kind of sadness or inability to find joy in spiritual work and doing good works. A person (usually a monk) feels despair and withdraws from good works, because they fill him with boredom and disgust.[25] Acedia is a psychological or spiritual condition that immobilizes a person in regard to the things that cause him or her sadness. It results in listlessness, loss of interest in life, a morbid inertia, and disinclination to action.[26] In the medieval world it was not a sin to be a beggar or to be lazy on the job, as long as one was not apathetic about life and God.

Work and Excellence

One of the most striking affirmations of work as more than mere labor appeared after the fall of the Roman Empire, at a time when the world around Rome was in ruins socially and physically. In 529, St. Benedict built his monastery on top of Monte Cassino. You can see a reconstructed version of it, surrounded by vineyards, farmland, and a war cemetery, on the road from Rome to Naples today. St. Benedict's monastery was completely self-sufficient. It consisted of farms, vineyards, and various workshops. The monks had a duty to care for the sick and the hungry. A book of rules prescribed how the monastery should operate. The *Rule of St. Benedict,* written in 528, may well be the oldest and most continuously used management guide in Western history. The Benedictines have run their monasteries according to the *Rule* for almost fifteen hundred years. Among other things, it tells the abbot how to organize an abbey and provides instructions on when monks should work, how much they should work, and when they should pray.

Before St. Benedict's time, monks did hard and painful labor to seek atonement for their sins. However, Benedict gave a more positive spiritual meaning to physical work. The theme of his Rule is *ora et labora,* "prayer and work." Benedict encouraged his monks to pursue excellence as part of their devotion to God: "And first of all, whatever work you begin to do, beg of Him with most earnest prayer to perfect it." The *Rule* describes an organization in which people lead lives of work, prayer, reading, meditation, and service.

John Cardinal Newman believed that St. Benedict's mission was to restore the Roman world that in his time lay in shambles. As Newman saw it:

> The Benedictines' work was not the work of science, but of nature. They went about it not as if setting about to do it, not professing to do it by any set time, or by any rare specific or any series of strokes, but to do so quietly, so patiently, gradually, that often till the work was done, it was not known to be doing."[27]

Newman notes that the monks did not speak or draw attention to themselves, yet eventually the swamp became a hermitage, a farm, an abbey, a village, and then a city. For St. Benedict, work was not a job or a calling, but a kind of visible prayer. Imagine the impact that these silent Benedictine monks had on medieval villagers as they farmed, cleared trees, drained swamps, and built mills, and also copied the manuscripts they salvaged from ruin. Benedictine orders fanned out all over Europe and played a pivotal role in developing the medieval towns and cities.

Although the Benedictines were among the most skilled farmers, craftsmen, and engineers of the early Middle Ages, the Church considered them the lowliest order of monks because they labored. The early Christians, while they had not valued work itself, had seen some relationship between work and faith. The work ethic that emerged from the Benedictine legacy applied Christian spiritual virtues to crafts and other vocations. It encouraged people to work with care and diligence, but was still wary of the riches that came from work. These values of quality and craftsmanship were shaped and enhanced by the craft guilds that later emerged in twelfth-century Europe. Nonetheless, it took about a thousand years for the idea of work to ascend in priority from Benedict's ideal of "prayer and work" to the Protestant notion of "work and prayer."

Occupational Sins

In the twelfth and thirteenth centuries the Church began to take a different view of human volition, and this view in turn gave work new significance. In the early twelfth century the theologian Peter Abelard wrote that sin is less about what is done in the observable world than what is in a person's heart. Good and evil were choices based on an individual's dispositions and experiences. Abelard's view of human nature helped shift the Church's focus from the sin itself to the psychology of the sinner. By the thirteenth century the Church had become more interested in a person's disposition to sin, which was rooted in concrete social and work-related situations. As historian Jacques Le Goff points out, "For them, the demon took the form not so much of the seven deadly sins as of the countless offenses against God that a trade or group might foster in a variety of ways.[28]

Prior to the thirteenth century priests had used penitential manuals, which were like case law books. These manuals helped priests decide if a person had sinned and what the penance should be for the sins. In 1215 confession became mandatory for all Christians, and priests needed help in understanding the moral dangers of various occupations. New confessional manuals replaced the old penitential manuals. There were three basic themes to these books. First, they defined every Christian in relation to his or her occupation. Second, they asserted that all labor deserves compensation, vocation, and money. Third, they justified all occupations based on labor.[29]

Confessional manuals played a key role in forming occupational consciousness. They regarded sin as a type of occupational hazard. One such manual, the *Summa confessorum* by John of Freiburg, began with a section on sins common to all people and was then arranged by sins common to fourteen occupational categories, ranging from bishops and their vicars to manual laborers. The confessional manuals told priests what sins to look for and what questions to ask in confession. For example, one manual says, "A knight must not be questioned about the sins of a monk, or vice versa."[30] It was assumed that work not only identified people, but identified their potential virtues and vices. Priests were told to keep an eye out for signs of lust in innkeepers, bathhouse keepers, and tavern keepers. Cooks were potential gluttons, while the dishwasher's and laundryman's contact with the unclean made them generally suspect and put them near the bottom of all work categories. The manuals also urged priests to watch merchants and lawyers closely for signs of greed. Some wealthy merchants bought confessional manuals, which were very expensive, and used them as business ethics guides. The manuals contained advice on all sorts of things, such as fair pricing, moneylending, and doing business at fairs on the Sabbath.

This new emphasis on the relationship between spiritual life, intentions, and vocation theologically connected personal identity and morality with work. Meanwhile, with the emergence of craft guilds, identity with one's work was already growing. In the early middle ages, people had only first names, such as Mary, William, and John. Their identity came from their patron saint, their father, or their town. A person might be named after St. Mary, or might be named "John's son" or "William of Stratford." By the twelfth century, surnames that identified a person with his or her work came into use. Consider the number of common last names that derive from trades, like Baker, Carpenter, Thatcher, Smith, Weaver, Goldsmith, and Cook. They come from a time when you would call on Margaret Thatcher to fix your roof and James Baker for a loaf of bread.

As new individual and group identities based on occupations formed, Church policies changed to accommodate the demands of the guilds and the middle class for a more respectful attitude toward their work. The Church was willing to be pragmatic. For example, it invented purgatory around this time as a halfway house for the growing middle class. Purgatory gave the middle class their own piece of spiritual real estate between heaven and hell, the powerful and the poor, and the clergy and the laity.[31] The idea of purgatory didn't really catch on until the fifteenth century, when it turned out to be a terrific, albeit disastrous, fund-raising gimmick, celebrated in the ditty, "As soon as the coin in the coffer rings, The soul from purgatory springs."[32]

Work Deserves a Fair Wage

The late twelfth century marked the beginning of the great cathedral-building era. Merchants, craft guilds, and professionals provided financial support for Church construction projects. Guilds often donated windows in honor of their craft, which is why we see so many scenes of carpenters, weavers, and the like on the windows of the great medieval cathedrals in Europe. When the cathedral of Notre-Dame was being built, a group of prostitutes approached the bishop of Paris and, in imitation of the guilds, offered to donate a window depicting the Virgin Mary (rather than a scene from their trade). The embarrassed bishop turned down their offer. A decision on this case was later written by Thomas of Chobham and included in a confessional manual. This rather odd decision illustrates the importance of the Church's policies on work. Prior to this time the Church did not approve of wage labor because it gave one person undue control over another person's well-being. In retrospect this looks like an odd idea for a Church that tolerated slavery and serfdom. Thomas of Chobham bends over backward to affirm both the right to be paid for one's work and the Church's old policy on the value of "good works."

> Prostitutes must be counted among the mercenaries. They hire out their bodies and supply labor. Whence this principle of secular justice: she does evil in being a prostitute, but she does not do evil in receiving the price of her labor, it being admitted that she is a prostitute. Whence the fact that it is possible to repent of practicing prostitution while keeping the profits of prostitution for the purposes of giving alms. If, however, prostitution is engaged in for pleasure, and the body hired out to experience ecstasy, then one's labor is not being hired and the profit is as shameful as the act.[33]

Thomas of Chobham then pushes on to consider other potential problems with the prostitute's trade, such as truth in advertising, fair price, and again the redeeming quality of good works and charity.

> If the prostitute perfumes and adorns herself so as to attract with false allures and gives the impression of a beauty and seductiveness which she does not possess, the client buying what he sees, which, in this case, is deceptive, the prostitute then commits a sin, and she should not keep the profit it brings her. If the client saw her as she really is he would give her only a pittance, but as she appears beautiful and brilliant to him, he gives a handsome sum. In this case, she should keep only the pittance and return the rest to the client she has deceived, or to the Church, or to the poor.[34]

Later in the passage Thomas of Chobham seems to come to his senses and notes that prostitution is wrong in itself (*ex natura*), which negates everything that came before it, except for the Church's desire to respect paid work. While work was no longer disparaged by the Church, the key social distinction between "respectable" people and the rest of society still rested on who did manual labor and who did not. For example, butchers were often the wealthiest people in town, but were still considered very low in the social order. Despite the growth of craft guilds and the Church's new affirmation of work, all physical work was still considered contemptible and the serfs of the feudal system replaced the slaves of antiquity as the laborsaving devices of those who could afford them.

The Renaissance Man

In the Middle Ages the Church gave people a choice between God and the world. Potential threats to the soul lurked behind all beauty and pleasure in earthly life. A tension existed between discipline and pleasure, the moral and the aesthetic values. Work teetered ambiguously between these opposites—people had to work to live, but profits and living too well were morally dangerous. By the close of the Middle Ages, there seemed to be a kind of aesthetic and material craving, which art alone could not satisfy. Between the fourteenth and seventeenth centuries trade grew across Europe. Markets were filled with exciting and exotic goods. An increasing number of people were able to live with the luxuries of the nobility. The nouveau riche of Renaissance Florence wanted to surround themselves with beautiful things, and in the process of doing so they glorified the makers of beautiful things.

One way that the increasingly powerful new middle class satisfied this urge was with elaborate dress.[35] For example, in fourteenth-century Florence the wives of merchants and bankers paraded through the streets decked out in dresses made of the finest silk, brocaded and bias-cut. On their heads they perched jeweled tiaras—the crowns of the newly emerging middle class. Needless to say, the Church got nervous about this conspicuous and immodest display of wealth. So the Florentine government passed sumptuary laws, forbidding tiaras, along with dresses made of striped, embroidered, or bias-cut fabrics. The government also forbade wearing more than two rings on one finger. These women, looking like Christmas trees, refused to obey, and the city gave up.[36] This display of material goods produced the positive kind of "envy and strife" that Hesiod had said drove a person to work. In other words, people work more when there are more things available to buy. All types of fashions emerged at this time. However, by the end of the eighteenth century the dress of the workman emerged as the standard male costume.[37]

Our most beloved picture of work came from the Renaissance: that of work as creation. God created man, who was a creator of art, music, and other things of beauty. Wealthy merchants and bankers had the ancient Greek classics dusted off, translated, and reinterpreted. The myth of Prometheus took on new significance. Prometheus, whose name means "foreseeing," stole fire from Zeus so that man could use it to forge the articles of human life. For the ancients, Prometheus was a trickster who doomed humanity to hard labor. By the Renaissance he was a hero who had allowed mankind to seize hold of fate. The value of work grew as more people began to feel that they could control their lives rather than wait around for divine providence. Fourteenth-century Florence gave us the image of man as a creator who molds the world and reshapes nature, the *homo faber*. The Renaissance man educated his mind, spirit, body, and hands and produced things of beauty and worth. If religion was the opiate of the Middle Ages, creativity and beauty were the amphetamines of the Renaissance.

The Renaissance had its own rendition of the work ethic. St. Antoninus of Florence and St. Bernardino of Siena condemned idleness and extravagance and lauded activity. Wealth was all right as long as the rich man did something with his money and did not cling to it like a miser. The fifteenth-century philosopher and architect Leon Battista Alberti praised laboriousness because it "fills so well the slow passage of the hours."[38] Time was something used and filled, not simply passed. Alberti was considered one of the first universal, or Renaissance, men. He believed that life was about doing things, not waiting for them to happen. To the ancient Greek belief in training the body and the mind the Renaissance added training the hand. When we think of the Renaissance, we usually remember the great artists like Sandro Botticelli and Leonardo da Vinci, even though they were not the lone artists that we imagine. Many of the greatest works of art came out of workshops of craftsmen who executed parts of the drawings and filled in the outlines of the paintings.

Writers of the era saw new possibilities everywhere. One of the earliest was the fifteenth-century humanist Lorenzo Valla. Valla attacked medieval traditions and papal claims to temporal authority. In his book on the nature of the true good, *De voluptate,* he redefined pleasure and virtue to establish a middle ground between the Epicurean who endorsed a life of pleasure and beauty and the Stoic who prescribed simplicity and self-restraint. Predating the utilitarian philosophy of Jeremy Bentham, this work argued that virtue was the "calculus of pleasure."

Pleasure was not a bestial impulse, but a principle of reason and discernment. Virtue was a talent and the ability to endure.

Sir Thomas More and Tommaso Campanella both created utopias that included careful directions on the organization and distribution of labor. More's *Utopia,* written in 1516, called for a communistic society based on utilitarian principles. In his Utopia criminals and slaves did all the work that citizens find menial and degrading, such as cleaning, butchering, and hunting. This left the more interesting work to citizens, who worked only six hours a day. Like the ancient Greeks, More's Utopians used slaves to free up their time for leisure and intellectual pursuits.[39]

Campanella's *La Città del Sole* (City of the Sun), written in 1602, emphasized a social order based on communal living and science. Campanella makes all classes of society equal in his utopia, and everyone in it loves working because all have jobs that are suitable to their character. However, Campanella tells us that the most noble people are those who work at more than one trade.[40] The person defines his or her work, not vice versa—the man makes the work rather than the work the man. What we call the Renaissance man is someone interested and accomplished in many areas and in control of who he is and what he does. The ideal of the Renaissance man stands in sharp contrast to the modern view. While we still admire well-rounded people, we tend to encourage and reward those who excel in one profession or area of work.

The Command

Work became a more important activity because of the Renaissance and the Reformation. A proliferation of laws prohibiting suicide by workers between the sixteenth century and the eighteenth century serves as a gruesome indicator of the increasing value and despair of laborers.[41] Like the Renaissance humanists, the Protestant reformers were opposed to the world of the cloister and fully committed to life in this world.[42] Both Martin Luther and John Calvin wrote extensive commentaries on the Book of Genesis in which they interpreted work as God's commandment *to* us, not his curse *on* us. Luther made work not only a service to God but a universal moral obligation for everyone.

The moral and spiritual ascendancy of work was marked by the descent of the beggar from a figure worthy of compassion to a lazy free-loader, from the first one to enter the pearly gates to the last. There was massive unemployment across Europe in the sixteenth century. In England the enclosure laws turned communal land farmed by peasants into private pasturage for nobles. This forced peasants off the land. Those who couldn't find work became vagrants and beggars. Some scholars estimate that the population of Europe doubled during the sixteenth century, outstripping the job market and the land available for people to farm.[43] Beggars and vagrants appeared in great numbers in cities from Rome to London.

As we look back at this history through the lens of modern economics, we can easily explain why ranks of the unemployed swelled and understand why displaced people migrated into cities. But this was not the way that Luther and other religious leaders of the time saw the world. In their view, vagrancy and unemployment were not the result of economic conditions; they were the result of a personal moral deficiency. Luther railed against lazy beggars and vagrants that he saw on the streets. He believed that the reason people were poor and homeless was that they didn't want to work (a view still held by some today).[44] His attitude was a radical departure from the traditional views of other major religions. In the Koran, for example, the bible beggars are part of the natural order of the world and almsgiving is a moral and spiritual duty.

Luther wasn't alone in his condemnation of beggars. Alarmed by vagrants in sixteenth-century Rome, Pope Sixtus V denounced people who *feigned* poverty in order to live off the community without labor. In 1536, Henry VIII of England outlawed begging except by "old and deserving beggars," who were issued begging licenses.[45] Charity to the poor was not abandoned in the sixteenth century, it just became more discriminating. The able-bodied beggar was out, but the blind cripple was still worthy of receiving alms. The world of work had become everyone's monastery. There was no sympathy for those who were capable of work but living on the outside.

We credit Calvin and Luther with the idea of work for work's sake and the abhorrence of rest and pleasure. This is but one of the many renditions of what is called the work ethic. For Calvin, work was a token of grace and the means of salvation. In contrast to the aesthetic views of the Renaissance, Calvin's call to work demanded a worldly asceticism that limited indulgence in pleasures and luxuries but did not completely exclude them. The accumulation of wealth was a sign that you were among God's chosen. Laziness and poverty indicated that you probably were not. One of the Calvinists' favorite biblical passages was Proverbs 22:29: "Seest thou a man diligent in his business? He shall stand before kings." According to Calvin, the wealthy burghers of his time weren't supposed to spend their money on excessive consumption, but rather to save and reinvest it. But the emphasis on work, saving, and investment nonetheless resulted in a richer and more diverse material world that was, as Calvin and the Catholic Church feared, very seductive. Little did Calvin know that despite his warnings against luxurious consumption, the work ethic would, for some, mutate from the belief that we were born to work into the belief that we were born to shop.

One distinctive feature of the Protestant work ethic was that it expected people to have the same reverence for all kinds of work and workers. However, Luther was distrustful of trade and moneylending. He did not believe in social mobility and thought that everyone should be happy with his or her place in life. The old distinctions of physical versus mental, dirty versus clean, and liberal versus servile work did not, in theory, matter to him. Luther articulated this attitude in his sermons to his congregation in Wittenberg. "The carpenter at his bench, the shoemaker at his last, the housemaid at her cow—all of them were to find in the humble tasks of daily duty an authentic vocation from God himself."[46] The ditchdigger and the doctor both had the same spiritual purpose, albeit with different ways of attaining it. The most lasting stricture of Luther's and Calvin's work ethic is the belief that people who work hard are good and those who don't work or don't work hard are morally inferior.

Work That Calls

The Protestant work ethic also implied that through work you could find yourself and discover your salvation. Work provided a means of discovering and creating oneself. For believers unsure of salvation, work was a quest for identity and signs of God's favor. As Max Weber pointed out, the Reformation left modern man with "an unprecedented inner loneliness."[47] In the Middle Ages, the Catholic could attain grace with the help of priests and the sacraments. The Calvinist and

Lutheran had to go it alone; no one could change what God had already decided.

The Reformation had defined *all* work as *Beruf,* a "calling."[48] A calling did not refer to a type of work, but to an attitude toward work. In the "Apology of the Augsburg Confession," Luther articulates the Reformation view: "The monastic life is no more a state of perfection than the life of a farmer or an artisan. These too are states for acquiring perfection. All men, whatever their calling, ought to seek perfection [in their calling]."[49] The idea that all work was God's commandment promised everyone a sense of meaning in his or her work no matter how painful, unpleasant, and ill paid it was. This promise remained even after the notion of a calling was freed from its religious mooring. The Protestant idea of a calling gave work a spiritual dimension. It never said that work would bring happiness. If anything, the asceticism that a calling brought to the mundane affairs of life placed serious limits on the pursuit of earthly happiness. The notion of a calling faded from common speech, and it is now used mainly in reference to religious occupations. Callings became secularized into vocations. While we sometimes use *calling* and *vocation* interchangeably, there is a difference. God determines your calling; you discover your vocation on your own.

From the time of Calvin and Luther, the work ethic was more likely to make sense to middle-class craftspeople, farmers, small businessmen and businesswomen, and professionals. When these people worked diligently they got something out of it—a better life, respect, and satisfaction—whereas for slaves, indentured servants, and early industrial workers, there was little to gain from working beyond what was necessary, except exhaustion. The Protestant work ethic took hold in the northern European countries and among the early settlers of the northern United States, but not in the predominantly Catholic countries, such as Spain, Italy, and France, or in the American South during the time of slavery. Writing in the early twentieth century, Max Weber observed, "The Protestant prefers to eat well, the Catholic, to sleep undisturbed."[50]

We have been looking at how religion shaped the moral value of work. The ancients saw work as a necessity and a curse. The medieval Catholic Church bestowed on work a simple dignity; the Renaissance humanist gave it glamour. But the Protestants endowed work with the quest for meaning, identity, and signs of salvation. The notion of work as something beyond mere labor, as work-plus, indeed as a calling, highlighted its personal and existential qualities. Work became a kind of prayer. More than a means of living, it became a purpose for living. Work went from curse to calling, and as we will see in the next chapter, it took on a number of other positive personal and social connotations.

4.

Romantic Visions

When you detach the work ethic from its religious moorings, there isn't much to recommend it. Why should people work hard, if there is nothing in it for them? Why is it that the man who works at a job that pays subsistence wages is considered good and not stupid? It's possible to believe abstractly in the work ethic, but if one was to live by it, the ethic had to make sense. For most people, work had to promise something a little closer to home than heaven.

The work ethic that we have inherited is not a single concept but an amalgamation of three ideas. The first and oldest is a principle of fairness and social obligation. Able-bodied people have a duty to provide for themselves. This idea is not unique to the Protestants but, as we have seen, is found in Hesiod and Aesop as well as the Bible. Nor is the second element, the idea that one should perform one's work to the best of his or her abilities, which we have seen in the Benedictines, and which has probably existed among craftspeople throughout the ages. The third idea, distinctive to Luther and Calvin, is that work *itself* has moral and spiritual value and everyone is called by God to some kind of work in life. In this view, work is good no matter how menial and regardless of pay. A hardworking person is an admirable and disciplined person—"He's a good man, he works hard." Out of these three basic ideas about fairness, personal excellence, and personal goodness grew romantic ideas of work as something that went beyond drudgery and carried with it the hope that through work one could find happiness.

Work on a Desert Island

Daniel Defoe's novel *Robinson Crusoe* is about the adventures of a man in search of his vocation. He tries out many jobs but isn't satisfied. At the beginning of the novel Crusoe says, "Being the third son of the family and not bred with any trade, my head began to be filled very early with rambling thoughts."[1] If the young Crusoe obeys his father he will receive an inheritance and will never have to be "embarrassed with the labors of the hands or head." Young Crusoe rejects his father's view of a comfortable life and heads off to sea in search of his calling. When his ship wrecks, he is stranded on a desert island. A large part of the story is Crusoe's journal of his life on the desert island. He is eventually rescued from the island and returns home, but then he heads out to sea again.

Crusoe's conflicting attitudes toward work reflect romantic and pragmatic views of work as a calling. He is torn between adventuring and creating, between the desire to make profits and the desire to make a life.[2] In the beginning of the novel, Crusoe tells us how he became a wealthy planter in Brazil. However, he complains, "I was gotten into employment quite remote to my genius and directly contrary to the life I delighted in, and for which I forsook my father's house."[3] Crusoe doesn't know what his "genius" is, but throughout the story we see that it is work itself, not the wealth it brings, that makes him happy. By "genius" Crusoe means his calling or what it is that he is supposed to be doing. However, the tension in the book is between the personal questions "What am I good at and what do I want to do?" and the Protestant question "What does God want me to do?" The pride and enjoyment that Crusoe takes in his work are reflected in the way he talks about his experiences on the island. Crusoe describes in loving detail not how he made clothes, tables, and pots, but the human capacities that went into making these things. He describes table-building this way:

So I went to work; here I must observe, that as reason is the substance
and original of the mathematics, so by stating and squaring everything by reason, and by making the most rational judgment of things,
every man may be the master of every mechanic art.[4]

In his journal Crusoe documents and celebrates the work that he does
every day. All of his exertions are utilitarian because they serve to make
his life more comfortable. However, his greatest joy is in his ability to
make things. Crusoe creates his paradise, he glories in his work, but he
still does not discover himself. Despite meeting up with a companion
named Friday, Crusoe is compelled by inner loneliness and restlessness
to leave the island.

Published in 1719, *Robinson Crusoe* became a model for the modern economic man found in John Locke and Adam Smith—a conceptu-
alization that was later criticized by Karl Marx. Alone and providing for
his own needs, Crusoe makes choices based on self-interest and utility.
He not only embodies all the virtues of the Protestant work ethic but
also personifies the belief that through work and self-sufficiency one
discovers happiness. Today we share in Crusoe's legacy. The "rational
economic man" is an island; he quests for meaningful work and he is
forever unfulfilled and in need of something more. Crusoe has a practical and romantic vision of what he will do and what he will be. For
Crusoe, work promises to supply the means to life *and* the meaning of
his life.

Work, Wealth, and Civic Virtue

The Protestant work ethic was brought to America by the Puritan ministers who helped settle the Northern states. It was a stark and ascetic
view of work and wealth as homage to God. In the eighteenth century
Benjamin Franklin remade the work ethic by tempering the Protestant
view with enlightenment ideals. He believed that people should strive
for wealth so that they can use it in a humane way to help society.
Anticipating Adam Smith's articulation of enlightened self-interest in
The Wealth of Nations, Franklin argued that wealth was morally justified because it benefited society *and* would bring happiness to individuals. He emphasized work as a social obligation, not a religious duty.

Max Weber thought Franklin took the *ethics* out of the work ethic.

The ethics of Franklin's work ethic rested on two moral concepts. The first was utilitarian: personal goodness is based not only on individual action but on the way in which the individual uses the fruits of his or her labor to benefit society. The second moral precept was that usefulness is an end in itself. Weber claims that for Franklin the appearance of being honest, not honesty, is adequate behavior.[5] According to Weber, the pursuit of wealth without moral underpinnings is often frivolous and empty:

> the idea of duty in one's calling prowls about in our lives like the ghost of dead religious beliefs. . . .
> In the field of its highest development, in the United States, the pursuit of wealth, stripped of its religious and ethical meaning, tends to become associated with purely mundane passions, which often actually give it the character of sport.[6]

Franklin secularized the work ethic, but he didn't ignore traditional Christian virtues. The way to wealth for Franklin was through prudence, industry, and frugality. Good character was necessary for success. In his autobiography Franklin lists eleven virtues that one needs for success: temperance, silence, order, resolution, sincerity, justice, moderation, cleanliness, tranquility, chastity, and humility. He preached a worldly asceticism, but he also believed that money was a means to an end—and that end was the freedom to enjoy life.[7]

Franklin published his ideas about work, thrift, and diligence in *Poor Richard's Almanack* under the pen name Richard Saunders in 1732, and later repackaged the maxims from the *Almanack* into *The Way to Wealth*. His popular *Almanack* was filled with short, pithy, easy-to-remember sayings like "Early to bed and early to rise makes a man healthy, wealthy, and wise." Franklin's maxims were repeated for generations and reiterated in children's stories.

Spreading the Word

Since the work ethic of Calvin and Franklin did not come naturally to most people, it was conveyed to children through stories. The dual message of hard work and usefulness appeared in textbooks, magazines, and religious sermons. Between 1836 and 1900 at least half of all

Americans had read McGuffey's "Eclectic Readers." These readers rein-
forced the theology of John Calvin and glorified the ethic of hard labor,
industry, and thrift. They expressed the idea that God made some people rich so that they could help the poor. The stories in the readers
showed how children with the right character got ahead, while the
morally weak and undisciplined went away empty-handed. In "Waste
Not, Want Not," written by the Anglo-Irish writer Maria Edgeworth in
the late 1790s, the main character, Ben, saves a piece of whipcord that
his brother John had thrown away. The two boys are in an archery contest. John's bow breaks during the contest and he goes down in defeat.
Ben's bow also breaks, but he is able to fix it with the whipcord that he
had prudently saved, and he wins. At the end of the story John issues
the moral, for anyone who missed it: "I'll take care of how I waste any
thing hereafter."[8]

Jacob Abbott, a minister and educator from Maine, started writing
stories about a character named Rollo in 1832. His stories were clear
articulations of the Protestant work ethic, set in traditional patriarchal
families. For example, in "Rollo at Work" Rollo's father makes him
spend an hour sorting nails. When Rollo complains that the task is very
dull, his father tells him, "You should have the power of confining
yourself steadily and patiently to a single employment." Boys "mistakenly expect work to be as much fun as play." According to Rollo's father, a real man knows that work "requires exertions and self-denial"
and it "will be laborious and tiresome."[9]

By the mid-1850s, at the onset of industrialization, children's stories began to change. Authors such as Edgeworth and Abbott showed
children how to grow up on a farm or in a village, but subsequent writers were unsure about how to convey the moral value of work to those
who lived in the emerging industrial cities. Perhaps because writers
didn't know what to do in this new setting, they turned to adventure.
One of the most popular writers of the late nineteenth century was
William Taylor Adams, a school principal from Massachusetts who
wrote under the pen name Oliver Optic. Optic wrote stories about or-
phans and widows' sons who were forced to take on the role of men.
The hero of his story "Work and Win" is a vagabond orphan who is
bold, daring, and impulsive but doesn't like to do boring work. After a
series of harrowing adventures that include rescuing drowning maid-
ens from a sea of sharks and being shipwrecked on a Pacific island, he
emerges a new man. By the end of the book, he becomes industrious,
useful, and reliable.[10]

The advent of the dime novel in the mid-1800s forced Oliver Optic and a number of children's writers like him to change their tune. Overly moralistic tales would not sell as well as the full-blown adventure stories that Optic had begun writing about crime, lost relatives, and Indian fighting. In the preface to *In School and Out; or, The Conquest of Richard Grant,* Optic is almost apologetic about the "many exciting incidents" in the story. However, he assures the reader that these adventures are merely the canvas for the real story, which is the moral reformation of the main character. Optic's new heroes were still moral models, but their code had shifted from diligent work to deeds of daring, from personal restraint to impulse. Instead of preaching to young people, writers like Optic tried to capture their hearts though a good story. A master of this genre, Optic served as a mentor to Horatio Alger, Jr.

Alger was an odd but in some ways perfect person to have his name become synonymous with the American success of the self-made man. The son of a Unitarian minister, Alger graduated eighth in his class from Harvard College in 1852. He tried to make a living as a writer but didn't earn enough, so he became a minister. In 1866 he was accused of, and didn't deny, performing "unnatural acts" with young boys. With his father's help, he escaped prosecution after promising the judge that he would never seek a ministry again. Alger then moved from Brewster, Massachusetts, to New York City, where in 1868 he wrote his first and only best-seller, *Ragged Dick,* the story of a shoeshine boy who became a "handsome young gentleman."

Alger, like many of his contemporaries, wrote basically the same story over and over about the poor boy making good. His heroes were honest, industrious, kind to children and the elderly, and always attractive boys. They did not aspire to great wealth. All they wanted out of life was a steady job, an adequate income, and respectability. They wanted a chance to wash their faces every day, save money, and plan for the future. In Alger's novels there was plenty of room for his characters to improve themselves as office boys and clerks.

Alger did not lionize the industrialist. His stories argued for "judicious economy." Some of Alger's characters used the interest from their savings accounts to help the less fortunate, hence transforming the act of investment into a moral act. In Alger's world, money could enhance moral respectability.[11] But perhaps the most enduring message in Alger is his articulation of the work ethic as the American dream: With virtue and hard work, anyone can make it.

Neither the Protestant reformers' spiritual glorification of work nor Franklin's catchy sayings about work and civic virtue fully account for why the work ethic became a compelling part of American life. Land, natural resources, political and social equality, and mobility made America a land of possibilities. Crusoe had to go to sea to find himself. America was the place where one could make and remake himself. In Alger's stories every good boy's dreams came true, even if this was not always the case in real life.

The Noble Businessman

These moralistic children's tales about work never really took hold in the South. There, one aspired to own land and slaves. Blood was more important than money. Individual hard work, with its moral value, just wasn't part of the picture for those who owned slaves. Historian C. Vann Woodward points out that after the Civil War there was a concerted effort by Northern businessmen to depict the glamorous side of business so that people in the South would want to emulate them. Writers and journalists portrayed businessmen as hardworking exemplars of success and progress.

William Makepeace Thayer specialized in biographies about chief executive officers, showing how character formed early in life is important to success. Like his contemporary Alger, he wrote success stories, but he used biography instead of fiction. In his "From the Log Cabin to the White House" series, he followed four presidents from their humble beginnings to the executive mansion. Washington went from the farmhouse to the White House, Garfield hailed from the log cabin, Lincoln from the pioneer house, and Grant from the tannery. The fifth book in the series was about Ben Franklin. Since Franklin never got to the White House, Thayer called this biography "From Boyhood to Manhood."

Thayer went on to write biographies of business leaders. His *Turning Points in Successful Careers* consisted of fifty biographical sketches. These sketches focused on incidents that had transformed the subjects from mediocre people to successful ones. For the wealthy Philadelphia editor George William Childs, the turning point was when he left the navy to work in a bookstore; for Leland Stanford, it was when his law library burned down and he got started in the railway business; for Horace Brigham Claflin, it was when he quit studying Latin and Greek in college and became manager of the largest dry goods house in the world. In Thayer's biographies, as in Alger's stories, luck and coincidence move the plot along. But Thayer denied that luck played a part in people's lives. His biographies were clearly aligned with the Protestant ethic; incidents such as fires and changes of heart came from divine providence, not luck. Thayer told his readers, "Man deviseth his own way, but the Lord directeth his steps."[12]

As the number of business journalists increased, many of them set out to lionize the businessman. The Scottish immigrant Bertie Charles (B. C.) Forbes later raised the celebration of the virtuous businessman to an enduring art form, which carried on Franklin's message that work, virtue, and wealth lead to happiness and social benefit. When he started *Forbes* magazine in 1916, he described it as "a publication that would strive to inject more humanity, more joy, and more satisfaction into business and into life in general."[13] Forbes even offered readers his own Franklin-like aphorisms, such as "ASPIRE—then perspire," "TAKE the broom and sweep out gloom," PUT the I CAN in American," and "ANOTHER way of spelling success:—s-w-e-a-t."[14]

The mythology of the heroic businessman remains popular, even though not all businesspeople are philanthropists or morally virtuous or believe in enlightened self-interest. Some people simply enjoy reading about how someone became rich. Today the romantic vision of the business hero is more likely to be in the first person than the third person. (Consider, for example, the popularity of autobiographies by Lee Iacocca, Donald Trump, Bill Gates, and Sam Walton in recent years.)

Acres of Diamonds

Along with Alger and Thayer, Russell Herman Conwell was arguably one of the most influential apostles of the work ethic and the American dream in the late nineteenth and early twentieth centuries. Conwell, a Yale graduate, was a Baptist preacher who founded Temple University in Philadelphia in 1888. He was one of a long line of what people today call motivational speakers. He delivered his famous "Acres of Diamonds" speech some six thousand times. Fees from this speech netted him over a million dollars, which he donated to a charity for poor boys. His famous speech was about a man who sold his land to search for diamonds, only to discover that there were diamonds in his own backyard. Work was part of a quest in life, but in America you didn't have to travel far. His advice was simple: "Keep clean, fight hard, pick your openings judiciously, and have your eyes forever fixed on the heights toward which you are headed."

Reverend Conwell mixed moral advice with sound business advice. The best way to make a fortune, he said, is to find out what people need and then fill that need. He cautioned: Above all don't go into politics. He said, "Greatness consists not in the holding of some future office, but really consists in doing great deeds with little means."[15] Conwell frequently said that it was better to be the son of a poor man than a rich one, because the poor boy had more opportunities to develop moral fiber on the road to success.

The eighteenth- and nineteenth-century advocates of the work ethic preached that strong moral character was the key to wealth. In the early twentieth century the emphasis would shift to personality, as in Dale Carnegie's 1936 classic *How to Win Friends and Influence People.* Psychology, not morality, became the key to success.

Business Is Best

Many of the success writers and preachers and even some politicians of the nineteenth century disparaged political service, while glorifying business. For example prior to becoming president, James A. Garfield told the 1869 graduating class of a Washington business college that colleges that taught classical learning were an "absolute" failure in preparing young people for business life. He admonished students never to work for the government civil service. After a rousing speech on how to be successful, Garfield drove home the foundational belief of the American dream, equality: "Even the lowest is free to mingle with all others, and may shine at last on the crest of the highest wave. This is the glory of our country. . . ."[16]

Arguably, in no other culture in history were business and work held in such high esteem. Europeans who visited America in the nineteenth century were amazed by American energy and industry. In particular, they were surprised to learn that there was no leisure class. The Viennese immigrant Francis Grund noted that business was the chief source of pleasure and amusement in America. He commented:

Active occupation is not only the principal source of their happiness and the foundation of their national greatness, but they are absolutely wretched without it, and instead of the *"dolce far niente,"* [the sweetness of idleness] know but the *horrors* of idleness. Business is the very soul of an American: he pursues it, not as a means of procuring for himself and his family the necessary comforts of life, but as the fountain of all human felicity . . . it is as if all America were but one gigantic workshop, over the entrance of which there is a blazing inscription, *"No admission here, except on business."*[17]

We Are More Than Our Work

In the past people identified with and even named themselves after their work. However, two new visions of work and personal identity evolved from the Protestant work ethic: through work you could either find yourself or make yourself. Not everyone believed this, especially not slaves and Southerners. This was fine for Robinson Crusoe or Ragged Dick, and maybe for the farmer, professional, craftsman, or small-business owner, but not for the scores of wage earners who flocked into cities to work in the new factories of the industrial era. It was not at all clear that good character and hard work would lead to wealth in this line of work.

There are two kinds of stories about work after industrialization. The first is the enlightenment tale: science and knowledge would lead to progress. Prior to industrialization, work was harsh and physically degrading toil. Mechanization of labor led to tremendous material progress in the modern world. Work became cleaner, safer, easier, and less physically exhausting. The second story, offered by critics such as Jean-Jacques Rousseau, was that work had fallen from some state of grace, where autonomous craftsmen used their skill to produce useful and beautiful things and apple-cheeked farmers led quiet, happy lives planting and harvesting lush green fields.

Writing in the eighteenth century, Rousseau foresaw some of the problems with work in an industrial society where the majority of people worked for wages. Rousseau believed that the human race had fallen from a golden age when they discovered that they could get advantage from the work of others. He said the primitive man is spontaneous and naturally wants to work and be creative. When people are made to work for someone else, they lose their creativity and their desire to work. They are no longer free citizens. In *Emile,* Rousseau emphasized craftsmanship as the best way of life. His romantic ideal was a man who worked like a peasant and thought like a philosopher, dwelling on truth and beauty while shoeing horses—a pastoral Renaissance man.

Rousseau's critique influenced nineteenth-century critics of work like Karl Marx and the British designer and social critic William Morris. While it was clear that work had long been considered part of a person's identity, it was not clear that this was good for the worker in a world where organizations narrowly defined jobs.

Marx believed that work should be regarded as a human need that could be enjoyed for its own sake, because the very essence of man was that he was a producer of goods. According to Marx, private property and capitalist production alienated people from the creative and social rewards of work and the pleasure of using the goods that they produced. Marx saw the dangers of being identified with work, especially when people had little choice in their occupation and did a very specialized job. His ideal was a world where people could earn a living and still be free enough to become accomplished producers in many areas. Echoing Rousseau, Marx says this kind of world would

> make it possible for me to do one thing today and another tomorrow, to hunt in the morning, fish in the afternoon, rear cattle in the evening, criticize after dinner, just as I have in mind, without becoming hunter, fisherman, cowherd, or critic.[18]

It's not clear whether these people would be amateurs who just dabble, or Renaissance men and women who pursue a variety of interests with equal enthusiasm and desire for excellence. The main point is that people not be locked into the identity of one occupation. If we take Marx's views of work and identity seriously and to the limit, there are no painters, only people who paint. At first blush Marx's idea looks like pure dilettantism. It is, if you consider that the word *dilettante* comes from the Latin word for "to delight." Dilettantes, then, are people who do things because they take delight in them. Would Marx's ideal world be one where there are no singular experts? Would there be no doctors, only those who heal? Marx's point is this: If you are employed as a cleaning woman, but you are also head of your church group and a sculptor, would you like it if people identified you mainly by your paid employment? Think about the struggle of the proverbial "actor" who is a waiter—or perhaps more accurately, in many cases, the waiter who is an actor. Marx realized that the stories of people's lives contain more information about their work than the chapters on their paid employment.

Worthy Work

William Morris was a latter-day Renaissance man and, from the descriptions of his contemporaries, a workaholic. He excelled as a designer, craftsman, poet, and translator. In 1884 Morris founded the Socialist League and began to attack industrialists and the capitalist system of labor. While he shared Marx's ideas on socialism, Morris was also concerned with the aesthetic values of work itself. In a letter, Morris wrote:

> Over and over again I have asked myself why should not my lot be the common lot. . . . Indeed I have been ashamed when I have thought of the contrast between my happy working hours and the unpraised, unrewarded, monotonous drudgery that most men are condemned to.[19]

Appalled by the thick smoke and ugly buildings of industrial England, Morris made proposals for beautifying the workplace with gardens. He also railed against the ugliness of manufactured goods. He thought machines should save labor but not take over the "thinking hand." He believed that the aesthetic values of work itself come from the satisfaction of producing goods that are not only useful but beautiful.

Morris was a part of the Romantic movement in England. While that movement idealized the Middle Ages, in his own designs Morris did not aim to copy Gothic architecture but rather to copy the way the builder and craftsman handled tools and materials in the Middle Ages. Morris believed that work could become beautiful if you liberated the worker from stultifying routine and allowed him or her to use the natural properties of the materials to produce beauty without the intervention of art.[20] Perhaps one of Morris's most lasting legacies was the Arts and Crafts movement, which in the late nineteenth century reinstated craftsmanship in home furnishings during a time of mass production.

One of Morris's most interesting insights into the meaning of work was his description of "worthwhile work." Morris said that work can be either a "lightening to life" or a "burden to life." The difference lies in the fact that in the first case there is hope while in the second there is none. According to Morris, it is hope that makes people want to work and makes work worth doing. He wrote: "Worthy work carries with it the *hope* of pleasure in rest, the *hope* of pleasure in our using what it makes, and the *hope* of pleasure in our daily creative skill."[21]

The concept of hope is a useful one for understanding the necessary conditions for a good job. In the Protestant work ethic, work held out the hope of salvation, but it didn't matter what kind of work it was. Morris's characterization of worthy work is about a certain kind of work. The idea of worthy work is subjective in the sense that hope is a potential that people have, but may or may not actualize. Not everyone gets to use the object that they make. But Morris's point is that if they did, they would take pleasure in using or owning it. Also, people all have different hopes for what they will do with their leisure and different creative skills. Worthy work is objective, in the sense that most people would like to have jobs that offer adequate leisure, useful high-quality products, and the opportunity to exercise skill.

In the industrial England of Morris's day, not all jobs had these qualities or could be made to have these qualities. Morris knew that unpleasant work had to be done, but he believed that even such jobs should be made more humane. He wrote: "If work cannot be made less repulsive by either shortening it, making it intermittent, or having a special usefulness to the man who freely performs it, then the product of such work is not worth the price."[22] So even though some workers may have to do a terrible job, the job itself should be structured so that they do not have to lead a terrible life because of their job.

The Ideals of Craft and Profession

When it comes to the actual work that a person does, there are two ideal types: that of the craftsperson, or those who work with their hands, and that of the professional, or those who work with their minds. Through most of history the artist and the craftsperson were the same. The distinction between an artist and a craftsperson is fairly modern.[23] The etymology of the word *craft* is uncertain, but *The Oxford*

English Dictionary suggests that the word itself came from the word for strong. The original meaning it lists for *craft* is "strength, force, power, virtue." The second meaning is "intellectual power, skill, art." Some of the oldest crafts were painting, sculpture, and pottery. Craftspeople have always been admired because they create things that are beautiful and functional. What they create is a direct reflection of what they are—their skill and intellect, but perhaps most important, their personal drive for excellence. When we admire the craftsmanship of an object, we admire the knowledge, skill, and commitment of the maker. Craftspeople learn their trade and the quality standards of their trade from one another, and because of this, they share a common bond.

The earliest craft guilds appeared in Europe around 1100. Guilds are one of the most important developments in the history of work, because they gave workers greater control over their lives. The guild's main function was protection of the trade, protection of its members, and protection of the customer. Guilds offered independence from town authorities and the Church. They were mutual aid societies that offered a kind of workmen's compensation and buried their members. For example, the Braeler's Decree stated; "If any serving man who has behaved himself well and loyally towards his masters, shall fall ill . . . he shall be cared for by the good folks of the trade until he have recovered."[24] Guilds also held craftspeople to moral and professional standards. The "trademark" was an assurance that the product had been made properly according to the standards of the guild.

The word *professional* comes from *profess,* which was originally used to mean a public declaration made by someone entering a religious order. It later came to mean a business or occupation about which one makes a solemn public promise or vow. In the Middle Ages the only professions were those of the cleric who was usually also a scholar, a lawyer, and a doctor. At the core of professions were—and are—three criteria. The first was that all professions require formal technical training and some institutional certification process to validate the training—doctors, lawyers, and clergy all have to go to a university. The most important part of this training is that it requires mastery of the cultural traditions of the profession. Doctors learn the importance of doing no harm. Lawyers learn the responsibilities of defending one's client. The second criterion was that skills have to be developed for use in the profession. Lawyers learn how to prepare cases, doctors learn how to do medical procedures and so on. Third was that a profession must have some institutional means of making sure that the profession is put to socially responsible uses—and is so organized to ensure the ethical conduct of its members. Such is the purpose of bar associations and the American Medical Association.[25]

Perhaps the most distinctive elements of a profession are autonomy at work and disinterested service. Sociologist Talcott Parsons argued that a business manager could never be a professional. He wrote: "The business man has been thought of as egoistically pursuing his own self-interest regardless of the interests of others, while the professional man was altruistically serving the interests of others, regardless of his own."[26] This was written fifty years ago. Today many business managers would disagree with this statement. They want to be like professionals, and then try to become so by focusing more on the integrity of the product or service they deliver than solely on profits. This is difficult in business because one ultimately still has to think about profits.

Ideally, professionals are not paid for their work. As we said earlier, a professional doesn't "do jobs" but is "subsidized" by pay to carry out his or her work.[27] This idea may cause some readers to laugh, given the number of scandals concerning unethical and greedy doctors and lawyers and reports of plagiarism and falsification of research among scholars. The reason the public is so outraged over the unethical behavior of professionals is that professionals still are regarded as having an implicit "public vow to society."

Problems arise when professionals act or are made to act like business people. We consider it unsavory for a doctor to let self-interest or economic interests override the interests of the client. In his book *Death of the Guilds,* Elliott Krause argues that professions have become nothing more than a way to make a living. As a result of this they have not only lost the privileges of professions, but they have also abandoned the moral virtues that were just as much a part of crafts and professions as skill.[28]

We compliment people for acting like professionals even when they don't belong to a profession. When we say, "She is a real professional," we mean she does the job well and with integrity. People in all sorts of occupations either are or want to be considered professionals. By "professing" or taking the public vow of a profession, public relations people, nurses, administrators, investment consultants, and real estate agents make a statement about their colleagues' integrity and expertise. They do it to court public trust and respect.

The less noble aspect of professionals and craftsmen is that their complicated procedures for training and entry serve to give their group a monopoly on certain kinds of knowledge. In the Middle Ages the masons were intent on keeping their building techniques secret, and guilds eventually became town monopolies. One way that professionals in law, medicine, and the academic disciplines remain exclusive is by creating their own language (or using a dead one, like Latin). For example, if you put legal documents into ordinary language, you might eliminate the need to hire a lawyer in some cases. Academics use specialized language to protect and reinforce membership in their disciplines. Often, academic writing and research about topics of interest to the public can be understood only by other scholars—and at times not even by them. In some universities there are informal sanctions for the academic who dares to write for wide audience. Colleagues who write prose that even "the public" understands can't be very bright.

Craftspeople and professionals have much in common as ideal types of workers. First, they do not make sharp distinctions between work and leisure—both reflect a continuity of life and work. Second, their work is a direct extension of what they are. They are what they do and are proud of it. Third, because of their commitment to their work, they are often respected by others in society. Fourth, and most important, both are independent. No one tells them what to do when they are engaged in doing the work at hand.

In short, the romantic vision of work that we get from the professional or craftsperson encompasses autonomy, creativity, status, respect for individual skill, disinterested service to others, and freedom from the constraints of managerial control. Professionals and craftspeople have a desirable identity. This is not to say that everyone wants to be a craftsman or professional, or that all craftsmen and professionals fit this description. What I am saying is that these two models have usually been recognized as the best kinds of work.

The Work Ethic Revisited

One curious thing about the work ethic is that members of almost every generation think that the next generation does not want to work as hard as they do. This revelation usually strikes people about the time that they reach middle age. If each generation were right, then the work ethic would have died out a long time ago. The forty- and fifty-year-olds who run business and government today were some of the long-haired hippies of the late 1960s and the 1970s. Back then, few parents would have guessed that their longhaired son and miniskirted daughter would end up working longer hours than they did. Perhaps the reason we worry so much about losing the work ethic is that most people never really embraced it in Luther's or Franklin's moralistic form. Yet the idea of the work ethic still exists in a secularized ideal. Even though many don't live by it or think it makes sense, most Americans know that they are *supposed* to work hard and do their best regardless of pay.

Our enthusiasm for work depends on what we do and what we aspire to be or to have. Morris was right that work should give us hope, but we also need to have some hope or belief in the future in order to want to work. For the slave and the serf and those who are desperately poor, uneducated, and powerless, the work ethic may never have made sense, and this leads us to the ultimately romantic vision behind work and the work ethic. When Luther and Franklin thought about work, they thought about the small farmer, shopkeeper, or craftsman. When people around the water cooler today fantasize about another job, they rarely fantasize about working for someone else. They fantasize about owning a small vineyard, opening a shop, working as an independent consultant, or starting a private practice. Everyone has his or her own dream, whether it's making a living as a jazz musician or setting off on a quest of discovery like Robinson Crusoe.

The equation of hard work and a better life is more difficult to see when we work for other people, because in doing so we give up control of what we do. Here Rousseau was right when he noticed that the problems with work started when people realized that they could take advantage of another's labor. The struggle for freedom and power or control has long been the struggle between masters and slaves, lords and serfs, and employers and employees. It is the central problem of work. Not all romantic visions of work are fantasy; however, the ability to reap the personal, moral, social, and material benefits that work offers depends as much on where, for whom, and under what conditions people work as it does on what they actually do. That is why the next four chapters examine the problems of working for others.

PART TWO

WORKING
FOR OTHERS

5.

Work and Freedom

In America people prefer to be employers, not employees. The long-treasured ideal of work is that of the independent farmer, businessperson, craftsperson, professional, or entrepreneur. Not many people live out this dream. Most Americans are employees. They do not have the means or wherewithal to set out on their own, but few would deny that the idea is attractive. Cultural values such as independence, freedom, and equality make the idea of working for others almost "un-American." This does not mean that Americans don't like to help each other; they just like to do so on their own terms. It is perhaps because of this fierce independence that work in America evolved into arrangements that are antithetical to its democratic ideals. Most workers leave their constitutional rights in the parking lot or on the bus when they go to work.[1] While employers don't explicitly prohibit these rights, when at work it is usually unwise to exercise rights such as freedom of assembly, freedom of speech, or the right to bear arms. In America the rights of those who make money take precedence over the rights of those who earn it.

Why is it that the most democratic nation in the world does not have the most democratic workplaces in the world? Perhaps the answer to this question lies in national characteristics. You need a strong hand to manage fiercely independent people. A still better reason why America didn't develop democratic workplaces lies in the American dream. America was and is still perceived as a land of opportunity. Settlers and immigrants came here, lured by the promise of land and a better life. Even today, people from Mexico, Haiti, Cuba, and Cambodia risk their lives to get to America. They are still willing to suffer inhuman working conditions because of the dream. In the early 1900s an immigrant factory worker could work sixty hours a week and hope for an upwardly mobile life, if not for himself, then for his children. This is historically unique. Throughout time the poor have worked hard all their lives and, for the most part, stayed poor. When work promises to pay off big, in terms of land, home ownership, and higher education, people pay less attention to power and freedom in the workplace and more attention to power and freedom in the marketplace.

Power is a word unsaid—or only occasionally whispered—among the managerial ranks. Nonetheless, managers have power over the economic well-being of employees. Elevation to a managerial position rewards a person by conferring not only a higher status and, usually, higher pay, but also more power. The power of a manager's position comes either from his or her own freedom *from* the oversight of other people or from his or her power *over* other employees. The supervisor always has direct face-to-face power over people, whereas the high-level manager sometimes disappears into the background, out of sight of the people he or she ostensibly manages. In either case, power and freedom are prized possessions in the workplace. The manager is free from certain constraints, although he or she takes on new responsibilities. When power over other people is awarded as a prize, it is often tempting to abuse that power. As Rousseau noted, "It is better to award people with honors than with privileges."[2] Today businesses frequently reward the best engineers, teachers, or account executives with managerial or administrative positions. Some of these people don't make good managers, but few turn down the prizes: more money, power, status, and freedom.

The meaning of work done for a wage is often shaped by the relationship between employers and employees. The relationship is usually one of unequal power, and this causes problems for both sides. Employers or managers have always faced the temptation of forcing their will on employees. Employees throughout the ages have struggled to maintain their personal autonomy and dignity at work. The principle of freedom is at the heart of this relationship and is fundamental to how we think about work—freedom *to* work, freedom *at* work, and freedom *from* work.

Slavery

It may seem melodramatic to start a discussion of freedom with slavery. Yet slavery is the oldest and most certain way to get people to work. *Slavery* is a pejorative for *work*—it signifies human degradation, work at its worst. Even today workers often say, "He treats me like a slave," or "I'm not her slave," or "He's a real slave driver." Slavery represents a repulsive but seductive managerial ideal: total ownership and control of the worker. We associate work with necessity. Slavery represents the most extreme form of necessity. Most people work "for a living"; the slave works to stay alive.

Aristotle noted that some people have slavish personalities and are meant to be ruled. These are people who don't want to make choices and do want to be bossed around. Others become slaves because of their circumstances.[3] They were captured in a war, or sold into slavery, or born to slaves. While Aristotle approved of slavery, he wrote that slavery makes people less than human because they are unable to exercise the capacities that make humans distinct from brute beasts, such as the ability to make choices, deliberate, and plan for the future.[4] Slaves, he wrote, have no share in happiness because they have no control over their lives,[5] which consist mostly of work, punishment, and food. Despite his chilling definition of a slave, Aristotle saw that the most effective way to motivate slaves is to offer them freedom as a prize sometime in the future.[6] Once slaves gain their freedom, the ones who are slaves by circumstance, not personality, recover their ability to choose and plan for the future. Hence, according to Aristotle, they again become human.

One wonders what Aristotle would say about the last century of work. Some people have been denied the opportunity to exercise choice, deliberate, and foresee the future at work. They are not self-sufficient without a job. They can't choose when to go to work and what to do at work. They do not deliberate on management policies or decide how to do the task at hand. Worst of all, many still can't plan for the future because they don't know if they will have a job. Yet even under the most draconian working conditions, modern employees can't really be compared to slaves. Unlike the slave, they can always quit and they usually have to wait only eight hours to regain their freedom at the end of the day. But *can* they always quit? What if there are no other jobs in town, they can't move, and they have families to support? *Are* people always free from work when they leave the workplace? What about people who go home at the end of the day but are attached to the office by beepers, car phones, and faxes? Do service workers find it hard to stop their professional smiling or turn off their phone voices when they get home from work? Do some people feel more fully human or more themselves when they leave the office, shop, or factory?

Unfortunately, slavery is not altogether a thing of the past. Britain's Anti-Slavery Society, the United Nations Working Group on Slavery, and groups such as India's Bonded Liberation Front report that slavery still exists in Asia, Africa, and Latin America. These groups consider anyone a slave if the person is unable to withdraw his or her labor voluntarily. This includes bonded laborers who work for nothing to pay off moneylenders, serfs who cannot leave the agricultural estates where they work, and exploited children who are taken from their families or sold by their families and work for nothing.

On the Arabian peninsula chattel slavery was not officially abolished until the 1960s. In Sudan after independence slavery grew quickly as the result of civil war. In February 1988, you could buy a Dinka child in Sudan for $90. (That same year, in Bangkok, Thailand, you could buy a child for $130.) By 1999 the price for a Dinka child was down to $50, or the price of two goats.[7] Latin America has approximately eight million bonded laborers, India more than five million. This form of bondage often occurs when a person takes out a loan at a very high rate of interest. The person's labor is never enough to pay off the loan, so often children inherit their parents' debt.[8] A detailed study of India's Uttar Pradesh carpet belt in 1989 estimated that the area's fifty-five thousand looms employed more than a hundred thousand boys, many of whom were six years old. Owners bought outright about 15 percent of these boys.[9]

Slavery isn't confined within the borders of developing countries. A week before Christmas in 1997, police raided a slave auction in Milan. There they found women standing half-naked on auction blocks and selling for $500 to $1,000 each. The women had been abducted from countries in the former Soviet republics. They were being sold to brothel owners, who would then confiscate their passports and confine them to work in bars and brothels in Italy, Germany, Japan, and Israel.[10] Asian women have long been bought and sold in this way, as brothel workers. Like their Asian sisters, desperate and often naive young women from Russia, Latvia, and the Ukraine were seeking work. Since there were no jobs at home, they answered employment ads for models, secretaries, dancers, domestics, and waitresses overseas, only to find themselves sold and forced to work as prostitutes. Those who resisted were often beaten and raped, and were sometimes killed. The new white slave trade has grown rapidly in the past few years and is run mostly by Russian crime gangs. Yitzhak Tyler, chief of undercover police operations in Haifa, says a person can buy these women cheap and make a million dollars a year. "No taxes, no real overhead. It's a factory with slave labor. And we've got them all over Israel."[11]

Some observers and slave holders argue that slavery and child labor are inevitable elements of the turmoil of economic development. A better way to understand slavery is as the temptation of those who have economic power and other forms of dominance to force those in desperate need to work for them. Slavery brings out the worst in everyone. Fear and powerlessness compel the slave to work. For the master, the slave is, as the ancients put it, a "talking instrument" (*instrumentum vocale*) that the master uses to produce value. Total control over another person's life or economic well-being can be intoxicating, and few can handle this unbridled power without themselves becoming morally degraded. In 1829 a North Carolina judge named Thomas Ruffin expressed the need for total power of the master over the slave, echoing Aristotle's description of the slave. In his decision excusing a man who had intentionally wounded a slave, Ruffin wrote:

> With slavery . . . the end is the profit of the master, his security and the public safety; the subject, one doomed in his own person, and his posterity, to live without knowledge, and without the capacity to make anything his own, and to toil that another may reap his fruits. . . . Such services can only be expected from one who has no will of his own: who surrenders his will in implicit obedience in the consequence only of uncontrolled authority over the body. There is nothing else which can operate to produce the effect. The power of the master must be absolute, to render the submission of the slave perfect.[12]

One of Ruffin's major premises is that slaves have no reason to work, hence no inclination to work. That is why the *only* way to make them work is to take total control of their physical being. As we'll see later, assumptions about whether people naturally do or do not want to work affect how employers treat them.

Suffering and Redemption

The fantasy of working long hours at a job you hate so that you can start your own business is not new. Many of the first settlers in America sold their freedom and labored as indentured servants in hopes of owning their own land when they were free. In seventeenth-century America there were so many opportunities for skilled tradesmen and for land ownership that few people wanted to work for wages. Labor was one of the few resources from England for which the colonists willingly paid top price. Seventeenth-century shippers loaded their hulls with indentured servants, whom they regarded as a profitable commodity. Potentially profitable or not, it was not uncommon for one-third of the servants to perish before the ship arrived at an American port. Propaganda for the new world promised "bread and freedom" and characterized America as a place where hunting, fishing, and land were free.[13]

Despite these lofty promises, a majority of the early white settlers did not come over as free people. Wealthy landowners not only wanted cheap labor, they wanted to purchase labor for a one-time fee. This was not a country of equals. For the indentured servant, the social contract was actually a legal contract in which the employer had most of the power and rights. More than half of the early white settlers outside New England came to America as indentured servants or redemptioners. They had to work before they could gain their freedom. Employment was a temporary slavery that might eventually lead to freedom and opportunity.

The Virginia Company established the practice of indentured servitude as a way of supplying planters with labor. This was the only way that poor people could get to the colonies. Usually indentured servant contracts were from four to seven years, longer if the servant was a child. Servants worked for a master and the master fed, sheltered, and clothed the servants. After their contract was up, the servants were free. Maryland and Virginia offered fifty acres of land for every free man, indentured servant, or redemptioner. In practice, however, few of these people were ever able to prove their right to the fifty acres, and the land went to their masters. Of the five thousand servants who came to Virginia between 1670 and 1680, fewer than thirteen hundred ever got possession of their piece of the promised land.[14] If the servant ran away, there were strong penalties, such as beatings, extensions on the years that he or she had to serve, and in some cases death. Masters frequently overworked and misused indentured servants.

Redemptioners were mostly German and Swiss families who had only enough money to make the trip down the Rhine but not enough money left to pay for passage to America from Rotterdam. These people agreed to work to pay the shippers the balance of what they owed for passage to America. Unscrupulous Dutch shippers turned their passengers into a lucrative business. They would delay the journey and demand payment for their passengers' upkeep. Eventually most passengers would sell their belongings to pay the shippers and then, when they had nothing else to sell, they would sell their freedom. When the Dutch ships and their passengers landed in ports such as Philadelphia, only the passengers who had paid in full could disembark. The ones in debt had to stay on the ship until a friend or relative paid for them or until their service was purchased by someone. Their contracts varied in length depending on how much money they owed, but usually lasted three to six years.[15]

The German redemptioners did not make good servants. They had not planned to be servants when they left their country to come to America and they were not used to acting like servants. They made excellent colonists, however, because they were hardworking and usually came with their families.[16] Indentured servants, on the other hand, were a mixed bag. Some had fled England because they were poor; others were convicts, adventurers, people escaping religious persecution, or people who needed to get out of town fast. Unlike redemptioners, most indentured servants were unmarried when they came to the States.[17]

In his nonfiction book *Bound Over,* novelist John van der Zee draws colorful profiles of indentured servants. Included in their number are several prominent Americans who either had some association with indentured servants or were at one time indentured servants themselves. They include James Madison, Alexander Hamilton, Thomas Jefferson, Samuel Adams, and Benjamin Franklin. Describing the beginning of a voyage on the *London Packet,* van der Zee writes: "The resemblance to

enslavement began at least at [the ship's] embarkation, where both voluntary and involuntary emigrants were herded on board . . . and then
crammed below decks in unsanitary conditions with insufficient provisions.[18]

These were the conditions under which Tom Paine arrived in
America. Paine's experience as an indentured servant must have had
some impact on his passion for rights. In 1776, in the first of his *Crisis*
papers, Paine used familiar images to rally Americans: "These are the
times that try men's souls. . . . Britain, with an army to enforce her
tyranny has decided that she has a right (*not only* to TAX) but 'to BIND
us in ALL CASES WHATSOEVER,' and if being *bound in that manner* is
not slavery, then there is no such thing as slavery upon earth." The
British government sanctioned indentured servitude as a means of set-
tling the colonies. Private shipping companies, as noted, often made
more money selling labor than they did selling other goods. John van
der Zee argues that it was because of indentured servitude that writers
such as Samuel Adams, John Adams, James Otis, and Thomas Jefferson
frequently used words like *tyranny* and *slavery*.

While indentured servitude seems a practice of the past in America,
only a few years ago investigators uncovered a Thai employer using indentured servants in a sweatshop in Los Angeles. They found seventy-
four women from Thailand sewing clothes for seventeen hours a day.
The employer locked the women in an apartment and threatened to
beat them and harm their families if they tried to escape.[19] Just as it
took the early American settlers years to pay off their boat tickets to
America, the Thai women had to work up to seven years just to pay
their employer for their airfare. Some of the women in this case said
that they did not mind the way they were treated. All they cared about
was bringing money home to their families. There have been scandals
also in the treatment of au pairs in this country. Au pairs, young foreign
women who come to the States to live with a family and care for the
children, are sometimes mistreated, overworked, and underpaid. They
come willing to work cheap for the excitement of being in America—
sometimes only to find themselves not much better off than an indentured servant.

Slaves and Wage Slaves

Slavery and indentured servitude represent a desire to own rather than
rent the labor of others. White indentured servants came to America

before the massive influx of African slaves, which began around 1650 and escalated in the 1800s. By 1860 there were 4,442,000 African slaves in America. Southern planters liked African slaves much better than white servants because they considered them better adapted to the climate and more docile, but most important, the master owned them.[20] In some colonies runaway indentured servants were hanged, but hanging runaway slaves was considered wasteful because they had the value of capital.[21] The practice of indentured servitude faded but did not disappear as slavery became more prevalent and the country became more populous.

Slaveholders who defended slavery claimed that slavery in the South was no worse than the situation of wage slaves in the North. If anything, they contended, slaves were better off. Masters provided for their slaves and slaves worked shorter hours in the healthy outdoors, unlike the industrial hireling who worked inside a dark and dirty factory. The Northerners countered by pointing out that, unlike the slave, the wage earner was free to choose his occupation and he received cash compensation for his work. Horrible working conditions that included long hours in locked factories, child labor, unsafe machines, and unhealthy air tended to weaken some Northerners' moral arguments. Friedrich Engels compared British industrial workers to American slaves. He wrote: "They are worse than the Negroes in America, for they are more sharply watched, and yet it is demanded of them that they shall live like human beings, shall think and feel like men."[22] He argued that they are subject to the same, if not worse, indignities because of the degrading mode of production. So the argument against the Northern industrialist was that the *freedom* of the wage laborer did not make up for inhuman labor practices.

The Southern plantation owner and the Northern industrialist both shared a desire to dominate labor. Southerner William Gregg argued before the South Carolina legislature that slavery "gave capital a positive control over labor." He observed that in the North "labor and capital were assuming an antagonistic position."[23] Employees were willing to complain about working conditions and wages and they would do things like slow down work when they were unhappy. Gregg believed that the paternalistic relationship of the plantation owner and his slaves was superior to the wage incentives used in the North.

Historian Eugene Genovese argues that the Southern plantation owner had a greater interest in maintaining his lifestyle than in extracting huge profits from his slaves. His view is similar to Aristotle's distinction between household economy, production for self-sufficiency, and production for trade or profit. As was mentioned earlier, Aristotle noted that the wants of a household economy are finite, whereas the wants of the trade economy are infinite. Genovese maintains that although the slaveholder may have had greater control over his workers, he did not need to have the kind of control over production that the Northern capitalist needed in order to extract huge profits from his workers.[24]

Genovese's argument raises some questions. Slavery was the economic mainstay of the South, and by the nineteenth century plantation owners were well aware of the need for profit and investment and of the ways in which markets functioned. Slaveholders too needed to get the most out of their workers. So it is hard to believe that most behaved like Aristotelian householders, working *only* to keep their plantations going. They wanted profits, but the question is, Did they want or need less profit that the Northern industrialist?

Exploitation of Need

The fact that a person can choose his or her work does not necessarily justify ill-treatment by an employer. Part of the question is how many options a person really does have. A common myth is that all people really have a wide range of choices when it comes to making a living. The most important part of the American dream was that anyone could become anything. This was a land not only of opportunity but of options. But what about the destitute person whose only options are degrading ones?

The practice of self-enslavement had been around for a long time. It was common among the Germanic and Anglo-Saxon peoples in the Middle Ages. A person in need of support and/or protection would sell himself to another. This choice, though more or less freely made, was grounded in the same fears of starvation and violence found in other forms of slavery. Self-enslavement raises some interesting questions. Does a frightened and starving person *freely* choose to enter into a contract with someone who can provide him or her with food and safety? This is a question that lies beneath the way Americans think about employment.[25] Is any kind of work or any set of working conditions okay as long as a person freely chooses it? We may be quicker to defend people's right to do any job they want to do, but what about the right of employers to hire people for physically dangerous or personally demeaning work?

The philosopher John Locke offers some insight into these questions. The desire to be free from the yoke of one's master or employer is at the heart of some of our most treasured political ideals. In the first of his two treatises on government, Locke asks, "And how is it that property in land gives a man power over another?[26] Here Locke is disputing the natural right of kings over property and their subjects. Locke argues that people own the work of their hands and the labor of their bodies. He also notes that we have a moral obligation to help those in need and not take advantage of them: "Charity gives every man a title to so much out of another's plenty, as will keep him from extreme want, where he has no means to subsist otherwise; and a man can no more justly make use of another's necessity, to force him to become his vassal, by withholding that relief."[27]

Locke then goes on to raise one of the biggest tensions of the employer-employee relationship. He writes that "the subjugation of the needy does not begin with the consent of the Lord, but with the consent of the poor man, who preferred being his [another person's] subject to starving."[28] So, it's wrong to force a needy person to be your slave, but it's not wrong for the needy person to choose to be your slave or indentured servant. Are the two really that different? This is like the employer who says to a single mother of four, "If you don't like working here you are free to leave" or "If you didn't like the working conditions here, then you shouldn't have taken the job in the first place." A single mother who lives in a small town and has four children to support has the freedom to choose where to work, but little to chose from. When it comes to work, everyone has freedom of choice, but not everyone has viable options.

The actual difference between the indentured servant and the slave rests on his or her consent, even if a person really has only one viable choice. The indentured servant's bondage may be short-term and tempered by the voluntary contractual arrangements between the two people. The slave's bondage is involuntary and long-term, and there is no restriction on the master's power over the slave. In theory at least, it is not wrong to take away a person's freedom as long as he or she consents to the arrangement. This begs the larger question of exploitation. How much freedom and human dignity can an employer morally justify buying because someone is willing to sell it? The fourteen-year-old runaway on Sunset Boulevard in Los Angeles is willing to sell his body to buy the drugs he desperately needs. To what extent does he "freely" enter into the transaction? The answer to a question like this has always been hotly contested. Some would argue that the boy could choose otherwise, others that given his physical and psychological condition, he is not free.

Monkey Labor

It is easy to slip into a logic of exploitation that says that those in need who are exploited are better off than they would be if they weren't exploited. *The Economist* ran a tongue-in-cheek report on working monkeys that illustrates this logic. In southern Thailand several thousand monkeys are "employed" every year to pick the 1.5 million-ton crop of coconuts. Village families train the monkeys and rent them out to plantation owners. The monkeys "earn" about twelve dollars per month in "monkey wages" of eggs, rice, and fruit from the plantation owner. Working monkeys are given names; they are groomed, bathed, and fed three times a day. Sometimes their owners even give them a ride to work, on the back of their motor scooters. When a monkey is ill, it gets the day off. When it is too old to work, it "retires," either back into the wild or as a family pet. The downside of the monkeys' work is that they are kept on chains and not allowed to breed at will. However, the article points out, this practice of "employment" keeps some species such as the crab-eating macaque from becoming extinct because their habitat is being destroyed by humans.[29]

There is a striking parallel between this case and the way that colonists—and some people today—have justified their treatment of indigenous or tribal people in Africa, the Americas, and Australia. They would argue that although the farmers take away the monkeys' freedom, the monkeys are "better off" than they would be on their own in the wild, especially since their habitat has been largely taken over by the farmers. We don't know what the monkeys think. Would they prefer to give up their monkey wages, their names, their daily baths and motor scooter rides to take their chances in the wild? The justification for this arrangement is simple. It's okay for farmers to take away the monkey's freedom because they supply the monkey with what *they* think the monkey needs, even if it is not what the monkey wants.

This extreme (and, to some, frivolous) case illustrates how the logic of exploitation justifies taking advantage of those in need by arguing that one is taking care of people's needs. Exploitation is also about using one's power over others to determine what people need and what they *should* be willing to trade to have their needs filled. Similarly, the farmer decides that the monkey *needs* three meals a day and assumes that the monkey is willing to give up its freedom for them. As we'll see later, sometimes employers fill "needs" that employees do not have or want.

Wages for Time and Freedom

We own our labor and we own our freedom. Freedom, like labor, is something that we can barter. Most paid employment involves some loss of freedom for the employee. All of us must sell, in varying degrees, our work and our time to earn a living. Both John Locke and Adam Smith realized that employees are not really paid for what they produce. Smith said workers receive compensation for their loss of freedom at work, not for the product they make. Here loss of freedom means a restriction of their liberty to do and say or not to do and say certain things during the time that they are working. Usually when we take a job we implicitly or explicitly agree to do it when, where, and how our employer wants it done. For instance, think about a receptionist's job. She has to sit at the front desk all day, greet people, and answer the phone. She is not totally free to come and go when she pleases. Someone has to cover for her when she goes to the rest room, or takes a break for coffee or lunch. *Being there* is a fundamental part of her job. She is paid for her time as well as for what she does. She can't say what she wants when she answers the phone, she has to be polite and say the name of the company. Today managers would argue that she is paid for the value she adds to the organization—her "value added."

The idea that wages are compensation for loss of freedom also leads to some absurd possibilities. Would this mean that the less freedom a person has on the job the more he or she should get paid? Quite the contrary: jobs with more surface freedom tend to signal higher status and pay more money. In his book *Class*, Paul Fussell argues that the amount of freedom one has on the job is a better indicator of class than salary.[30] The idea of selling freedom often goes hand and hand with selling labor, especially when a person is in desperate need of a job and has little choice.

The Power of Knowledge

If the instrumental necessity to work makes working seem too bleak, let us consider the ways in which many employees hold on to their freedom and manifest power at work. Skill and knowledge make a worker valuable and give him or her more power in the employer-employee relationship. Consider the clerk who is the only person in the office who knows where everything is and how to get necessary tasks done. She is extremely valuable in some organizations and has a type of informal power. In a large bureaucratic organization this person has power, based on know-how, not position. The irony is that in bureaucratic organizations some people derive power from their positions, which may or may not be based on skill and knowledge about the job. Others gain power and influence because of their personalities and contacts. Knowledge of the job is not always enough in modern organizations, even though futurists claim knowledge will be everything in the new "learning organizations." For some, knowledge about people and relationships serves them better at work than knowledge about their job.

People are willing to sacrifice time and money to gain specialized knowledge so that they can have more control over their work lives. For example, young men used to spend years as apprentices to craftsmen, virtually indentured. In America apprentices signed labor contracts to work with a craftsman. The English apprenticeship system came to America, but the guilds that governed that system did not. As a result of this, there were no standards of quality or certification. Anyone could call himself a master artisan. Without a guild there were no restrictions on the number of apprentices that one could have and no definition of the obligations that the master had to train them. This state of affairs gave early American craftsmen a reputation for shoddy workmanship. Apprentices often performed menial chores and did not get proper training. Many ran away and had little problem securing work elsewhere, because labor was in short supply.

Benjamin Franklin apprenticed in his brother's print shop in Boston. He ran away because his brother did not treat him well and Franklin figured that he knew the trade well enough to do better elsewhere. His flight from boredom, rebellion against authority, and success as a businessperson made Franklin a hero to abused apprentices. Runaway apprentices became particularly common after the American Revolution. The chaos of the revolution left the apprentice and the master questioning the benefits of their contractual relationship. Tradition and respect for the craftsman's knowledge were the main forces in the colonial apprentice system. The revolution raised questions about the value of that tradition.

American craftsmen profited from the economic boom that started in the late 1780s. It was a particularly good time for printers. The literacy rate rose and the growing number of American-produced newspapers, magazines, and books displaced foreign publishers. Between 1783 and 1799 twelve states enacted legislation concerning apprenticeship. Most of the laws favored the master.[31] Boston printer Isaiah Thomas did a particularly good job of training his apprentices and groomed them for his franchise. At the end of their training he would set them up in their own businesses with him as a half partner. Thomas's reputation and his franchising system made parents eager to place their children with him. By the late 1700s he had more applicants than he could take, which gave him an advantage when it came to setting the terms of the indenture contract. In 1756 Thomas's apprentices received lodging, board, cash, and clothing. They also got two "freedom suits." These were suits that the young man would wear when he was finally free from his indentured contract. In 1785 Thomas promised to furnish apprentice James Reed Hutchins with "lodging, board, and part of his wearing apparel with good hats shoes & close bodied coats, his other clothing to be provided by his said guardian."[32] This contract no longer included cash or the traditional freedom suit.

By the nineteenth century, respect for the specialized knowledge of the craftsman was fading. After the American Revolution young people took on a republican attitude about life and work. They wanted to strike out on their own and they weren't ready to submit to any authority at work. Their elders complained, as elders have throughout history, that young people have no respect for authority and don't want to work.

Sharing Secrets

In the early part of the nineteenth century, Americans considered employment a temporary situation on the road to staking their claim, plying their trade, setting up shop, starting a business, or hanging out their shingle. Until the mid-1800s this was a realistic goal. Rapid industrialization at the close of the century diminished this possibility. To create the kind of workforce necessary for industrialization, industrialists had to redefine the social values of independence and self-sufficiency.

The craftsman's value and power came from his knowledge of how to make something. Fathers passed on the secrets of a craft to their sons and masters passed them on to apprentices. Keeping the secrets of the craft was as important as transmitting knowledge of the craft to apprentices. Secrets gave the craftsman power and autonomy, but in America there was no strong guild system to enforce secrecy. Literacy among craftsmen and the ever widening dissemination of information through books and other publications led some craftsmen to sell their secrets to the public in print. How-to books such as *One Thousand Valuable Secrets* (1795) offered information on engraving, ironmongering, varnishes, cements, sealing wax, glass, paint, and gilding. In 1800 Batty Langley's architectural pattern book for carpenters first appeared in America. It revolutionized building by giving carpenters easy rules for creating popular building styles. Sometimes these books contained more information than a particular master had to give.

Perhaps the most interesting thing about these books was that craftsmen, after a long tradition of secrecy, eagerly shared the tricks of their trade. One wonders whether their new openness resulted from a desire to make money as authors or from a desire to democratize the crafts. Was it a way for the craftsmen to promote their expertise and wares, or did the disclosure of their secrets express a desire to share with the world the skill and pleasure of craft? Perhaps craftsmen gave up their secrets because industrialization was devaluing their skills. Whatever the reason, they began the tradition of how-to books that still flourishes today. They left behind the how-to tradition that offered everyone access to personally and aesthetically rewarding work at home, at a time when work outside the home was becoming more and more mindless, boring, and ugly.

Industrialization, not how-to books, tamed the power and authority of the craftsmen and radically changed the meaning of their work. During the height of the industrial revolution that took place between 1870 and 1929, the physical output of American industry increased fourteenfold. Mechanization not only made work more efficient, it also deskilled some jobs and made people easily replaceable, like the parts of machines. Given the value that workers placed on autonomy and freedom, it was a major power struggle to convert American workers into industrial laborers.

6.

Taming the Worker

Industrialists in late nineteenth- and early twentieth-century industry had to contend with what amounted to an "attitude problem" of skilled American labor. Skilled American-born workers wanted to do the job *their* way and at *their* pace. Industrialists wanted work done their way. Workers at this time were neither "docile obedient automatons" nor were they "upwardly mobile individualists."[1] They collectively worked with pride and skill to maintain control of production, for they realized early that it was this control that was the key to their dignity and relative freedom. In the contest for control over production, employers had to discover new ways, ones that did not openly conflict with basic American principles of freedom and equality, to assert control over labor. Hence, at the turn of the century business began its ongoing quest for the magic motivators that would make employees work.

As mentioned in the last chapter, one source of power for a worker is his or her specialized skill. The other source of power lies in associations of workers. While America did not have as strong a craft guild tradition as Europe, it had a variety of craft unions for skilled workers such as shoemakers, hatmakers, dockworkers, and cigar rollers. A craftsperson had always had leverage with an employer because he or she had skill. This was not the case for the unskilled worker. Unions for unskilled workers were arguably the most important development in the history of work. For the first time, unskilled labor was given an independent voice and power in the employer-employee relationship. This was particularly important as mechanization slowly deskilled the work of craftspeople.

In America the first such organization was the Knights of Labor. In the 1880s anyone over the age of eighteen who worked for wages could become a member. But the organization rules stated that "no person who either sells, or makes his living from the sale of intoxicating drink, can be admitted, and no lawyer, doctor, or banker can be admitted."[2] Eventually the Knights of Labor joined forces with skilled labor and formed the American Federation of Labor. Samuel Gompers served from 1886 to 1924 as its first president. Unlike his European counterparts in the International union, Gompers did not want to overthrow the capitalist system. He believed that the purpose of a union was to redress the balance of power between employers and employees so that employers received a "fair" return on their capital and employees received wages that enabled them to make a decent living.[3]

Unions struck fear into the hearts of industrialists and the twentieth century became a pitched battle for control of the hearts and minds of the American worker. Between 1900 and 1930 three innovations and initiatives fundamentally changed the nature of work and shaped the workplace as we know it today: scientific management, welfare capitalism, and the human relations approach to management. All of these not only tamed the workforce but also made work into a far more complicated social and psychological experience than it had ever been before.

A "Manly Bearing" Toward the Boss

In the late 1800s industrial workers organized themselves along the general lines of craft guilds. The iron rollers of the Columbus Iron Works kept excellent records of how they practiced their craft between 1873 and 1876. They worked in twelve-man rolling teams that constituted a union. The team negotiated the quantity of iron they would roll, how long it would take to roll it, and their fee rate. They then decided collectively what portion each member of the team should get.

Essentially the boss, or owner, bought the equipment and raw materials and then sold the product. The actual management of production was up to the team.

The iron rollers trained their own members and instilled values related to the team and the work, not the employer. A strong moral code gave the iron rolling teams their sense of autonomy. The first and most important part of this code was that workers do only the amount of work agreed upon by the union, which was called the "stint." Employers were constantly trying to make employees work faster. Most workplaces had a stint, and those who failed to maintain it by doing too much or too little were ostracized. Workers who upheld the stint despite the curses of their boss earned reputations as "good men" and trustworthy masters of the trade. The worker restriction of output symbolized "unselfish brotherhood," personal dignity, and "cultivation of the mind."[4] One reason why the stint was important is that workers wanted control over the amount of time that they worked. Businesses at this time often ran factories around the clock and then shut them down for months at a time.

Another interesting part of the workingman's moral code was having a "manly bearing" toward the boss. In the nineteenth century this popular expression was an honorific signifying dignity, respect, and egalitarianism. A person earned this honorific by refusing to work while the boss was watching. It is useful to reflect on the difference between *only* working when the boss is watching and *not* working when the boss is watching. They are both gestures of defiance, but one is about keeping one's job and the other is about keeping one's dignity. The first says, I don't want to work, but I will, because *you* are watching. The second says, I'll work because *I* want to, and not because you are watching. The time-study engineer Frederick Winslow Taylor devoted himself to stamping out both gestures of defiance.

Knowing "the Rule"

Taylor came from a wealthy Philadelphia family. He dropped out of Phillips Exeter Academy and turned down a chance to go to Harvard in order to work in industry. In 1876, at the age of eighteen, Taylor got his first job as an apprentice at Ferrell & Jones, a steam-pump manufacturer in Philadelphia. When he started work the head of the shop took him aside and asked, "Do you know the rule?" Taylor replied, "What rule?" The man repeated the question a few more times and then took out a foot-long ruler with lines but no numbers on it. He placed his knife on one of the lines and asked, "What is it?"[5] Taylor couldn't answer, because he did not know the measurements on a ruler without the numbers or without counting the lines.

Taylor then observed that the skilled mechanics in the shop could put a piece of wood on a lathe and turn it accurately to any dimension they wanted without the use of gauges or other measuring devices. These skilled craftsmen made a strong impression on young Taylor, but it wasn't what one might expect. Taylor admired the craftsmen's ability to measure without a ruler, but he went on to spend his life reducing the need for people with such skills in industry. As Taylor saw it, the balance of power was tipped toward workers because they knew more than the foreman.[6] The key to gaining control over workers and the pace of production was to design work so that almost any person could do any job with maximum efficiency.

"Speedy Taylor" and Schmitt

In 1878 Taylor took a job at Midvale Steel and quickly worked his way up to foreman and then chief engineer. While at Midvale he began to study how to improve industrial productivity. He was so obsessed with this that his coworkers called him "speedy Taylor." Taylor's most famous illustration of scientific management is the case of a Pennsylvania Dutch immigrant named Henry Noll, to whom Taylor gave the name "Schmitt" in his research. Taylor "scientifically" selected Schmitt to carry out his experiment because Schmitt was foreign and did not have close ties with the other workers. He was also known to be thrifty, strong, and industrious. In *The Principles of Scientific Management,* published in 1911, Taylor portrays Schmitt as a typical, and not very bright, worker, but in fact Schmitt appears to be exceptionally energetic and a cut above the ordinary. We are told that Schmitt jogged to work every day (before jogging was chic), and that he could read and write. In his free time, Schmitt was a volunteer fireman, a charming ladies' man, and a heavy drinker. He even owned a plot of land and had built himself a house on it.

Taylor calculated that Schmitt could load 47 tons of pig iron a day if he did it properly. The current rate was 12.5 tons per day. In *The Principles of Scientific Management,* Taylor reconstructs his dialogue with Schmitt. He begins by asking Schmitt if he is a "high-priced man or one of those cheap fellows." Then Taylor asks Schmitt whether he would like to earn $1.15 a day or $1.85. Schmitt chooses the latter, and then Taylor gives the condition of a high-priced man (or a man who deserves to be paid more) in this chilling little dialogue:

> Now you know just as well as I do that a high-priced man has to do exactly as he is told from morning to night. . . .
>
> If you are a high-priced man you will do exactly as this man tells you tomorrow, from morning till night. When he tells you to pick up a pig and walk . . . then you pick up a pig and walk . . . when he tells you to sit down and rest, you sit down. Now a high-priced man does what he is told and no back talk.[7]

Schmitt followed orders and carried 47.5 tons of pig iron in one day. For 60 percent more pay, he did 400 percent more work. However, soon other workers were willing to do the same either out of fear of losing their jobs or for the money or both.

Schmitt became the most famous worker in the world after Taylor's publication of *The Principles of Scientific Management.* The book was an immediate best-seller and was soon translated into twelve languages, including Esperanto. Taylor's system was hailed as a great advancement all over the world. His critics heaped disdain on the Schmitt experiment and Taylor's description of it. Given its rigid control over labor and production, it is not surprising that some of Taylor's biggest fans included Vladimir Ilyich Lenin, who annotated the Russian version; Adolf Hitler; and Benito Mussolini, who once met Taylor's widow and asked her for a picture of Taylor.

In 1912 there was a Congressional investigation of scientific management. Some witnesses testified that most people could not work like Schmitt for very long without suffering physical or mental harm.[8] Taylor wanted to prove that his system didn't physically harm workers. So he tracked down Schmitt (Henry Noll). When Taylor found him, he had the forty-four-year-old man examined by a doctor, who gave Schmitt a clean bill of health. Apparently the only problems Schmitt had stemmed from women and liquor, not scientific management.[9]

From Pig Iron to Biscuits

The four basic elements of scientific management profoundly changed the relationship of employer to employee. First, scientific management was based on centralized planning and routing of the successive phases of the work. Taylor wrote, "In the past the man came first; in the future the system must come first."[10] Second, scientific management broke each operation down into its simplest parts. The third element of scientific management called for workers to be trained by management and then for each worker's performance to be supervised closely. Taylor knew that he had to change the values of the workers as well as the structure of their work. Since workers not only learned their trade but learned the mores of "keeping the stint" and "manly bearing" from one another, it was better for the company to train employees to do things its way.

Breaking the stint was Taylor's biggest challenge, because of his concern for speed. Hence the fourth element of scientific management rested on wage payments that were carefully designed to induce the worker to do as he was told. In his essay "Why Manufacturers Dislike College Students," Taylor wrote that cooperation meant workers "do what they are told when they are told, promptly and without asking questions or making suggestions." Taylor thought the best way to get obedience and break the stint was to appeal to workers' self-interest by paying them more.

Taylor believed that the same principles of scientific management could be applied in the management of homes, farms, work in the trades, governmental agencies, and philanthropic institutions. By the mid-1920s the logic of scientific management found favor in almost every industry. A book on scientific management in education was commissioned in 1907 by the Carnegie Foundation. Mary Pattison, a housewife from New Jersey, read Taylor and, in 1911, wrote a book about how to "scientifically" manage housework. All the tasks described in her book were timed to the second. Her recipe for biscuits read, "Add salt and baking powder—10 seconds. Stir and mix dry ingredients—62 seconds," etc.[11]

Resistance

Workers did not give in easily to scientific management. Unions called Taylor's system "the speedup system." Immigrant workers in the early 1900s had a simple response to speedups initiated by scientific management—they would just walk out and quit. Many workers were so alienated by work in industry that they moved from job to job, hoping for a better deal. During the economic boom of 1912–1913, the annual turnover rates of workers in industry ranged from 100 to 250 percent. Between October 1912 and October 1913 the Ford Motor Company, with its famous production line, hired a whopping fifty-four thousand men to maintain an average workforce of thirteen thousand employees.[12]

Workers from the Watertown Arsenal in Massachusetts thought that scientific management was an affront to their dignity and that it went against American ideals. Consider the language in this letter written by Watertown employees in 1915, protesting the presence of a time-study man at the arsenal:

> It is humiliating to us, who have always tried to give the government the best that is in us. This method is un-American in principle, and we most respectfully request that you have it discontinued at once.[13]

Workers there also argued that the quality of their work would suffer if they were under pressure to work faster to meet incentives.

Replacing Animosity with Kindness

At the end of World War I, labor strife broke out in America. Between 1915 and 1918 labor productivity dropped 10 percent and industry was plagued with absenteeism, strikes, and aggressive, militant unions.[14] The steel strike of 1919 involved three hundred thousand workers. It was crushed after three and a half months, and after twenty people died. The government was no longer friendly to organized labor. Industrial leaders engaged in an all-out assault to diminish the power of unions. At the same time, large employers wanted tranquil labor relations and they were willing to make life better for workers in order to get it. Impressed by the way that patriotism had motivated people to work together during World War I, some employers began to wonder if they could foster that kind of spirit and commitment in their organizations.

The inspiration for welfare capitalism came from many sources, including fear of labor unrest, the cost of high turnover rates, philanthropic institutions, and public relations. There were also some business leaders who genuinely wanted to improve the way that they treated their employees. The general idea behind welfare capitalism was to keep workers happy and draw them into a community in which their interests were aligned with the employers' interests, not their own as a class. Charles M. Schwab was head of Bethlehem Steel through some of its worst years of labor unrest. After he retired he became an advocate of welfare capitalism. In 1928 he told an engineering audience that engineering problems are not the real challenge of industry. He said, "Industries' most important task in this day of large-scale production is management of men on a human basis."[15] Financial leaders such as George W. Perkins of J. P. Morgan advised industrialists to treat their workers well in order to maintain good public relations. Members of the emerging investigative press, whom businesspeople of the time called "muckrakers," were starting to expose businesses that did not treat their workers well.

Some of the early welfare plans were paternalistic schemes designed to control the lives of workers, such as the model town that the sleeper car manufacturer George Mortimer Pullman built for his workers outside Chicago in 1880. Pullman was not only their employer but their landlord and the owner of their local store. Workers there staged a violent strike in 1894 when Pullman reduced their wages but not the rents that they paid. Other plans offered workers a stake in the firm and more security. E. K. Hall of American Telephone & Telegraph acknowledged the insecurity of life for workers. He told a business audience, "We must find ways and means to help our workers get their worries out of their minds so they can get on the job 'rarin to go.' "[16] In 1923 companies such as Procter & Gamble and IBM began guaranteeing employees forty-eight full-time workweeks per year. Procter & Gamble also started a profit-sharing plan in 1886, and Sears Roebuck implemented one in 1916. By 1927, eight hundred thousand employees had invested over a billion dollars in these profit-sharing plans, or what we call employee stock ownership plans (ESOPs), and they too suffered when the stock market crashed in 1929.[17] In 1911 International Harvester was among a number of companies that started a pension plan. Other innovations at the time included health insurance, improved safety standards, and amenities such as company cafeterias.

The American Plan

In January 1921, members of employers' unions from twenty-two states met in Chicago and joined together under the so-called American Plan.

It was called the American Plan because post–World War I employers held that the open, or nonunion, shop was an important American freedom. But in fact most employers were more interested in freedom from unions than freedom for workers. Employers hoped that under the American Plan they could win employee loyalty and cooperation by incorporating many of the tenets of welfare capitalism.

One feature of the American Plan was workers' councils, or shop committees. These were company unions, designed to hear grievances and foster cooperation. John D. Rockefeller Jr. implemented one in 1915 after the brutal suppression of strikers at the Colorado Fuel and Iron Company in which militiamen set fire to workers' tents and a number of women and children burned to death.[18] After World War I, 317 companies, including Youngstown Sheet & Tube, International Harvester, and Goodyear Rubber, had workers' councils, or company unions. Many of these councils focused on work grievances about company policy; however, they spent most of their time solving production problems. These company "unions" were basically quality circles run by management. Workers had a say in them, but it was on management's terms. Years later, in 1935, the National Labor Relations Act ruled that quality circles and other similar participatory schemes are illegal unless employees have the right to choose their representatives and have a genuine voice in decisions. The act prohibited "sham unions," or in-house unions formed by employers who were attempting to keep out real unions. Employers today often blame this act for prohibiting the implementation of participatory schemes in union workplaces.

Employers who joined the American Plan paid membership dues. In return they had access to labor spies, strikebreaking services, and blacklists of labor organizers. The services were supplied by private agencies that hired out armed hoods as strikebreakers and security guards. Union-busting was big business. The annual income of the three largest agencies supplying these services in 1920 was an estimated sixty-five million dollars.[19] If declining union membership was a measure of the American Plan and welfare capitalism, then these initiatives were an enormous success. In 1920 union membership peaked at over 5 million; by 1923 it was down to 3.6 million.[20] Labor historians differ as to whether labor participation in unions went down because of economic prosperity, heavy-handed antiunion tactics, poor union leadership, or the new benefits given to workers. It was probably a little of each.

Welfare capitalism and the American Plan reached a pinnacle in the 1920s and died a quick death when the Depression hit in the 1930s, leading one critic of the time to conclude that "obviously the welfare of wage earners cannot be left to employers."[21] A number of companies really had a strong sense of responsibility for their employees. The plan's demise during the Depression highlighted one of the major impediments to trust and loyalty between employers and employees. Except in times of illness, an employee can always hold up his or her side of the bargain with an employer. Businesses cannot or will not always hold up their end when the economy turns sour and profits are down.

Furthermore, some business leaders believed that the new benefits did not improve employee performance. At a management conference in 1935, Chester Barnard, president of New Jersey Bell, said that welfare capitalism did nothing to develop the employee or to foster collaboration.[22] Other management programs of the time focused more on the individual and group psychology of workers.

Watching Workers

Scientific management and welfare capitalism were not the only management initiatives around. The 1920s were a decade of industrial innovation and experimentation *and* union repression. The human relations approach to management focused on how the attitudes and feelings of workers affected productivity. In this approach, in contrast to scientific management, work was seen not just as a physical process and motivation was about more than money. The human relations management technique did not replace scientific management, it complemented it. One critic called human relations and industrial psychology "the maintenance crew for the human machinery."[23] This approach to management emphasized the importance of the relationship between supervisor and workers and the dynamics of the groups formed by employees. Managers had to learn how to understand employees, and most important, they needed to know how to talk and listen to workers.

From 1920 to 1927, researchers at the Hawthorn Works of the Western Electric Company set out to discover the effects of lighting on productivity. Working under the direction of Dr. C. E. Turner, a professor of biology and public health at MIT, they assumed that physical changes in the workplace would affect output. In one experiment they divided workers into a test group and a control group. The control group worked under consistent illumination. In the first experiment the test group was subjected to three levels of lighting. Productivity went up in the test room, but it also went up in the control room. Next the researchers lowered the lighting in the test room, but kept it the same in the control room. Curiously, productivity again increased in both rooms.[24] Researchers were baffled.

Fritz Roethlisberger; his colleague at the Harvard Business School, Elton Mayo; William J. Dickson, from Western Electric; and others sought to unravel the mystery of the experiments at the Hawthorn Works in a research project that lasted from 1927 to 1931. In the now famous test room experiment, Roethlisberger and his colleagues placed a group of five women who assembled telephone relays in a separate room for five years. During this time they experimented with temperature, lighting, and rest breaks. They also monitored how much the women slept at night and how much food they ate. In the latter part of the experiment, they increased the number of rest breaks and decreased the workday by one hour.

During the first half of the experiment the women were happy. They enjoyed the attention from top management. More rest breaks and shorter hours improved their working conditions; their productivity increased; and they earned more money. Some researchers began to think that these results proved their hypothesis that fatigue was the major factor limiting output. To test their hypothesis the researchers restored the original working conditions to the test room. So the women went back to forty-eight-hour weeks without rests breaks and other perks. The results presented researchers with yet another mystery. The women's output did not go down as expected, but maintained the same high level as before.

Roethlisberger offered a simple explanation for these puzzling results. He said that people, unlike stones, know that they are being experimented on, and their feelings toward the experiment and researchers determine how they respond to the tests. The women in the test room were reacting more to the change presented by the experiment itself than to the experimental innovations.[25] This response came to be known as the Hawthorn effect. The most important feature of the Hawthorn effect in the workplace is that it is usually temporary and is often simply a reaction to special attention. Elton Mayo, who was not directly involved in the experiments but played a key role in analyzing the results, added a Freudian twist to Roethlisberger's explanation. Mayo explained the Hawthorn effect as a form of transference. Positive transference is like falling in love, and as in any love relationship, people use the elements of power in the relationship for good or evil.[26] The women in the test room responded positively no matter what the situation, because they felt good and had a strong attachment to the authority figures involved in the experiment. Interestingly, neither Mayo nor Roethlisberger ever seriously entertained the possibility that employees might be deceiving them intentionally during the study.

Listening to Workers

Roethlisberger and his fellow researchers weren't content to stop at these conclusions. In the second phase of their work they began interviewing employees. They soon discovered that other variables affected productivity but were not detectable in "scientific" experiments. Some of the variables were so obvious that they seem almost silly, whereas others were more subtle and seem somewhat questionable. For example, one worker, who had been reprimanded for not keeping up his usual pace, explained in an interview that on the night preceding the day of the incident his wife and child had died unexpectedly. A woman who had trouble with her supervisor discovered in the interview process that the reason why she didn't like the supervisor was that he resembled her detested father. Mayo confidently claimed that once the worker discovered her "wholly irrational" dislike of her supervisor, she had an easier time working with him.[27] He didn't consider the fact that sometimes the supervisor who reminds you of your detested father *really is* detestable.

From this phase of interviews Mayo and Roethlisberger found other "curious" results. One woman complained at great length about the food in the company restaurant. Within a few days she ran into the interviewer and thanked him for conveying her feelings to management and securing prompt action. The interviewer hadn't said a word about the food, but the food tasted better to the woman. Mayo concluded that employees responded favorably for therapeutic reasons; when they complained about work it was not because they wanted change, but because they needed emotional release.[28]

It is interesting to compare Roethlisberger's and Mayo's later reflections on the Hawthorn studies. While they both agreed that work is a psychological and social process of individuals and groups, Mayo saw people as simple and malleable, whereas Roethlisberger realized that everyone is different. He was fascinated by the question of what work means to individuals. Mayo was far more sanguine than Roethlisberger about the scientific approach to studying work and the ability of managers to change and control the behavior of workers. Years after the experiment Mayo wrote an upbeat description of what happened to the women in the test room. The words might have come from a management book today. He said the women in the test room "became a team and wholeheartedly cooperated in the experiment." As a result of this, "they felt themselves to be participating freely and without afterthought, and were happy in the knowledge that they were working without coercion from above or limitation from below."[29]

Roethlisberger's later reflections on the Hawthorn studies were more ambivalent. He said it was difficult to generalize about people and that researchers "should abandon the idea that the meanings people assign to their experience are logical and give up on the model of 'the economic man,' a man primarily motivated by economic interest, whose logical capacities were being used in the interest of this self-interest."[30] Of the two interpretations, Mayo's was far more attractive to business because it was simple, unambiguous, and optimistic about the use of psychological techniques to manage workers. Mayo believed that psychology could help managers capture the loyalty of workers so that they would direct their energies to the good of the organization. The Hawthorn studies became a permanent part of the management canon.

Criticism from a "Crazy" Woman

There were lively debates about the findings of the Hawthorn studies. One of the harshest critics was Mary B. Gilson, a researcher who worked with Mayo but was later cut out of the Western Electric studies. In her review of Roethlisberger's book *Management and the Worker* in the *American Journal of Sociology,* she said the most provocative question about the conclusions of the Hawthorn studies was, "Why does big business fund social research?"[31] She pointed out that between 1933 and 1936 the Western Electric Company paid nearly twenty-six thousand dollars for espionage in its plants. (It was a common practice at the time for companies to hire out spies to sniff out union activity.)

She said, "We know of no instance where spies have been employees without some fear of unionism on the part of management."[32] Gilson also found it odd that Mayo and his researchers interviewed twenty thousand workers and none of those workers criticized the company or talked about unions. The Hawthorn studies completely ignored unions. In the 1920s many large companies required employees to sign what were called yellow-dog contracts, stating that they would not join a union. Under these agreements, inducement to join a union was a breach of contract, and although employees had a right to strike, they did not have a right to instigate a strike. Given the labor environment, it's understandable why employees would not bring up unions in the interviews, or if they did, why some researchers would not report it. Gilson wondered whether Mayo and Roethlisberger had been used by Western Electric. She suggested that their research simply told the company what it wanted to hear.

Gilson also criticized Mayo and Roethlisberger for not raising questions about power, authority, class, and workers' rights in their analysis. She asserted that the Hawthorn research ignored other studies and left out important facts. Gilson, who had done extensive research on women workers, found Mayo and Roethlisberger's explanation for why women did not talk about job advancement as much as men in the interviews silly. The authors did not mention that women were not allowed to advance in the company in the first place. Also, the researchers operated under the assumption that women didn't work to support families; they only worked for pin money. Here Gilson refers to a Department of Labor study done during that time, which showed that most women who work support their parents' family or their own family, or they are widows. The majority do not work for extra money or "pin money." One of her most scathing comments about the research was that perhaps someone ought to do a study on "Research in the Obvious Financed by Big Business."

Roethlisberger was hurt by Gilson's review, but Mayo was quick to dismiss her criticisms, using some time-honored arguments. In a letter to Roethlisberger he wrote:

> Don't let Mary Gilson worry you—everyone knows that she is crazy as hell. . . . She hates all men—thinks women are "badly put upon"—and nothing of the discussion can shake this compulsion. After attacking me for not employing, promoting, advocating the cause of women, she suddenly changed her tune and said that she had told me

everything in *Management and the Worker* a long time ago. Then she
went off on the tack that she had really done the work and that I, like
the usual man, had taken *her* work without acknowledgement. . . .
The poor lady really should be put away somewhere.[33]

He then went on to conclude that the more successful you are the more
people misrepresent your opinions. Gilson may well have been crazy,
but her criticisms of the Hawthorn studies were not.

Over the years of experiments at the Hawthorn Works, Roethlisberger noticed that the supervisor role had changed from that of a
hard-nosed autocrat to that of jargon-ridden and seemingly friendly
men eager to increase their control over employees by using some of
the new psychological insights. Ten years after Gilson's critique,
Roethlisberger acknowledged that she was right about some things. At
the time of the Hawthorn studies he had not seen how interviewing,
counseling, social-skill training, and equilibrium in social relations manipulated workers "into believing that they belonged to a work community that was best managed by the authoritarian model of modern
industry."[34] This raises the question of whether the human relations approach to management was really an improvement or whether it fur-
ther complicated the relationships of people at work. It hadn't changed
some things. Managers still saw cooperation as doing what the boss
wanted, and the focus was not the skills of cooperation but the aims of
cooperation.

Mayo's and Roethlisberger's work on the Hawthorn studies became
a permanent fixture in management texts. Roethlisberger's and Gilson's
concerns appear rarely and, if at all, as footnotes; yet they both foresaw
many of the problems in today's workplace that are a consequence of
the human relations approach to management. Managers tend to
smooth over or squash conflict, employees are suspicious of manipulation, and the language and ideology of the workplace make it difficult
to articulate the problems that arise. Moreover, employees have been
subject to a variety of faddish motivational programs that have produced a series of Hawthorn effects. They are psychologically jump-
started, but their batteries run out after a few miles.

The Trade-offs

Many people today don't like to think about unions. For some, they
conjure up images of a corrupt special interest group that is lazy and

overpaid. Others like to blame unions for ruining America's ability to compete in the global market through their greed and low productivity. In spite of these negative perceptions, polls consistently show that most Americans believe that unions are effective in improving members' wages, protecting job security, and protecting workers against unfair employer practices.[35] Employers often consider unions a sign of their failure, a personal insult, and an allegation of distrust. Despite corruption and excesses in the history of unions, they are still *the* most important innovation in the relationship between employer and employee in history, because they address the imbalance of power between the two parties. At their best, they not only protect the health, security, and dignity of members but they often convince or frighten businesses into paying a living wage and improving working conditions for everyone, not just their members. Union membership has gone up and down throughout the twentieth century. It grew in the 1930s and under the New Deal, when government took on more responsibility for social welfare. In 1950, 40 percent of nonagricultural wage and salary workers belonged to unions. During this time the American dream was still alive and well.

The growing sector of white-collar work required new applications of the human relations or psychological approach to management. Those who did mental work in clean, attractive offices were willing to put up with the little indignities of work, such as submergence of self and acquiescence to authority in order to pay for houses, cars, and shiny chrome kitchen appliances. They were willing to trade freedom in the workplace for freedom in the marketplace. Whereas the indentured servant and the industrial laborer traded long hours of physical labor for their slice of the American dream, the "organization man" had to give up a piece of his soul.

7.

How Did Work Get So Confusing?

By the middle of the twentieth century, the problem of work in large corporations was the problem of alienation. For most people the work was boring, and often employees didn't see the final product of their labor. Industrial organizations uprooted people and disconnected them from their families and community life. Many prominent business theorists believed that corporations could solve the problem of alienation. Elton Mayo thought that corporations could mend the torn fabric of society.[1] Peter Drucker, in his groundbreaking book *The Concept of the Corporation,* published in 1946, argued that the corporation was *the* representative institution of society because it was best suited to fulfill the aspirations and beliefs of the American people—what was "good for General Motors" really was good for America. While Drucker acknowledged that the majority of people did not work in corporations, he argued that work in corporations sets the tone for work in other areas of society. Corporations should give status and function to the individual worker and create good industrial citizens.

From the Hawthorn studies, Drucker drew the following conclusions about alienation. First, "It is not monotony and routine which produce dissatisfaction but the absence of recognition, of meaning, or relation of one's own work to society."[2] Drucker and other theorists had been very impressed by the energy and pride displayed by industrial workers during World War II. After the war, management thinkers began to wonder how to instill the motivation and commitment of the war effort into peacetime work. Second, the problem of alienation in an industrial system could not be solved by giving more benefits, security, or wages. It could be alleviated only by giving people the responsibilities and dignity of an adult. Meaningful work was primarily about the social and moral qualities of a job, not the particular work that one did.

In his first book, *The End of Economic Man,* published in 1939, Drucker had blamed fascism on the collapse of "economic man." He said that European capitalism had failed to prevent fascism because economic freedom led to inequality, and the fascists had seized on this idea and reasoned that if freedom interferes with equality, then people have to give up freedom. Yet seven years later, in *The Concept of the Corporation,* Drucker disparaged the economic man as a worker. He wrote that "a man who works only for a living and not for the sake of work and of its meaning, is not and cannot be a citizen."[3] Furthermore, Drucker described the fascist notion of "freedom" in Europe as the right of the majority against the individual.[4] Later, in his criticism of organizational life, he charged corporations with constructing a "social ethic" that legitimates the interests of the corporation against personal interests and undermines the autonomy of the individual.

Drucker, perhaps the most respected management theorist of the twentieth century, has long made the case for socially responsible corporations. He said that the means we use to strengthen the corporation and make it more efficient should also promote the realization of the beliefs of our society.[5] However, Drucker may have been too optimistic about giving profit-oriented and inevitably self-interested corporations the heady responsibility of fulfilling human aspirations and developing industrial citizens. Drucker argued that corporations, as representative social institutions, have to deliver on their promise to live up to society's values and aspirations. But there are several stumbling blocks to corporations' delivering on these promises. As Louis Brandeis pointed out in 1914 in his article "Other People's Money," and Adolf Berle and Gardiner Means argued in their classic from the 1930s *The Modern Corporation and Private Property,* it's not easy for corporations to behave responsibly when the people who own the firm (stockholders) don't run it and the people who run the firm (managers) don't own it.[6] On the one hand, corporations demand loyalty and are the source of jobs, wealth, and technological creativity. On the other hand, they can be disruptive social forces that pollute the environment, corrupt the political process, promote addictive products, and ruin people's lives. Furthermore, in a global economy the health and destiny of a corporation is sometimes not in the firm control of the mere mortals who run it. That is why it is so important for management to control the internal environment of the organization.

Using management techniques and organization theories honed during World War II, large white-collar organizations began to mold their employees into *their* image of a good corporate citizen. Each company had its own image, and the good corporate man (they were mostly men in those days) was not always the good family and community man. The quest for the magic motivator had come a long way from Taylor's simple equation of pay for performance. Management researchers began to dig deeper and deeper into the human psyche in their search for the "ghost in the machine"—that elusive spirit that inspired enthusiastic human action and commitment without concern for external rewards and without asking for more. Corporate managers also had to find a cause, a mission, or a set of ideals that would give work a social meaning and create the kind of commitment that they had seen in the war effort. The meaning of work for an individual in a large organization was shaped as much, if not more, by the organization as it was by the job one did. Work in these organizations became socially and psychologically more complicated. It was somewhat confusing because work was no longer supposed to be simply an economic transaction. It was a personal and social transaction. Work was a place where corporations molded employees into corporate citizens. Corporations battled alienation between work and life and sometimes won by making work a larger part of one's life.

The "New Little Man"

In the 1950s, social critics such as C. Wright Mills worried about the influence large corporations had on their employees. He painted a gloomy picture of white-collar work in large bureaucratic organizations. For Mills, the golden age of work was the 1850s, an era of family farms and small independent shopkeepers. He wrote that back then work was well integrated into life and it gave people deep roots in their community and society. This may have been so for the craftsman or shopkeeper who lived and worked at home, but it probably wasn't the case for everyone. Mills also assumed that it is inherently good to have work integrated into life and that alienation is a bad thing. He believed that the meaning of work for industrial and white-collar workers had diminished to the point where work no longer gave them inner direction and connection to society.

For Mills, white-collar work was in some ways worse than un-skilled labor. He said "paroles" suffer physically, but at least they are free when they go home, whereas white-collar workers not only sell their time and energy, they sell their personalities."[7] He called the white-collar worker the "new little man" who is politically apathetic, has shallow roots and no loyalties, and is always in a hurry but doesn't know where he is going. According to Mills, the new little man is un-heroic, is unaware of his history, and has no golden age he can recall in time of trouble. Willy Loman, the main character in Arthur Miller's 1949 play *Death of a Salesman,* personified Mills's "little man." Mills tells us that Loman is "a man who by the very virtue of his moderate success in business turns out to be a total failure in life."[8]

The counterpart of the new little men were what Mills called the "new men of power" in corporate America. Since these new men of power lived in a democratic society that valued freedom, equality, and self-determination, they needed to keep employees happy in order to remain free of unions and hostile government regulations. Mills was concerned that the human relations industry offered corporate leaders the promise of finding new symbols that would publicly justify this vast inequity of power and cultivate loyal and enthusiastic workers.

According to Mills, organizations focused on employee morale because the Protestant work ethic of individual self-improvement (or salvation) through hard work was not viable in large complex organizations, where so much of the work was fragmented and meaningless, and there was little room for mobility and improvement. Personnel departments took the place of the Protestant work ethic, and morale had replaced morality as the motivation to work.[9] Employers could not depend on their employees' having a moral commitment to work. Mills said the goal of the personnel department was to develop cheerful and cooperative subordinates. Employees' feelings would be on the organization's terms and in the organization's hands. By controlling the sentiments inside the workplace, employers could maintain and justify their power without alienating workers.

Mills argued that the white-collar man was psychologically whipped into shape by the organization to suit its purposes and then doomed to lead a shallow and petty life outside of work because he had sold his personality. The man at work became the man at home. In this case the integration of work and life that Mills applauds in the nineteenth century is disastrous in the twentieth. Work, as Mills describes it, ruins rather than enhances home life and life in the community. What Mills failed to notice is that alienation can be either the problem or the solution. The separation of work and life that he disparages might be the healthiest response to work in the modern organizations that he describes. Perhaps Willy Loman would have been a better person if he had led the double life of salesman and family man. The real concern of critics like Mills was that too much emphasis on work ruins a person's life, not only because of the time it takes, but because of the influence of the organization on the individual. The flip side of this argument is the employer's concern that the way people live their lives outside work might detract from their lives at work. That is why organizations try to mold employees into their image. Both sides call this problem alienation—either work alienates people from life or life alienates people from work.

The Organization Man

White Collar was published in 1951. Five years later, in *The Organization Man*, William H. Whyte echoed some of Mills's concerns, only Whyte zeroed in on people's need to belong. Whyte builds upon a type that David Riesman had described in his book on American character, *The Lonely Crowd*, published in 1950. Riesman observed the ways in which business values were starting to dominate society. He wrote that life for many people in America had become mobile, expanding, profit oriented, and full of choice. "Inner-directed" people are able to cope with this world because they have direction and goals implanted in them by their elders. "Other-directed" people, found mostly in big cities, are shallower, freer with their money (because they often have more), friendlier, and more uncertain of themselves.[10] They take their cues about values and goals from the outside and they want to fit in and be liked.

In his chapter "The Other-Directed Round of Life: From Invisible Hand to Glad Hand," Riesman argued that a society dominated by other-directed people emphasizes manipulative skill over craft skill and expense accounts over bank accounts. Business is supposed to be fun and managers are supposed to be glad-handers who joke with secretaries and charm their bosses and clients. According to Riesman, the other-directed person tends to belong to the company first and has shallower roots in the family, church, and community. This is the character type behind Whyte's organization man.

The workplace of the late 1950s is both radically different from and strikingly similar to the workplace of today. Both emphasize group work and place a premium on loyalty and commitment. Whyte focused his criticism of organizations on a "social ethic" that he said made morally legitimate the pressure of society against the individual. This ethic rationalizes the organization's demand for loyalty and gives employees who offer themselves wholeheartedly a sense of dedication and satisfaction. Such an ethic includes the belief that the group is a source of creativity, belongingness is the ultimate need of the individual, and psychologists and sociologists who work in management disciplines can create ways to achieve a sense of belongingness.[11] Whyte's critique of the social ethic is similar to current critiques of communitarianism. Community-oriented life looks awfully good from the outside, but from the inside it may be oppressive and authoritarian.

Whyte feared that psychologists and social engineers would strip people of their creativity and identity. He expressed concern about the inherent dishonesty of the psychological approach to management, and he criticized the social engineers' search for "the magic term which will combine manipulation with moral sanction."[12] He attacked the use of personality tests to weed out people who don't "fit in" and challenged the notion that organizations should be free from conflict. But perhaps Whyte's worst fear was that organizations would become "antiseptic hells" where the enemy was not up-front like Big Brother's henchmen in George Orwell's novel *1984,* but "a mild-looking group of therapists who, like the Grand Inquisitor, would be doing what they did to help you."[13]

In the 1950s social critics worried about people's conformity to institutions and the values of burgeoning suburban life. Today we worry about the lack of a consensus of values and the breakdown of urban and suburban communities. In the workplace there still is an increasing effort to build "teams" and emphasize the value of groups. No one seems worried about loss of creativity and submission of individual identity to group identity. Managers care more about the problem of the individual who isn't a team player. Like so many of their predecessors, the majority of management theorists today believe that groups and teams are the foundation of all that is good and productive.

Whyte disagreed. He wrote: "The most misguided attempt at false collectivization is the attempt to see the group as a creative vehicle."[14] Contrary to popular management thinking today, Whyte did not believe that people think or create well in groups. Groups, he said, simply give order to the administration of work. In his book Whyte describes an experiment on leaderless groups done at the National Training Lab. The idea of the exercise was that when the group "jelled," the leader would fade into the background and be consulted only for his expertise. These groups resulted in chaos but, as Whyte tells us, the trainers hoped that the resulting emotional exhaustion of the group would be a valuable catharsis and a prelude to agreement.[15] The individual, according to Whyte, has to enter into the process somewhere. However, he wondered, should we openly bring individuals into the process, or "bootleg" them in an expression of group sentiment? Basically, Whyte saw the leaderless group as intellectual hypocrisy. The power and authority of the group simply camouflaged the real power and hidden authority of leaders.

Since Whyte's book, there has been a tremendous amount of research on groups, as well as endless writings on the glories of teams. The rhetoric of organizations today includes words like *team, partner, family,* and *associate.* But cohesive groups and teams aren't always the best way to work or make decisions. Researchers such as Irving Janis have alerted us to the disadvantage of "groupthink," a condition in which members of a group begin to think alike and fail to see other perspectives on a problem. Incidents such as the 1986 *Challenger* disaster, in which seven astronauts died when the space shuttle exploded seventy-three seconds after takeoff, illustrate the disastrous consequences of a decision that was made by such a group. The group of scientists and administrators who made the decision to launch the shuttle were a "team," unified by their work and their desire to launch the shuttle on time. They were not swayed by the few dissenting engineers who doubted the safety of the O-ring seals on the solid-fuel rockets.

Organizations no longer give the personnel tests that Whyte discussed in his book, but they do give others, like the Myers-Briggs test. This test is used to describe a person's personality traits. For example, some people are extroverted intuitive thinking judgers, or ENTJs. According to the test, these folks are natural leaders. Some people actually enjoy taking the Myers-Briggs test because it tells them something about themselves. It puts them on a map and makes for good conversation. Sometimes companies get carried way with the results of these tests. Several years ago Allied Signal in Virginia thought it would be a good idea to have its employees wear color-coded badges indicating how they scored on the Myers-Briggs test. This system was supposed to help people communicate better by allowing them to know about an interlocutor's personality up front.[16]

Some organizations still use tests to select conformist workers. For example, in 1988 after taking one such test, a woman was surprised to get a job at Ethicon hospital supply firm. The company tested applicants to see how well they worked in groups. In one test applicants were asked to build bridges with sticks while a facilitator stood by and took notes. The woman later said she didn't offer suggestions on how to do the job and usually went along with the group.[17] She was amazed that the company wanted her, because she didn't feel that she had done her best on the exercise.

Today companies sometimes use tests such as the Gordon Personal Profile to predict management success. These tests look for leadership qualities and the ability to make decisions without a group. For Whyte, personality tests were an affront to a person's autonomy and privacy. But many employees see them as a tool for self-knowledge and development. Psychological tests, like horoscopes and magazine quizzes on sex appeal, promise to shed light on the inner self. The problem is that when one takes these tests at work, self-knowledge comes at the price of self-exposure and perhaps unfair pigeonholing. While many things have changed since Whyte's time, his general critique of the corporation probably still holds true, but most employees either don't care or simply accept these tests as part of the job.

At the end of his book, Whyte exhorts the reader to "fight the organization" and not get caught up in its demands for conformity. He advises his reader to cheat on personality tests and offers instructions on how to do so. In the belief that "the dice are loaded in favor of The Organization,"[18] he offers these instructions as a means of leveling the playing field for employees. Whyte recommends that people fight the organization by tricking it or simply failing to capitulate to its demands.

The Man in the Gray Flannel Suit

Another illustration of the struggle against the organization is in Sloan Wilson's novel *The Man in the Gray Flannel Suit,* published in 1955. At the beginning of the novel a personnel manager asks the main character, Tom Rath, to write an autobiography in which the last line reads, "The most significant thing about me is . . ." Rath, disgusted by the personnel manager and the exercise, debates whether to say what the company wants to hear or tell about his most significant memory—of a woman he met during the war. Between truth and fiction, Rath holds on to his dignity by stating the facts—his place of birth, his schooling, and the number of children in his family. He writes that the most significant thing about him is the fact that he is applying for the job. He also notes that he did not want to write an autobiography as part of his application. Rath etches a fine line between himself and the organization. This scene in Wilson's novel still resonates with readers today because all of us at some time decide how much of ourselves we are willing to reveal to an organization. In the modern workplace it isn't always easy to draw this line. This thin line is not about the quantity of work you will do. It is the boundary that you draw between your private life and inner self and the more public aspects needed to do your job. Some workplaces prefer that there be no line between the two. Deciding how much to give and how much to withhold can be confounding and confusing.

Needs Nobody Wants

The real confusion about work in large organizations began in the 1960s, when the model of the authoritarian boss gave way to that of the "sensitive" manager. In 1960 MIT management professor Douglas McGregor articulated two views of work and management. Theory X management was authoritarian. It rested on the same assumptions that Taylor had about workers: people are lazy, lack self-discipline, respond only to material rewards and punishments, and want security but not responsibility in their jobs. Theory Y management was participatory. It assumed that people like to work (or don't dislike it), are self-motivated, have self-control, and want to have responsibility for their work.

Around the same time that McGregor's book, *The Human Side of Enterprise,* was published, the National Training Labs had developed T-groups, or training groups, which would eventually evolve into a variety of other forms such as "sensitivity training," "encounter groups," and "integrity groups." Research on group dynamics had been around since the 1930s. The body of knowledge on how people worked together in groups grew significantly through the next two decades. However, by the 1960s and 1970s the emphasis of group research shifted from the study of how people worked together in groups (group processes) to how groups could change individuals.[19] A number of large companies used these training groups ostensibly to transform bossy managers into participative ones. After much crawling around on the floor together and getting in touch with their inner feelings, few managers were transformed. While participatory management and initiatives to make managers more sensitive sounded good, they could also make work more complicated. Friendly, caring managers didn't necessarily negate the lines of power and authority in an organization, they masked them.

Managers not only had to be "nice," they had to make work fill people's needs. Needs sometimes motivated people to work and sometimes kept people from working. The trick was to satisfy some and cultivate others. In *The Affluent Society,* John Kenneth Galbraith argued that the desire to find meaning in work is not a basic human need but rather the aspiration of people in an affluent, well-educated society.[20] But the management industry was more interested in needs than personal preferences. The ubiquitous drawing of a pyramid depicting Abraham Maslow's "hierarchy of needs" still graces the pages of most management textbooks. According to this scheme, people move "up" from their most basic physiological needs for food and shelter to the needs for safety and security, belongingness and love, and then self-esteem. The highest need on Maslow's scale is self-actualization. Management texts use the pyramid to describe employees' needs and explain how to fulfill them in the workplace. The lowest physiological needs are the most potent and, as we have seen earlier, are what have always driven people to work. Once the organization supplies the means to fill employees' physiological needs, it focuses on other needs, e.g., for belongingness, self-esteem, and self-actualization. These are the ones that, in theory, animate the "ghost in the machine."

The pyramid, often taken out of context, does not do justice to the ideas of humanistic psychologist Abraham Maslow, whose work became prominent in the 1960s. Maslow acknowledged that some people's needs do not follow the order of the diagram. Indeed, taken at face value, the order of Maslow's hierarchy contradicts some of our observations of people. Often those we admire most are the ones who prefer to starve or face death rather than give up their dignity or beliefs. The lovers who risk their lives and inheritance to be together, the lonely, hunted, hungry writer who chooses to write the truth about an oppressive regime—such people are not guided by their needs, but by what they value. These exceptions to Maslow's scheme represent what is distinctive about being human.

Clearly the needs at the bottom of the pyramid have always given employers leverage over workers. Nonetheless, to assume that needs are all that move people underestimates the power of human passions, ideals, and values. When people are free to make choices, they make their choices based on their values or what is important to them. That is why in chapter 1 we talked about how values and not needs determine how people chose their work. We choose what we value, but we can't choose what we need. Employees whose priorities don't follow the order of the pyramid are a manager's worst nightmare. They don't need what the organization has to give, e.g., belongingness and prestige.

Another needs theory focuses on the high end of Maslow's pyramid. David McClelland argues that people need affiliation, achievement, and power.[21] Unlike Maslow, McClelland doesn't believe that all people have the needs he enumerates but he does believe that through training you can cultivate these needs in them. This is a somewhat odd notion of need. If someone does not feel a need for power or achievement, why cultivate one in him or her? McClelland's work raises questions about the use of training to create needs that people do not have, do not want, and may be happier without. The monkeys who pick coconuts may not have wanted baths, monkey wages, and motor scooter rides, and they certainly did not need sick days and retirement before they started working. One way to assert power over others is to determine what people need or create needs for them, and then define what they have to do to have these needs met.

Blue-Collar Blues and White-Collar Woes

In 1971 Elliot Richardson, secretary of the Department of Health, Education, and Welfare (H.E.W.) under President Nixon, commissioned the W. E. Upjohn Institute for Employment to study work in America. One problem that the study addressed was what sociologists of the time called the "blue-collar blues" and the "white-collar woes." The researchers who wrote the study identified unrewarding work performed in authoritarian workplaces as the source of these "blues" and "woes." They reported that when the blue-collar worker came home, he was so fatigued that all he could do was watch television. Like Mills's "new little men," many workers were alienated from society and politically apathetic. Such people were dubbed the "silent majority."

Archie Bunker, in the television series *All in the Family,* was the Willy Loman of the 1970s. Both characters struggled with the demoralizing impact of work on life. Bunker had a bad case of the blue-collar blues, but his complaints about work were not unique to his class, income status, gender, or race. The show was popular with everyone even though Bunker was a bigot who was hostile to anyone different from himself. Every week viewers watched Bunker come home from work tired, frustrated, sometimes angry. After being bullied at work, he became the bully at home. Part of the show's popularity was that Bunker acted out what many people felt. He didn't have a great job, but there was hope for him as a human being as he fumbled and fumed his way through life with his family. We could laugh at Bunker, whereas Loman wasn't funny. Loman's failures in life led him to exaggerate his successes at work, but in the end, his job offered no hope or affirmation for the over-the-hill salesman. Bunker held no illusions about his work; instead, one night a week, he tried to salvage his life with his quirky family.

The H.E.W. study found that people wanted interesting work, a say in their work, and a chance to perform well in their jobs.[22] They wanted more from work than a paycheck: they wanted satisfaction. A few years earlier, psychologist Frederick Herzberg had argued that job satisfaction and dissatisfaction are not opposites, but two separate things. Job satisfaction is a function of the content or the intrinsic value of the job that you do. Dissatisfaction with work is usually a function of external factors, which Herzberg called hygiene factors, such as inadequate pay, dirty or unsafe working conditions, and mean, disrespectful managers.[23] If you improved the hygiene factors of the workplace— offered better pay and benefits, a physically pleasing workplace, and understanding managers—workers would not be dissatisfied; but this didn't mean that they would be satisfied. Herzberg believed that worker surveys in which people said they were *satisfied* with their jobs really meant that they were *not dissatisfied* with their working conditions. The workplace might have been pleasant and the benefits good, but employees still would not have been satisfied, and hence not highly productive, because the work they actually did had not changed.

The H.E.W. report cited a study by the Survey Research Center of the University of Michigan of 1,533 American workers across all occupational levels. When the workers were asked to rank the importance of twenty-five aspects of work, interesting work ranked first. The next three were help and equipment to get the job done, information to get the job done, and authority to get the job done. Good pay ranked fifth and job security ranked seventh.[24] The survey probably meant a number of things. First, to use the Maslow "needs" explanation, people were fairly well off, they had filled their lower needs, and they were seeking to fill higher needs. Second, work had become so tedious that, for many, interesting work had become a priority. Third, the 1970s were an introspective period and this "me generation" of workers really wanted more meaningful work. Fourth, given the tradition of the work ethic and the cultural climate of the times, people answered the questions the way they thought they should and were too embarrassed to admit that they'd take job security or higher pay over interesting work. Fifth, 1,533 workers is only a small snapshot in time.

Another conclusion of the H.E.W. study was that the workplace would have to change to fit the aspirations, attitudes, and values of workers. The report asserted that an interesting and satisfying job was as important as a job that paid well.[25] It recommended job redesign and increased participation of workers, arguing that these changes were necessary for America to be competitive. The study gave official recognition to the idea that many people wanted meaningful work. Implicit in this idea of meaningful or humanized work was the notion of freedom or participation. (Of course, the "many people" did not include the unemployed and below-minimum-wage workers who probably cared more about getting a job that paid a living wage.) Lastly, the authors of the study predicted that in the future people would increasingly trade money for leisure.

When the H.E.W. report was released, the initial supply of printed copies ran out in a few days. Academics, policy analysts, and the popular media discussed and debated it. *The Boston Globe* said that *Work in America* "may be one of the most important documents in years" and "there is no doubt that the facts in the report are right on target: the blue-collar blues are haunting the white-collar employee too." The report was well received by everyone but the Nixon administration. The findings contradicted Nixon's repeated assertion that Americans had abandoned the work ethic for the welfare ethic. A Labor Department official quipped that the problem of worker dissatisfaction would go away "if sociologists and reporters would quit writing about it."[26] Needless to say, the Nixon administration did not do much with the report, but the study triggered a Senate inquiry and fostered important research and experimentation in job redesign, worker participation, and workplace democracy.

Unemployment was below 5 percent in the 1970s and would not be that low again until the late 1990s. It was a reflective time when people were thinking about the nature of work and its affect on their lives. Studs Terkel's *Working* was a best-seller in 1972 and was later made into a musical. The book consisted of interviews with workers who ranged from a washroom attendant to a film critic. It offered a heroic and romantic picture of work. Terkel wrote that for some work is a "daily humiliation" and for others "salvation." Work was a search "for daily meaning as well as daily bread, for recognition as well as cash, for astonishment rather than torpor."[27] The overall message was very similar to that of the H.E.W. report. Most people wanted to work and wanted to do a good job, but their jobs or their bosses prevented them from doing so. They knew that they *should* have the values of the work ethic, but too many things got in the way of acting on those values at work.

The Bolivar Project

In 1972 Sidney Harman, owner and CEO of Harman International Industries, testified at a Senate subcommittee hearing on anger and alienation in the workplace. He told the subcommittee that the main reason why workers were unhappy was that corporate America treated them like replaceable machine parts. Irving Bluestone, a top official of the United Auto Workers (U.A.W.), was also at the hearing. Impressed by Harman's comments, Bluestone met with him afterward. The two men eventually agreed to try an experiment in giving workers greater control over their work at Harman Automotive, a maker of rearview mirrors, in Bolivar, Tennessee. They called the experiment the Bolivar Project.

The Bolivar Project gave employees increased job security and an active role in decisions concerning working conditions and training. The employees redesigned their jobs and made the production process run smoother. By 1975 managers, academics, and union officials were trekking to Bolivar to see this new wonder of industrial relations. Upon touring the plant one union organizer said, "What an experience to enter a factory where everyone is treated like an adult!"[28] In the 1970s this kind of program was called worker participation or workplace democracy. Today businesses call it empowerment. (As we'll see later, there's often a vast difference between the political ideals of these work-place democracies and what companies today pass off as empowerment programs.) Not only did Harman Automotive give employees a real voice in their work, the company also offered classes in the factory on topics ranging from welding to piano playing. Workers could attend these classes after they filled their production quotas for the day. This fresh approach to work even had an impact on the community, adding evidence that life at work affects life after work. The town opened its first day care center, and workers in the factory put together the com-munity's first interracial gospel choir. Productivity went up and ab-senteeism went down. Labor relations improved so much that the company completed the 1975 contract with the U.A.W. four months before the old one had expired.

Bolivar is the kind of experiment that some people secretly want to fail, and it eventually did. It made some union leaders and managers of similar businesses uncomfortable because, if it worked, it posed a chal-lenge to the legitimacy of their power and authority over members and workers. According to Sidney Harman, the Bolivar Project ultimately failed because managers were not equipped to manage a democratic workplace. He said the biggest mistake that they made was allowing workers to go home after they had met their production quotas. Employees eventually stopped going to the self-improvement classes and started cutting corners on their work to get out sooner. Some even put false bottoms on boxes so they could pack them with fewer mirrors to meet their quotas early in the day. Eventually workers regarded the shortened workday as an entitlement. By the 1980s Harman had to spend more money on quality control and the absentee rate went up again. The factory began a long decline in the 1980s and eventually shut down in February 1998.

With cases like Bolivar, it's often easy to blame the firm's failure on poor management and out-of-control employees. We might jump to the conclusion that theory X is correct—that employees don't want to take responsibility and exercise control. But perhaps the most important thing the case illustrates is that even with an engaged workforce and company educational programs, work sometimes cannot compete with the lure of *really* free time, especially when people have job security. Maybe the message here is that despite the best efforts of the organization, some people will always prefer to be on their own rather than at work. For them, work truly is pay for lost freedom, as much as employers want them to believe that they are paid for their "value added."

There are some even more compelling reasons why the Bolivar Project failed. The company was slow to move toward plastic-based technologies that were taking the place of metal for mirrors. Harman Automotive also changed hands and the new owners were not interested in the worker-empowerment experiment. Management might have stemmed the tide of irresponsible employee behavior. In the workplace as in a society, liberty does not mean license and laws are designed to protect one person's liberty from interfering with that of others and the common good. If the new owners had been committed to the experiment, they might have laid out the problems and asked employees to come up with a new policy on going home early. Employee problems are thorny but not intractable. Mistakes on how work is managed can be fixed or forgiven. However, the market shows no mercy to companies that fail to innovate and develop products that people want, even if the companies are well run.

The Bolivar experiment had a far-reaching impact on other businesses. The General Motors factory in Tarrytown, New York, was scheduled to close in the 1970s, but after an agreement to install labor relations programs like the one at Bolivar, the factory survived until 1996. The experiment also helped the U.A.W. convince the Big Three automakers to negotiate more power sharing with the union.

The case of the Saturn car company is similar to Bolivar, but may have a happier ending. In the early 1990s General Motors developed a separate car company that would go toe to toe with the Japanese in the compact car market. Saturn was another experiment in participatory management that produced impressive results—a good product and excellent labor relations. Soon researchers and car buyers were flocking to Spring Hill (also in Tennessee) to see the committed and enthusiastic people who made their Saturns. The factory and its friendly workers were even the basis of ads for the car.

In 1996 the small-car market started to shrink. People wanted bigger cars. Saturn workers had begged General Motors to let them start building a midsize car or sport utility vehicle, but the parent company said no. By 1998 Saturn's car sales were down by 20.2 percent.[29] Workers felt the downturn in their paychecks, because unlike the contracts of other U.A.W. members, theirs called for a lower base pay and bonuses. Furthermore, their union contract afforded them less protection against layoffs. By March 1998 there was dissension at Saturn. Employees were furious with General Motors, and some, fearful of layoffs, wanted to scrap their unique labor contract and work agreements for the standard protections of a U.A.W. contract. Two thirds of the union members voted to keep their unique labor arrangement, and the experiment continued for the time being.

One unforeseen problem with giving employees real power, based on an understanding of the business, is that they become frustrated and angry when management makes stupid strategic decisions.

Hell Is Other People

Work not only has a variety of meanings for people, but it also elicits a variety of emotions from them. When we work with others we usually have to manage our emotions at least some of the time. The persona that we wear and the emotional range allowed depend on the job. An important part of what it means to act "professional" is to have strong control over one's emotions. We admire the nurse, doctor, lawyer, or teacher who can stay cool and composed under fire. A professional stance requires a person to subordinate himself or herself to the job at hand. He or she wears a professional face in the office, and this can make reading emotional cues more difficult in professional settings. How professionals feel about their clients or how their clients feel about them gets pushed into the background. Some jobs, such as those in health care, require an acted emotional stance of care and concern plus the management of real emotions related to the job. A nurse who works in a ward for terminal patients may experience both genuine feelings of sadness for the death of a patient and the appropriate professional, emotionally distanced stances that are part of the job. In the first case he or she must manage real emotions of sadness, and in the second must affect professional expressions of regret in dealing with the family.

We expect professional behavior from all sorts of nonprofessionals too, especially from service industry workers such as bank tellers, salesclerks, and fast-food servers. For workers who do not engage in purely physical labor, the hardest part of their job is emotional labor, because, as a character in Jean-Paul Sartre's play *No Exit* notes, "Hell is other people." Women still carry the brunt of service jobs that require emotional labor, and in general do more emotional labor in the workplace. Women are expected to smile, be cheerful, show concern for people when they are ill, and laugh at the jokes of male colleagues. Part of this comes from their being in subordinate positions in organizations, but part of it comes from cultural expectations of women.[30] Men, on the other hand, have more leeway to swear and get angry at work. They aren't expected to smile and be cheerful all the time.

Organizations, like families and people in general, often bury conflicts and seek to remain pleasant and friendly, even though emotions like anger simmer beneath the surface. This control is particularly important for people in subordinate positions. Some people mistakenly feel that when they move higher up the corporate ladder they regain the license to yell and scream at others below them. In fact, the higher up one moves in an organization, the more one is expected to practice emotional control. Sometimes employees explode out of frustration, usually over a real or perceived injustice, such as sexual harassment, favoritism, or an unfair performance appraisal.[31] In March 1998 an angry employee of the Connecticut Lottery killed four supervisors and himself because he did not receive a promotion. A year earlier, basketball star Latrell Sprewell made headlines when he attacked his coach P. J. Carlesimo for taunting him. Like most problems in the workplace, anger at work has spawned a market for "anger consultants." There is even an "Anger Institute" in Chicago.

Almost everyone has to manage his or her emotions on the job, but in service work people not only have to control their emotions but must also convey a particular set of emotions. It used to be that service workers had to be polite; today they also have to be friendly. In her provocative book *The Managed Heart,* Arlie Russell Hochschild describes how businesses have transformed emotions into commodities that have market value. She argues that just as people can become alienated in goods-producing jobs, they can be alienated in service-producing jobs. People in goods-producing jobs feel alienated from their product because they do not use their intellect to produce it. People in service jobs feel alienated from their service because they do not always use their real emotions when giving the service. Both feel they are going through the motions of producing something that has little to do with who or what they are.

Emotional exchanges that we might avoid in private life become common in public life, though for the most part they're one-way. For example, a customer assumes the right to express hostility toward a flight attendant, who because of his or her job cannot yell back. In fact, airlines pay flight attendants to listen to rude and angry customers; that is as much a part of their job as smiling and saying "bye-bye" when you walk off the plane. As consumers of emotional labor, we feel outraged when a service worker yells back. Customers demand not only polite service but service with the appropriate emotional stance, whether it is infinite patience or sympathy with a problem or service with a smile. They often complain to a supervisor about an employee's expression of anger.

Every day we are exposed to commercialized feelings of personalization, good cheer, and friendliness (in some cases, though, they are quite genuine). The "happy face" view of service goes beyond politeness and civility. At the drive-up window of a NationsBank, there is a sign that reads, "The teller will greet you by name." Consider the Wal-Mart greeter whose main purpose is to make you feel good, which may, in some abstract way, inspire you to buy more or at least come back again. And many of us have cringed a little when the waiter in a restaurant introduces himself to us ("Hello, I'm Leon and I'll be your waiter . . .).

Hochschild observes, "All in all, a private emotional system has been subordinated to commercial logic, and it has been changed by it."[32] Some service employees are pushed to go beyond smiling service. Take, for example, a TWA computer screen that reads, "When people like you, they like TWA too." Part of the TWA employee's job is to be likable, which is far more complex and demanding than just smiling. But even the requirement to smile on the job can be sinister. Clerks at one supermarket have to wear name badges that say, "My Promise: A Smile or a Hello or You Get My Dollar." They are literally punished—or more precisely, humiliated—in front of the customer if they fail to smile.

Hochschild's study focused on flight attendants, who sell a variety of feelings such as security and comfort, and bill collectors, who specialize in producing fear and intimidation. The toll that these jobs take on people can be tremendous. The flight attendant complains that she can't stop smiling when she gets home; the bill collector can't always switch off the aggression. Hochschild says that a worker who identifies too much emotionally risks burnout. A worker who doesn't identify may denigrate himself or herself as a phony. Someone who sees the job as an acting job may be better able to cope with it, but may still have a certain cynicism about the work. As was pointed out earlier, maybe alienation is a reasonable reaction to work in the modern world. Alienation is usually caused by lack of personal control or freedom of choice over work. If work has nothing to do with you, why should you feel any connection to it? More freedom or power over the conditions of work is one remedy for alienation. With emotional work this might mean giving employees permission to yell at the customer once in a while. The problem today is that customers have come to expect smiling service no matter what. In this environment the emotional strain on employees who deal with customers promises to grow as their latitude for spontaneous emotional responses shrinks.

The bright side of service work is that people often do get satisfaction out of helping others and genuine emotions often do converge with emotions appropriate to the job. This usually happens when a person's personality suits the emotional stance of his or her occupation. Hochschild observed that the more we manage our emotions at work, the more value we put on "the unmanaged heart," or our spontaneous emotions. Hochschild draws the conclusion that the corporate use of guile and the organized use of training to sustain it have led us to value authenticity, or the truth of our own natural feelings, more. Ironically, it has also made it more difficult for one to convey genuine positive feelings on the job. Work has become increasingly confusing because it evokes feelings that must be suppressed and sometimes demands feelings that are not real.

The issue of emotions in the workplace takes us back to C. Wright Mills, William H. Whyte, and Sloan Wilson. All of them were concerned with the power of organizations and how they might negatively influence and dominate a person's life. Mills believed that people had to sell their personalities to work in bureaucratic organizations. Whyte was concerned with the toll of conformity on the individual. (Hochschild points out that people don't have to really change, they just have to learn how to act their emotional role.) In the opening scene of Wilson's *The Man in the Gray Flannel Suit,* Tom Rath is both sincere, in that he tells the truth, and authentic, in that he tries to come to grips with who he is. Nonetheless, the rest of the novel is really about his struggle to be truthful to himself. It's ironic that "the man in the gray flannel suit" became a term for a boring conformist organization man. Tom Rath is anything but that. He is a man wrestling the corporation and struggling to be honest with himself and others.

8.

The Promising Workplace

As we have seen, today's sophisticated corporate workplace is brought to us by scores of psychologists, sociologists, and management consultants, who have analyzed what people need and how they work in groups. There is no shortage of good intentions in its design. These specialists wanted work to be meaningful. They wanted employees to be fulfilled by their jobs. They wanted the workplace to have an enjoyable and friendly atmosphere. The ideal manager was not the mean and surly boss. He or she was a kind and caring leader who would inspire and "coach" employees. The number of new management fads exploded in the 1980s. Some argued that the manager's job was to "make meaning" for employees. While experiments in workplace democracy waned, many companies claimed to "empower" employees or give them more say over their work. Pundits predicted that more and more workers will be "knowledge workers" who will take pleasure in using their skills at work. By the 1980s work promised to be challenging, fun, exciting, and like a big happy "family."

Not only was the corporate workplace more interesting, friendly, and attentive to the welfare of employees, but many businesses began to emphasize the importance of shared ethical values in the organization. Real or sometimes feigned corporate interest in business ethics and the social responsibility of business flourished in the 1980s. Major business schools such as Harvard and Wharton began requiring courses in the subject. By 1986, 75 percent of Fortune 500 companies had mission statements or codes of ethics.[1]

The concern for business ethics emerged in the 1980s for several reasons. Some companies worried about bad press, scandals, lawsuits, and illegal activities. Others felt that a statement of shared ethical values was important because their employees came from diverse backgrounds and value systems. The desire for good public and customer relations spurred some businesses to pay attention or at least lip service to ethics. And lastly, there were corporate leaders who simply felt that a company should have a statement of ethics. Some codes were geared toward how employees should behave at work, while others stated the firm's ethical obligations to its stakeholders, including employees.

Some ethics statements expressed grand humanistic ideals. For example, in the early 1980s Borg-Warner, a conglomerate of automotive, financial services, and security service businesses, wrote its code of ethics. The Harvard Business School wrote a glowing case study of how its CEO, Jim Beré, developed the code.[2] Borg-Warner's code began with the statements "We believe in the dignity of the individual" and "We believe in the commonwealth of Borg-Warner and its people." It also said, "We must heed the voice of our natural concern for others" and "grant others the same respect, cooperation, and decency we seek for ourselves."[3] The code was framed and hung in the offices of Borg-Warner's various businesses. With all these innovations in the workplace and the ideals expressed in codes such as Borg-Warner's, the corporate workplace appeared to be an enlightened place that showed great concern for its employees.

After a history of slavery, indentured servitude, and scientific management, was the corporation of the mid-1980s the workplace El Dorado?

From Muscle Men to Holy Men

Popular management books have had a tremendous influence on management practices and to some extent on how people think. These books are often based on consulting experience or repackaged social science research, and are then written in a clear and enjoyable way. Often the ideas in these books lose something in the popular translation and lose even more in the way that companies actually implement them.

Small businesses can't afford to hire the expensive consultants. However, they can get a consultant's advice for free from a how-to management book. Furthermore, popular management books aren't bought only by managers, they are bought by employees who hope to be managers someday. These books contain the kind of language and encapsulated meanings that echo throughout the workplace. Most of the rhetoric of work today comes from popular management books and programs. As we saw earlier, the words that we use shape the way we do or don't make sense of the world. In this way, popular management books influence how people think about work. Often, because of their short shelf life and the wide range of competing ideas on the market at the same time, they send out conflicting messages about what work is and should be.

American management books are sometimes also popular in other countries. In 1985, for example, you could buy a copy of *In Search of Excellence,* by Thomas J. Peters and Robert H. Waterman Jr., in places as far away as Kota Kinabalu. American management texts are often used to teach M.B.A. courses in other countries. A number of foreign nationals get business degrees in the United States and carry popular management ideas home. Also, many of the big American consulting firms and well-known business professors spread "new" American ideas about management throughout the world. American multinationals carry the language of the latest management trend to foreign shores. While management ideas certainly translate differently in different cultures, the language of the latest American management theories is also spoken by businesspeople in other countries.

It is not surprising that the corporations that were repeatedly held out as models in best-selling business books in the 1980s were not only respected and successful businesses, like Hewlett-Packard, Johnson & Johnson, Levi Strauss, and AT&T, but also the major consumers of management research and employers of the consultants who write best-selling business books. On the one hand, these companies testify to the success of management innovations. On the other hand, the situation suggests that Gilson's question about the objectivity of management research that is directly or indirectly financed by big business is still relevant. We might also wonder why questions about power, authority, and conflict in organizations are rarely discussed in management texts or popular literature. These books and theories are for and about managers. Employees often appear in these books as theoretical constructs. Managers are told what employees need and how to deliver it.

Managers hungered for good advice in the early 1980s, when many businesses were devastated by inflation, stagnant growth, and global competition, mainly from Japan. The market was ripe for management fads designed to lift the spirits of managers and capture the hearts of workers. Management trends of the 1980s appealed to managers because they made them feel powerful and inspiring, but most important, they promised profits. In the 1980s the best-selling business books portrayed business leaders as masters of their corporate universe *and* lovable leaders. The lovable leader was an attractive image, especially given the lack of respect and trust for authority figures, particularly in business and government.

In 1981 Richard T. Pascale and Anthony Athos's *The Art of Japanese Management* was a best-seller. The "new" idea from Japan was job enrichment and "quality circles"—after all, these had worked for the Japanese (and, as we have seen, for some American industries at the beginning of the century). William G. Ouchi's *Theory Z* was also a best-seller that year. His book emphasized the Japanese practices of job security, careful evaluation of how the employee worked alone and in groups, and slow promotion within the organization. Needless to say, theory Z never really caught on. Ouchi admitted in his book that theory Z wasn't for every business. Both of these books intimated that managers needed the kind and gentle wisdom of a Zen master.

Another best-selling business book was Kenneth Blanchard and Spencer Johnson's *The One Minute Manager.* Written in 1982, this short adult fairy tale portrayed a kindly and therapeutic manager who inspired fealty and commitment. He was almost a caricature of the "mild-looking" therapist that Whyte feared would take over organizations. The hero of *The One Minute Manager* was a combination Mr. Rogers–Captain Kangaroo. Some companies required all of their managers to read the book, and it sold over three million copies. That same year, the enormously popular *In Search of Excellence* helped to elevate managers from muscle men to holy men who used emotion and inspiration to make employees productive. In the 1980s, as in the 1960s, many people believed that the key to making workers productive was to get to their feelings, or what Peters and Waterman called their "hot buttons." This was management without overt coercion, but not without impact. However, in the 1980s power and control of employees was cloaked in yet another guise, one that theorists called culture.

The "Discovery" of Culture

In Search of Excellence was arguably the most important business book of the decade. It was published in 1982, a year that produced a bumper crop of best-selling business books for a hungry audience of managers and wannabe managers who were tired of hearing that America was "managing its way into economic decline." In simple terms and pithy prose, Thomas J. Peters and Robert H. Waterman, Jr., told readers what American companies like Dana, Frito-Lay, and Texas Instruments were doing right.

When it came to managing people, Peters and Waterman believed that the role of a manager is to shape the "corporate culture" and "make meaning" for employees. By "corporate culture" Peters and Waterman meant the values, symbols, ideologies, language, beliefs, rituals, and myths of an organization. They didn't think excellent organizations produced the conformist described by Whyte. They assured us: "In the very same institutions in which culture is so dominant, the highest levels of true autonomy occur. The culture regulates rigorously the few variables that do count, and it provides meaning. Nonetheless, people in these organizations are encouraged to stick out, to innovate."[4] For example, they tell us, IBM has a strong commitment to service and "devotion" to the customer. This commitment provides the employees with great freedom, because "everyone, from clerks on up, is prodded to do whatever he or she can to ensure that the individual customer gets taken care of."[5] Peters and Waterman weren't prescribing workplace democracy, but rather the freedom to do one's job well within a controlled and well-orchestrated system. They emphasized the importance of paying attention to employees, finding out what excited them, and creating intentional and sustained Hawthorn effects within the organization.

Terrence E. Deal and Allan A. Kennedy's *Corporate Cultures,* also published in 1982, elaborated on how corporate culture shaped work.

Deal and Kennedy recognized what Mayo had noted almost forty years earlier: organizations *are* cultures, in that they have their own values, myths, rituals, and goals. Their book sang the praises of companies such as Xerox, IBM, General Electric, and Digital Equipment because they not only *had* cultures (in a sense every organization has a culture), they had *strong* cultures. The difference between a run-of-the-mill culture and a strong culture was simple: "A strong culture enables people to feel better about what they do, so they are more likely to work harder."[6] Successful companies have strong cultures and managers who understand their culture. Deal and Kennedy assured the reader that employees who work for companies with strong cultures will work overtime or go the extra mile because they are happy to belong to such a great organization. For them the ghost in the machine wasn't located in the person, but resided in the culture. The corporate culture ideal assumed that if you built a great place to work, great employees would come. Given this *Field of Dreams* philosophy, it's not surprising that two years later, in 1984, people were buying up copies of *The 100 Best Companies to Work for in America* (which has come out in several editions since then).[7]

Deal and Kennedy believed that, unlike workers ten or twenty years ago, the workers of their day were "confused" and this confusion was largely the result of "uncertainty." They explained that when workers feel cheated by their jobs, "they allow special interests to take up their time; their life values are uncertain; they are blameful and cynical; they confuse morality and ethics."[8] Deal and Kennedy thought that a strong corporate culture removed uncertainty from employees' lives by giving them what they needed: structure, a value system, and pride in belonging to a company of which they could be proud. However, some of the so-called problems that employees had weren't clearly explained. What are these special interests and why is it wrong to spend time on them? Are we supposed to be "certain" of our life values? Thoughtful people might constantly reevaluate their values and priorities in life. Lastly, what do Deal and Kennedy mean by the so-called confusion between ethics and morality? Is individual morality getting in the way of corporate ethics? This sounds like a restatement of what William H. Whyte called the "social ethic," which asserted that the moral claims of the group were more important than the moral claims of the individual. Perhaps the greatest uncertainty that corporate culture failed to alleviate was the same uncertainty employees had in the 1920s and, for the most part, have always had, uncertainty about their employment. But in the 1980s there still was a great deal of job security in corporations such as IBM.

By the 1980s corporate welfare programs and the corporate culture ideas of management made some corporations into the social and psychological equivalent of Pullman, Illinois, the town that George Mortimer Pullman built for his employees. However, instead of simply providing stores and houses, the company promised to take on the functions of other institutions in society. Large corporations offered employees "values," inspiration, social events, community, and friendship. The early efforts of welfare capitalism paled in comparison to what large corporations like IBM had to offer. Extraordinary benefit plans took care of employees' health, children, and elderly parents. Corporate employee assistance programs provided services ranging from substance abuse programs to aid for troubled families. Many large corporations were, or tried to be, the happy family and cohesive community that some people didn't have. The organization man wasn't dead, he—and now she—had just moved from suburbia into the company.

The great advantage of a strong corporate culture was that it was an all-inclusive, self-regulating social system. The disadvantages included the fact that it could be oppressive and resistant to change. But perhaps the greatest downside to it was that employees became increasingly dependent on work to fill needs—e.g., for friendship—that they might otherwise have filled outside of work. Hence, if you lost your job, you lost much more than your work and income.

The Enchanted Organization

In Silicon Valley, hi-tech firms such as Hewlett-Packard created a corporate culture that promoted creativity and collegiality. They tried to avoid the deadening bureaucratic trappings of hierarchy and privilege, which Max Weber had warned might lead to "a depersonalization of social life or a disenchantment of the world."[9] Robert Howard studied some of these firms, and in his book *Brave New Workplace* he argued that the new organization is an attempt to reenchant the workplace by making it more personal. He found that the "brave new workplaces" of 1985 seemed to work well for some people, but were disturbing for others. Organizations, portraying themselves as communities, were often highly divided between the professionals such as the Ph.D. programming genius and the secretary in the sales office. One of his interviewees reported that everyone from the head of the company on down went by his or her first name. This seemingly friendly, open atmosphere could be confusing, since the boss was still the boss who might at one moment be your beer-drinking buddy and at another be the one who fires you. Howard portrayed the brave new workplaces as organizations where emotions and power relationships are tricky because management cloaks the hierarchy in friendly, surface egalitarianism and achieves control over work through domination of meanings, values, and feelings.[10] Or, if all sensitivity and friendly feeling fails, it achieves control through a display of raw, naked power.

In Howard's brave new workplace social events such as doughnut breaks and beer busts are ways of improving communication. However, there is pressure to attend these events and pressure to be friendly. These mechanisms were put in place to produce a team spirit and commitment to the organization. For someone who prefers to work during the doughnut break or to buy groceries during the Friday afternoon beer bust, this forced socializing is a problem. Social events are also difficult for those who are simply different. The corporate culture may genuinely value a diverse workforce, but it still expects everyone to eat doughnuts together. The enchanted corporation requires people to do two kinds of work, the job itself and the work of taking part in its social life. People are often consciously or unconsciously evaluated on both. As etiquette writer Judith Martin ("Miss Manners") observed, "The chief purpose of business entertaining is to confuse people into applying social standards, such as loyalty regardless of merit, to business dealings."[11] She said that "business entertaining" is an oxymoron. It is neither business nor is it entertaining.

Inside the bleak and impersonal organization of Frederick Winslow Taylor, the workplace was not as pleasant, but the relationships of power and control were clear. Nothing much was required of the self, except to perform an assigned function. It is a plain behavioral world where people do more if you pay them more or threaten to pay them less. In a tougher, less sensitive working world, the incentive is, You get to keep your job. Taylor's pig-iron handler, "Schmitt," worked under physical and mental constraints but did not have to smile at the boss. He just had to move pig iron. Schmitt got his self-esteem at home and in the marketplace. He traded his satisfaction as a worker for his satisfaction as a consumer. He was the economic man, the drinking man, and the ladies' man; but he wasn't, and didn't have to be, the company man. There were few or no social requirements to his job. He was not asked to eat doughnuts with his coworkers and smile, or to talk about his innermost feelings in company training seminars. As Eldridge Cleaver pointed out in *Soul on Ice*, it is better to be a "field nigger" than a "house nigger" because the former does not have to suffer the added indignities of polite interactions with people he or she doesn't like.

The Mystic at Pacific Bell

Large corporations spent fortunes on consultants and training programs in the 1980s. Most of these programs were designed to make work more enjoyable and to give employees more of a say in their work, or "empower" them. The buzzword empowerment was also called "leadership." While giving people the power to do something is different from having them lead others, this difference is often ignored in management rhetoric. Many organizations were getting rid of middle managers and flattening out the organizational hierarchy. This meant responsibility was pushed down in the organization and employees were expected to take on more responsibility for their work. (This was another reason why business ethics training became a practice in some organizations.) However, empowerment or leadership programs were sometimes manipulative. Empowerment often meant making people do more work, or making them feel that they had more power when they actually did not. Sometimes these programs backfired.

In the 1980s, Pacific Bell was proud of its leadership development program. The program was intended to move the organization away from the old AT&T culture, give low-level managers more responsibilities, cut the number of middle managers, and become more customer focused. Of Pacific Bell's sixty-seven thousand employees, twenty-three thousand took the two-day training.[12] Charles Krone created the leadership development program that came to be called "Kroning." The stated aim of this New Age program was "to get all employees using the same language and thinking at all times about the six essentials of organizational health: expansion, freedom, identity, concentration, order, and interaction."[13] There is a certain obvious contradiction in a leadership or empowerment program that requires everyone to "think at all times" about the same things. The program was based vaguely on the Russian-born mystic Georgy Ivanovich Gurdjieff's "law of three," which teaches that there are no constraints that can't be reconciled. In 1987, the California Public Utilities Commission asked Pacific Bell to stop the training. After a two-month investigation of this forty-million-dollar effort, the commission reported that employees had complained that the program was an attempt to "brainwash" them. An employee survey turned up repeated references to "Big Brother," "thought control," and "mind restructuring." Employees also complained that the Krone program used obscure language and esoteric concepts that made some people feel stupid. The irony was that the investigation found that all employees expressed simultaneously a love of and commitment to Pacific Bell *and* a mistrust of its managers.[14] A survey of two thousand Pacific Bell employees concluded that top managers at Bell "blame the employees for the lack of productivity and are trying to make them think better; however, the Pacific Bell workforce already knows how to think."[15] These employees resented being told *what* to think.

Consultants or "Insultants"?

It's worth noting here that Scott Adams, the creator of the satirical Dilbert cartoons, worked at Pacific Bell around the time of the Krone program scandal. On the jacket of his first book, written in 1995, he is said to have spent "nine years as a necktie-wearing, corporate victim assigned to cubicle 4S700R at the headquarters of Pacific Bell."[16] The Krone program scandal helps us understand where he got some of his early material. Adams's cartoons often lambaste silly corporate training programs that insult the intelligence of employees. For example, in one cartoon the "renowned psychologist" Dogbert gives a team-building seminar in which Dilbert and his coworkers are asked to cut out paper dolls while blindfolded. Dogbert explains, "This may seem absurd. But soon cognitive dissonance will set in and you will cry and hug and think you learned something."[17] There really are outside firms that design silly training sessions. Sometimes these programs seem geared more toward elementary school students than toward the college-educated employees who make up a large proportion of corporate employees.

Thirty years after *The Organization Man,* corporations spent thirty billion dollars on training. (Today that figure has risen to fifty-six billion dollars.) Most of the training was in technical and management skills, but in 1986 about four billion dollars went to programs such as Krone's or Werner Erhard's rehashed est franchise called Transformation Technologies. In 1987, a California business magazine surveyed five hundred corporate owners and presidents and found that half of their companies used some form of consciousness raising, another form of sensitivity training.[18] These programs focused on the same themes espoused today, empowerment, leadership, and positive thinking. They were distinctive because they used unorthodox training techniques, such as meditation, biofeedback, and hypnosis. A company called Energy Unlimited promised to build self-confidence by escorting barefoot executives across hot coals.

While some managers get what they need from burning coals, others turn to horses for wisdom. In the mid-1990s corporate officers from Disney, Xerox, General Motors and AT&T flocked to seminars at Monty Roberts's farm in California.[19] Roberts, the famous horse gentler, immortalized in the movie *The Horse Whisperer* and the best-selling book *The Man Who Listens to Horses,* passes on the communication lessons that he has learned from horses to managers.

While many of these programs look ridiculous to the outsider, they gained serious followers among some corporate managers. Other managers just gave lip service to fads as they passed through the corporation. As John Micklethwait and Adrian Wooldridge point out in their book *The Witch Doctors,* there are so many management theories around today that they often contradict each other. For example, one theory will say the more distinctive a corporate culture the better, while another says the more multicultural a corporation the better.[20] One says quality is important, while another says that speed is what counts. They also note that today's companies change their management theories more rapidly. The life cycle of a management fad has shrunk from ten years to one year. The consulting firm Bain & Company took twenty-five popular management theories and did a worldwide survey on how many theories companies used in their businesses. In 1993 the average was 11.8; in 1994, 12.7, and the firm estimated that in 1995 the average would grow to 14.1.[21] Jack Welch, CEO of General Electric, thinks it is "healthy" for a company to try out different ideas of management.[22] But is it healthy for employees?

The impact of these programs on employees is unclear; however, anxiety, confusion, and cynicism are a few likely responses. Some frustrated managers invented the acronym BOHICA, or "bend over here it comes again," to describe this parade of management initiatives.[23] We rarely hear about cases in which employees complain about a company training program. That's why the Krone program scandal is distinctive. Most employees are a captive audience and their success in the organization is contingent on playing the game and using the language of these initiatives. Training programs sometimes create a short-lived sense of euphoria among participants or produce the so-called Hawthorn effect. Some raise the expectation that employees are going to be enriched and empowered; however, after the dust settles, everything seems the same until the next program.

The Krone program scandal was not an isolated incident. Many management fads make promises about empowerment on which they can't deliver or have no intention of delivering. On the one hand, Pacific Bell employees were being promised more power and control over their work, while on the other hand, some felt that they were being manipulated by the training program. The usual answer for why empowerment programs fail is that supervisors and line managers do not want to give up power or, as we saw in the Bolivar case, that they give up too much power. The impact of these training programs on employees is worth considering. For some people, rapidly changing management theories and their ideas about motivation and meaning may make work more exciting. However, others may find it successively more difficult to commit to a new management approach when they know management won't stick to it for very long. Finding satisfaction in work is difficult when the work is constantly being engineered by the next management initiative or training program. Work that stays the same but is continually redefined and renamed may eventually become meaningless.

In the 1950s employees conformed to the organization; in the 1960s and 1970s they went through sensitivity training; in the 1980s they went to company events to build corporate culture. In the 1990s training focused on team building. Rather than crawling around on the floor in a room, employees hung from ropes in the great outdoors. Outward Bound and programs like it aim to teach leadership and build teamwork by making people face scary physical experiences together. The organization man has given way to the team player, the man in the gray flannel suit to the men and women in Nikes. Who or what will they be next?

Through all this hoopla the ideal image of managers in organizations moved from the surly boss to the kindly, supportive, dynamic, inspiring, heroic, visionary, and powerful leader. In practice, some managers were still tyrants, but they were polite, smiled more, and had consultants to help them use the right language. On the one side are these "new" managers who maintain control without appearing to do so. On the other side are the workers who have had to go through all these corporate programs.

The workplace may have been more lively and filled with promise, but was it more honest?

Teamwork

The problem with management fads is that they are often uncritical and ahistorical. As a result, management theorists discover the same things about work over and over and are equally delighted every time they do so. Teamwork is one of these big "new" ideas that captured the imaginations of managers in the 1980s and 1990s. The word *team* brings to the workplace the idea of fun and the challenge and heroism of sport. The idea that we are all in this together and we've got to beat out the competition engenders excitement and caters to people's need to belong (if they have one). The other wonderful thing about the sports imagery is that it conjures up dramatic feats of excellence, noble commitment to a goal, and the desire for perfection. Micklethwait and Wooldridge note how ironic it is that business organizations today often encourage employees to act more like sports teams while sports teams act more like businesses. Professional basketball is hardly a model of teamwork when its big stars take over the games and payrolls of their teams.[24]

Teams, even more so than cultures, can be a powerful form of social control. In a team, peer pressure from the group keeps everyone in line, pulling his or her weight. The team affects the individual in a more direct way than the larger culture of the organization. If the group puts out a measurable product, they can "keep score" and hopefully be rewarded on their performance. After all, part of the attraction of playing on a team is the promise of winning. But what is it like to play on a team where the only prospect is staying in the game or losing? Professor Paul Osterman of MIT surveyed five hundred companies between 1992 and 1997 and found that companies that used teams to increase quality and productivity did not share their gains with the teams, unless they were unionized. He also discovered that the companies that used teams tended to have more layoffs that those that did not.[25] In these cases, playing on the team at work has little in common with playing on the neighborhood basketball team.

The idea of a team has become so popular in recent years that the word has become disconnected from the idea. As consultant Jon Katzenbach points out, most management teams aren't teams at all, but rather groups of individuals who use the term to feel good.[26] One company had a "team" of service representatives who spent all day in small cubicles talking on the phone. One wonders if being called a team really made them feel better about working alone together. Back in the 1950s even David Riesman recognized that the cult of teamwork in organizations was really "antagonistic cooperation," in which teamwork conceals the real struggle for survival within the organization.

Getting cooperation from employees has always been a challenge. That is why many companies invested in learning how to build and lead or "coach" teams. Here again the romanticism of teams and sports analogies are evident. Consider the reverence for the team leader in the book *Leading Self-Directed Work Teams*. The author, Kimball Fisher, emphasizes the importance of authenticity. He writes that the key values of a team leader are belief in the importance of work, a belief that work is life, a belief in the "aggressive" development of team members, and a determination to "eliminate barriers to team performance." This description is either inspiring or frightening, depending on whether you are the team leader or a team member. Would you want to work for this person?

Real sports coaches inspire, help, and encourage, but they can also sometimes act like obnoxious fascists who are lionized only if they produce winning teams. The relationship between a coach and a team player is usually paternalistic or materialistic. The word *coach* carries with it the romantic image of someone who has the interests of the individual as well as the team at heart. It promises care and concern. Authors like Fisher often combine the sports imagery of a coach and team with the Mr. Rogers and holy man model of management. Fisher tells us that team leaders have to be themselves, or authentic. He quotes a manager who says, "The distinction between the work person and the family person is unhealthy and artificial."[27] Whereas the team leaders have to be themselves, it's not clear who the team players are supposed to be. One thing we do know is that the word *team* promises a special kind of collaboration and cooperation and the possibility of winning.

If the word *coach* carries with it the promise of helping people perform better as individuals and together, what happens when such words are used but don't live up to their promises? Then the team is just a collection of people, the coach is just a boss, and employees smirk or give a sigh of resignation at the empty terms used to describe their work. A Dilbert cartoon sums up this attitude best. When Dilbert's boss tells his employees that he is going to reorganize them into "fast-moving teams," their response is, "Good plan. We'll never realize we're powerless, micro-managed serfs after we call ourselves a 'team.' "[28]

Information and Voice

The other insight about work that management theorists keep discovering is that if you give people information and a say in how to improve their work, they can produce impressive results. The fact that managers are constantly amazed by this tells us something about the respect that they have had for employees. Perhaps it is part of Taylor's legacy, perhaps it is a distortion that comes with having power over others, but in many workplaces today managers still underestimate the intelligence of their workers.

The case of Warner Gear, a subsidiary of Borg-Warner, illustrates the way that sharing information and giving employees a real say in their work and team building can turn a company around. In 1980 the management of Warner Gear, a builder of manual transmissions for cars and trucks, wanted to implement "employee involvement circles" (EICs). Their United Auto Workers union resisted, arguing that EICs were "just another form of management manipulation." At the time Warner Gear's labor relations were tumultuous. Before 1980, the U.A.W. constitution had sanctioned the trade-off of control for mutual gain. The company was in very bad financial shape. In desperation, management began sharing financial information with the employees. The union realized that they were all in the same boat and the boat was sinking, so it made generous concessions in the labor contract, especially in the area of health benefits.

By the end of 1980, the union agreed to take part in the EICs. Life at Warner Gear improved significantly. Grievances and production costs diminished. Morale and profits went up. The quality circles saved the company two million dollars in 1984, and all areas of production costs went down. By 1985 there were eighty EICs with eight hundred employees. Employees were enthusiastic about the circles and became knowledgeable about the business. One union member said, "When the quality circles first started, I thought that they were all bull, but not now. We have communication like we've never had before." Another commented, "I'm a union man. They wanted us to get involved. Now it's a way of life."[29]

Along with the EICs the company also instituted a profit-sharing program. In five years, Warner Gear turned itself around into a profit-making firm. Unlike the Bolivar case, where the company failed to innovate its product, Warner Gear had developed the shift-on-the-fly gearbox, which allowed drivers to go from two-wheel to four-wheel drive with the push of a button. For Warner Gear employees, work in 1984 was rewarding and filled with the promise of profits. In this case, as in the Bolivar case, knowledge of the business, genuine empowerment, teamwork, and "treating people like adults" paid off.

All was going well for Warner Gear in 1985. However, in July of that year, with no warning to the managers who had implemented the EICs, Borg-Warner decided to ship the marine and industrial manufacturing division to Kenfig, Wales. This meant that the factory would lose three hundred jobs. All the energy and commitment of the employees at Warner Gear didn't matter when it came to this business decision. While no one had promised employees that this sort of thing wouldn't happen, it struck at the very roots of trust and goodwill. The "team" that had helped save the company, had given up some of their health benefits, and worked in a place that had framed posters with the motto: "We believe in the commonwealth of Borg-Warner and its people" were out of work.

TQM: The Great Synthesis

Of all the management theories in the 1980s, few were embraced with the fervor or passion of Total Quality Management (TQM). Perhaps this was because people had learned TQM's guiding principle at their mother's knee—"Do it right the first time." This meant that quality control should be done along the way and not at the end of the process. TQM also rested on the old business adage "The customer is always right." To realize these two principles TQM was a synthesis of virtually all the useful management insights since scientific management. It rolled up Japanese management, quality circles, group dynamics, teamwork, leadership, corporate culture, and statistical quality control into one package. Managers enthusiastically adopted TQM because so much of it was familiar. However, this didn't stop management writers from proclaiming its newness. Many of its disciples emphasized that it was a "new philosophy" that required "business leaders to accept TQM as a way of life."[30] One textbook breathlessly explained that TQM is a "paradigm shift" and urged managers to make the shift to TQM, calling it "profound" on a personal and organizational level.[31]

There is little agreement on the exact definition of TQM, but the Total Quality Forum, a group of business leaders and academics who meet annually to study TQM and spread the word, offers up this jargon-ridden definition of Total Quality:

> . . . a people focused management system that aims at continual increase in customer satisfaction at continually lower real cost. TQ is a total system approach (not a separate area or program), and an integral part of high-level strategy. It works horizontally across functions and departments, involving all employees, top to bottom, and extends backwards and forwards to include the supply chain and the customer chain . . . [32]

In the 1930s W. Edwards Deming argued that, contrary to popular belief, if you increased the quality of your product you would increase productivity. Instead of doing quality control on the finished product, you did it along the way. Deming taught this process to the Japanese. So did management consultant Joseph Juran in the 1950s and 1960s.[33] Juran offered a simple definition of quality: it is basically a product's "fitness for use." The product or service should do what the customer wants, needs, and has a right to expect from it.[34] The U.S. military took notice of the ideas of Deming, Juran, and other quality theorists like Armand V. Feigenbaum and began to examine its practices in light of them. The actual name Total Quality Management was coined by a navy psychologist, Nancy Warren.[35] In 1988 the Federal Quality

Institute was established to introduce senior government officials to TQM and provide training, consulting, and information to their agencies.

The U.S. government embraced and promoted TQM. The Malcolm Baldrige National Quality Award was created by the Department of Commerce in 1987 to reward corporate performance and stimulate competitiveness. The core values of this award and TQM are customer-driven quality, leadership, continuous improvement, employee participation and development, fast response, design quality, long-range outlook, management by fact (this usually means hard data), partnership development, corporate responsibility, and citizenship. One can see by these values that TQM was more than a system of production, but also had implications for employer-employee relationships.

What's in It for Me?

In his book on TQM and leadership, Richard J. Pierce tells us that front-line supervisors must act like leaders; they must become "more participatory and less authoritarian." This entails listening to employees' ideas and, when appropriate, implementing the ideas. Pierce goes on to say that employees, too, have to change. They need to know that "improved quality performance on their part, while vital, may bring no added compensation ("What is in it for me"), but in the long run, productivity and quality improvement are necessary for survival."[36] While Pierce refers to survival of the company, implicit in this statement is survival for the employee in that company. Is this the stick (or veiled threat) replacing the carrot? Behind TQM is the noble idea of reinstating a craft ethic that includes pride in workmanship and the intrinsic value of a job well done. While this is a positive and rewarding model of work, it cannot be isolated from the context in which a job is done and the kind of work that is done. In this setting, the employers want employees to act and *feel* (as craftspeople often do) that they are not engaged in a solely economic transaction, while at the same time reminding them that management is engaged in a purely economic transaction.

In fairness to Pierce, Deming had argued back in the 1930s that business should abolish the practice of paying for performance. Since workers rarely control the resources that affect output, he thought they should not be rewarded or penalized on the basis of productivity.[37] However, in a participatory workplace, workers, at least in theory, have more control over the processes. Therefore they *are* responsible for the success or failure of their work. Like any idea in management, Deming's idea can be taken out of context and misinterpreted as an excuse for not sharing more of the profits with employees (and it often has been).

Consider the case of a small company named Ensoniq, where managers flattened out the pay structure. Initially the employees resisted this idea—"Why should I get paid the same as Joe when I produce more?" The "equity theory" of motivation predicts that in this situation, productive employees will lower their productivity to create a more equitable situation.[38] The authors of the case, management scholars Randall S. Schuler and Drew L. Harris, explain how Ensoniq got around this problem with its hourly workers this way:

> First the gestalt of quality helps. Managers have credibility; employees see through consistent action that management is not out to take advantage of them. So, employees listen to managers and think. Managers also provide repeated explanations of the effect of the overall system.[39]

They don't explain this "gestalt" of quality, but the view that there is some magic aura about quality is prevalent, even in the writings of management academics. There is also a kind of leap of faith: By implementing TQM your managers will do such a good job that employees won't care about pay for performance. This has been a managerial aspiration since the Hawthorn studies.

Ensoniq took a different approach for salaried employees. Wages are adjusted according to the market rates for the employees' skills. Employees were also given bonuses for the time spent with the company. Schuler and Harris tell us, "Because of the trust built into the system, employees seem willing to discuss options and offers from others with Ensoniq management before committing to those alternatives."[40] This may be the result of trust, but getting an outside offer also seems to be the only way to get a raise at Ensoniq. Nonetheless, Schuler and Harris conclude that the management system at Ensoniq works because there is little turnover. This doesn't really tell us much. The job market for hourly employees could be bad and the salaried employees may not leave because the company matches outside job offers.

TQM theorists were not content to stop at the idea of producing higher quality goods and services. By the late 1980s and into the 1990s, the words *trust, commitment,* and *loyalty* graced the covers of business books. Part of the "magic" behind quality was that it was not only an effective way to manage, but was good in some moral sense of the word. Corporate responsibility was one of the criteria for the Malcolm Baldrige award. Pierce asserts that quality is a matter of ethics and that quality requires ethical leaders all along the line and at the top, giving customers what they want. He concludes that "companies have a moral obligation to live up to the promises they have made in advertisements, product brochures, and annual reports."[41] This is a strong statement of ethical commitment to customers, but what about employees and other stakeholders?

Ethical commitment in TQM is more explicit in regard to the relationship between the company and customers than it is to the relationship with employees. It emphasizes the importance of ethical leaders along the line, but almost any management program will do so (if it mentions anything about ethics). What most TQM theorists imply is that employees are treated ethically because they are allowed to participate in decisions and management listens to their ideas. This is a fairly thin description of an ethical arrangement. Just because employees participate does not mean that their relationship to management is ethical. People can participate in fraudulent business practices or they may participate because they are afraid of losing their job or afraid of their manager. These would not be considered ethical relationships.

One of Deming's original fourteen essential points for quality managers was "Drive out fear so that everyone may work effectively for the company."[42] But what are people afraid of at work? In their study of fear in the workplace, Kathleen D. Ryan and Daniel K. Oestreich found that people were usually afraid of retaliation, reprisals, and retribution. Other sources of fear are found in the things that people in the organization are afraid to discuss, or the "undiscussables."[43] According to Ryan and Oestreich's survey of 260 people in twenty-two organizations, the boss's management style ranked as the number one undiscussable; next came coworkers' performance, and compensation and benefits.[44] If people are most afraid of talking about a manager's style of managing, then it may be very difficult to gauge what employees think about TQM, or any other management initiative for that matter. Increased productivity may be the result of factors that have nothing to do with "teamwork" and "coaching," such as fear.

Many businesses credited TQM for helping them bring better products and services to the market and be more competitive in the global marketplace. Those same techniques also helped make some government agencies run smoother. In 1991 the U.S. General Accounting Office concluded that "companies that adopted quality management practices experienced an overall improvement of corporate performance.[45] The Conference Board did a survey of twenty TQM studies and came to a similar conclusion in 1993. But that takes us back to the central question of this book: Did TQM and the management innovations before it make work better for people? In other words, did work become more enjoyable, meaningful, profitable? Did these new systems create an environment of trust? Did they deliver on all that they promised—empowerment, training, the joy of being a team member?

Doing More with Less

Reengineering was the last major management theory of the twentieth century and fittingly, the antithesis of scientific management. Whereas Frederick Winslow Taylor, and Adam Smith before him, believed that the most efficient way to produce was to break a task down into its parts, reengineering used new technologies to coordinate a series of tasks so that they could be done by one person. Scientific management turned workers into specialists and made work boring. Reengineering was supposed to make employees into generalists and hence make work more varied and interesting. To close the management theory circle of the twentieth century, both scientific management and reengineering were concerned with the speed of production. Time is still money, only now it moves faster and costs more.

Reengineering was the brainchild of Michael Hammer and James Champy. They called their 1993 book *Reengineering the Corporation: A Manifesto for Business Revolution.* They use several cases to illustrate how they put together work that scientific management had broken into small pieces. IBM had organized its credit department on the principles of scientific management. A credit request would have to pass through the hands of five different specialists before it was approved. The process took anywhere from six days to two weeks. Needless to say, this wasn't good for business. Two senior managers from IBM decided to take a financing request and walk it thorough the five steps, asking the specialists to stop what they were doing and process the request. They discovered that the whole process could be done in ninety minutes. In the end, IBM replaced the specialists with generalists, who would, with the use of computers, take each application through the five-step process. IBM cut its seven-day turnaround for each application to four hours and did it with a slight reduction in the workforce. At the same time the department was able to handle one hundred times more financing requests than it had in the past.[46]

Of all the management innovations of the 1980s and 1990s, reengineering held the promise of making the work that a person does more interesting. Information technology made it possible for one person to have access to the information of many workers. In addition, Hammer and Champy tell us:

> People who once did as they were instructed now make choices and decisions on their own instead. . . . Managers stop acting like supervisors and behave more like coaches. Workers focus more on the customer's needs and less on their bosses'.[47]

As you can see, they continue with the language of coaching. In their book, as in the TQM books, its not clear how these managers are transformed or why employees are no longer afraid of their bosses, but the underlying belief seems to be that if you change the system, people in it change too. Yet more often than not you need to change the people who run the system.

Two years after *Reengineering the Corporation,* Hammer spent a chapter in his *Beyond Reengineering* explaining why the modern football team is "an almost perfect model" for the reengineered organization.[48] He tells us the head coach sits on the sidelines and motivates and supports players, while the position coach nurtures and develops players so they can execute the coordinator's plays. But where do we get these "nurturing coaches" and "head coaches" who are willing to give up the power they have held in the past to stand on the sidelines? Do they take sensitivity training? Or do companies hire new managers with these traits? Nurturing, coaching, and the ability to refrain from using positional power are not skills or personality traits that people learn and develop in business schools. Most M.B.A. students take one or two management courses, and the rest of their curriculum focuses on other aspects of business, such as finance and advertising.

Hammer is quick to point out that reengineering, while more effi-

cient, is not the same as delayering, or flatten[...]
though they tell us it may produce a flatter o[...]
piece of logic, he vigorously asserts it is *not* t[...]
restructuring, which "only means doing less[...]
he tells us, "is doing more with less."[49] He fails to folio[...]
logical inference that in both cases you're still doing what you do[...]
less. Reengineering then, promises that work will become more varied
and maybe more interesting—but only if you still have a job.

The Workplace El Dorado?

This brings us to the question asked at the beginning: Are these "best
places to work" companies workplace El Dorados? When we look at
the big picture of work, life looks pretty good in these large organizations. In her book *Time Bind,* Arlie Russell Hochschild reports on a
study of four two-parent families and two single-parent families over
three summers at a Fortune 500 company she calls Amerco.
Hochschild found that life in the large organization was so good for
some people that they preferred being at work to being at home. She
had picked this company because of its excellent family benefits, such
as parental leave and time off to care for sick children or elderly parents. Like many such companies in the mid-1990s, Amerco was in the
process of implementing TQM. Hochschild gave TQM high marks. She
observed that TQM did for work what Benjamin Spock did for child
rearing, "It presumes that a worker is a capable adult, not a wayward
child."[50]

Hochschild had access to company employees and company surveys. From the climate surveys that the company used to get feedback
on its culture, and from interviews with the families she studied,
Hochschild discovered a paradox. At Amerco the average employee
worked forty-seven hours a week. The majority of employees reported
that they needed more time with their families. Amerco offered generous policies designed to give them more time with their families, but
no one who was strapped for time took advantage of these policies and
cut back on hours worked. Hochschild attempts to unravel this paradox.

She first eliminates the usual reasons why people might not want to
work less. It wasn't because of the money. People who made more

ere even less interested in cutting back on time than those
rned less. Nor was it the company's leadership. Workers be-
d that the CEO was sincere in his support for family-friendly poli-
s. While some middle managers did not like these policies, others
did. Nonetheless, even people who had supportive managers still didn't
take advantage of the family policies. Hochschild also rules out the
possibility that employees were "working scared"—they told her that
they were not worried about layoffs.

Linda, one of Hochschild's interviewees, is a shift supervisor and
thirty-eight-year-old mother of two; she is married to Bill, a technician
in the same plant. They both work overtime, on opposite shifts. Linda
says she usually goes to work early to get away from the house. The
workplace is more friendly and supportive than her home. Hochschild
observes that for many people, work has become home and home has
become work. Yet the idea of escaping to work isn't new. Men have always used work as a refuge from an unhappy marriage or a spouse and
children who do not offer him the same deference and adoration as his
employees. It's not surprising that women would also use work as an
escape, especially when they feel that they are not appreciated at home.
Not everyone Hochschild studied was escaping to work. Some were seduced by their own career ambitions, others simply enjoyed either
their job or their friends at work. Next to work, home life is boring for
some people.

If we were to end our story here, it would appear that Amerco had
reached the state of management nirvana organizations have searched
for since the beginning of this century. The company had harnessed the
"ghost in the machine" that made people *want* to work by enriching
jobs, flattening hierarchies, and empowering employees. From this
snapshot the Amerco workplace really did look like one big happy family of "team players." Amerco appears to be a triumph for the scores of
psychologists, sociologists, and management consultants who over and
over "discovered" that employees like to be treated as adults at work
and do best when they have some say over their work.

But the story doesn't end here. There was a specter haunting the
happy workplace, the specter of downsizing.

9.

Betrayal

For many Americans, the most frightening story in the evening news in the mid-1990s wasn't about genocide or a new killer virus, it was about middle-aged white men in suits, men who had been laid off by the "field of dreams" companies. The body counts were ominous. Sears got rid of 50,000 jobs; AT&T, 40,000; Kodak, 16,800; Boeing, 15,000; and IBM 63,000.[1] Many of these people didn't lose their jobs because they had done something wrong or their companies were going under. Some lost their jobs during an economic recovery—the stock market was booming and productivity was up. They lost their jobs because their companies had to "do more with less," so they were told, in order to be competitive in a global economy.

Women and minorities were also laid off, and there are far sadder stories of poverty and unemployment than the ones told by the white men in suits, but the stories of those men had a chilling effect. If the company men, who worked at "the best places to work," could be betrayed by their employers, then no one's job was safe anymore. They were the organization men, loyal to their companies. When they lost their jobs, they lost everything—income, benefits, friends, reputation, and sometimes even family. Their years of work didn't deliver what they thought the organization had promised. They'd had an unwritten social compact with their employer that if they did their job well, they could keep it until retirement.

Newspaper stories chronicled the stories of betrayal. *The New York Times* described how fifty-one-year-old Steven A. Holthausen's life unraveled after he lost his job. He had worked as a loan officer for a bank for twenty years and made a thousand dollars a week. After he lost his job, his wife divorced him and his children shunned him. He found work pumping gas and later got a job at a tourist information center making a thousand dollars a month.[2] When we hear stories like this, we wonder if maybe his family was in bad shape to begin with or maybe he wasn't a productive employee. A callous person might speculate that maybe he was just a loser. But what is clear is that his job had kept his life together. It had given him hopes and expectations for the future that were now dead.

There were also more cheerful stories, about people who recovered from the trauma of getting fired and started their own businesses or learned new skills and got better jobs. When forty-three-year-old Susan Batchelder lost her job as a district sales manager for a car manufacturer, she sought career counseling, and her friends were supportive. Batchelder said that she came to realize that losing her job gave her back her life. After looking into several career possibilities, Batchelder decided to go to school and get her real estate license. She now says, "I'm happier than I've ever been. Getting fired was good for me. Life doesn't end with corporate America."[3] But for each of these success stories, there are many more about people who will never have the same standard of living that they had in their old jobs. In 1995 the Labor Department estimated that only 35 percent of laid-off workers would get equal- or better-paying jobs.[4]

Farewell to Commitment, Loyalty, and Trust

Some would argue that there is nothing wrong with downsizing, as long as it is done right. Most of the "best places to work" companies offer extraordinary job placement services, training, temporary offices, and so on for the displaced worker. In 1996, when AT&T cut 40,000 employees, 34,000 were fired outright while the rest were given voluntary buyouts. When these cuts were announced, *Newsweek* printed a mug shot of AT&T's chairman, Robert E. Allen, on its cover. The caption read, "Corporate Killers."[5] The joke around AT&T at the time was that if they kept getting rid of people, AT&T would soon stand for "Allen and Two Temps."[6] That same year Chase Manhattan Bank merged with Chemical Bank, leading to another flurry of downsizing. Gallows humor at Chase included this quip: "Question: What do you call a Chase worker who is downsized? Answer: Chemical waste."[7] Companies like AT&T and Chase quickly learned the devastating impact on morale and public relations. When they cut the next 18,000 employees in 1998, AT&T softened the blow by offering middle managers lucrative buyouts. The "right" way to downsize, or as some like to say, "rightsize," is to pay people to quit or retire.

One of the great ironies of the 1990s was that business books and business rhetoric focused on "commitment," "loyalty," and "trust," while at the same time business practices stressed downsizing. Employers wanted trust, loyalty, and commitment from employees, but many employees knew that their employers were no longer willing or able to reciprocate. Organizations were trying to figure out how to maintain these values in an uncertain work world, a task that could not be done with smoke and mirrors, and in some cases could not be done at all. Frederick Winslow Taylor got around the problem of "cajoling" or gaining the goodwill of employees by paying them more to do more work, but that wasn't an option for businesses that were trying to cut labor costs.

"Commitment," has become a hot commodity, particularly in companies that had cut the workforce and doubled up employees' workloads. It is ironic that the less stability and loyalty companies have to offer employees, the more commitment they demand from them. However, as we saw in the Amerco case, for some companies commitment does not have to be a moral concept that entails belief in the goals and values of the company, but can be simply a matter of working longer hours.

When employees sense or know that the company will drop them in a heartbeat just to stay competitive, loyalty is absurd. Loyalty is a reciprocal concept. The affection and loyalty that Pacific Bell employees had for their company was genuine because the company had been loyal to them. This may have produced a workforce that was resistant to change, but there is no evidence that they were totally unchangeable.

How can companies expect employees to be loyal to them when they can't be loyal to employees? One way is to strip loyalty of its moral meaning. Employees will be "loyal" if you pay them more than they would make in other places. This seems to be one way Ensoniq maintained employees, although its managers also attributed it to the "gestalt of quality."

If you trust a person, you can do business with a handshake. When you don't trust someone, you try to get all transactions and agreements down on paper. When there is no trust in a society or an organization, people substitute rules, contracts, and laws. All of these require enforcers and lawyers. You can get cooperation with legal contracts, but running an organization without trust is not only cumbersome and lacking in goodwill but potentially dysfunctional. Trust is a moral and emotional relationship between people. It is difficult to get and difficult to give. It requires honesty, mutual respect, and a somewhat consistent track record of moral behavior. When we trust someone, we believe what he or she says. Philosopher Robert C. Solomon argues, "Without trust, there can be no betrayal, but more generally, without trust, there can be no cooperation, no community, no commerce, no conversation."[8] He goes on to say that trust also entails the suspension of certain fears. Trust doesn't mean that we can predict how a person or institution will act in the future, but it does create a set of reasonable expectations among people.

In his book *Trust,* Francis Fukuyama characterizes trust as the backdrop of a culture. It leads to what he calls "spontaneous sociability."[9] When cooperative groups of people—like rotary and garden clubs—pop up naturally in a culture that is spontaneous sociability. In the workplace, spontaneous sociability might be what management theorists have been trying to orchestrate and engineer since the beginning of the century. Spontaneous sociability is operating when people work as a team, not because management tells them that they are a team, but because they trust each other and agree to work together toward a common goal. A number of companies attempted to implement TQM while downsizing the workforce. Through arrogance, stupidity, or naïveté, they thought that they could build team spirit while employees were worried about their jobs and felt that they were competing with their "teammates" for their jobs.

When *commitment* is reduced to time at work, *loyalty* to something one pays for, and *trust* to a legal contract, these terms are emptied of moral meaning and the workplace becomes morally bankrupt. No matter how gentle companies were and how many services they provided their downsized employees, people suffered. Downsizing changed the unwritten social contract of work that had been bolstered by strong labor unions and had existed since World War II. As long as you did your job well and the business made some profit, over a period of time you would get the goods of the American dream—a house, a car, and a raise every year.

Downsizing had the social impact of making clear what workers had known or suspected for years. Employers and the economy are fickle and you shouldn't invest too much of yourself in the organization. As one survivor of Chase's downsizing commented, "People are a lot less amenable to being absorbed into the work culture. It's pay me, don't play me. Don't give me an employee picnic."[10] All that talk in the 1980s about making the workplace "one big family" was, as many workers suspected, false, because you can usually count on families. As Robert Frost wrote, "Home is the place where, when you have to go there, / They have to take you in."[11] We don't have workplaces that do that anymore, and employees know it.

Losing one's job is somewhat easier to swallow when the company was going bankrupt than it is when the company was doing well but says it needs to get rid of you to be more competitive in the future. With industrialization workers were treated like replaceable parts. Today they feel like obsolete or disposable parts.

Look Who's Got the Money

Downsizing was only the tip of the iceberg when it came to worker betrayal. For years we have heard how stiff the competition is in a global economy. Yet most workers have noticed that their pay has been stagnant while executives are getting paid more. The most central moral issue in the workplace is fairness. We tolerate inequities of pay, but over the past twenty years, in the name of competition, businesses became less willing to share their gains with employees and more willing to congratulate executives with huge bonuses and stock options for the company's victories in the marketplace and the stock market.

This ever-present fear of the competition made some workers willing to sacrifice pay and benefits for the good of the company. In return they were often promised a share of the profits when the company got on its feet. For example, in 1985 Columbia Falls Aluminum exacted a 15 percent pay cut from its employees and promised them a share of the profits. Brack W. Duker, the owner, told employees, "for every dollar in your pocket is a dollar in mine."[12] The company started making profits in 1986, and for the next five years Duker and his minority partner Jerome Broussard funneled most of the profits into an offshore bank account. For every dollar of profits they gave to employees, they gave themselves three dollars. For years the workforce didn't notice because workers were more concerned about getting their paychecks than about profit sharing. Then a bookkeeper at the plant, Roberta Gilmore, discovered the discrepancy and engaged the firm in a legal battle that lasted five years and ten months. In 1998 the court awarded Columbia Falls employees ninety-seven million dollars in profits owed. This is a case of egregious personal greed, but the same thing was happening to many other workers—their companies made more money while their paychecks remained stagnant.

Most economists today will agree that wages for middle-income earners have barely kept pace with inflation and wages at the bottom of the scale have fallen. They offer a variety of arguments for why this is the case. In his book *Fat and Mean,* economist David Gordon argues that the major source of our economic problems over the past twenty years is in the way most U.S. corporations treat their employees and the way that they have maintained their bloated bureaucracies. He estimates that by 1994 real hourly take-home pay for production and non-supervisory workers (who are 80 percent of the workforce) had declined by 10.4 percent from the postwar peak in 1972. Furthermore, he points out that real hourly take-home pay was four cents lower in 1994 than in 1967, but the real gross output per capita was 53 percent higher than in 1967.[13] In other words, over the past twenty years businesses have not shared their good fortune with employees. The public has watched corporate profits and executive compensation go up and their own wages stay the same.

The usual suspect hauled out to account for stagnant and lower wages is competition in the global labor market. But as Gordon points out, if cheap labor was driving U.S. wages down, it would probably affect other advanced economies. By comparing the growth of real hourly compensation in manufacturing in the United States with that in ten European countries and Japan, Gordon found that the United States was the only one with a growth rate close to zero.

Economist James K. Galbraith blames the growing inequality of pay and income as the result of failed government policies that have favored the rich and done a disservice to the middle class and the poor. These include a low minimum wage, rising interest payments to cover debts, and rising transfer payments to the rich and the poor. Galbraith says the labor market is essentially "rigged" by powerful companies that control wages as well as prices.[14] He also agrees with Robert H. Frank and Philip J. Cook, who argue that we live in a "winner-take-all society where the people, products, and companies compete for the few positions at the top where the winners reap huge rewards.[15] Similarly, educator Derek Bok gives a cultural explanation for the growing inequality of wages: powerful elites are insulated from competition and able to set their own terms because society no longer has any inhibitions about greed. In 1974 CEOs made about forty times as much as the average worker. Between 1997 and 1998 executive compensation, on average, rose 12.3 percent, whereas the average American worker's pay went up 3.5 percent. Roughly one in ten CEOs had pay packages worth twenty million dollars in 1998.[16] Paywatch, a trade union group, estimates that in 1999 the average CEO's compensation was 326 times more than the average pay of a factory worker.[17] Compensation specialist Graef S. Crystal notes that "C.E.O. compensation is going up so quickly that it has lost its shock value for many people."[18]

Managerial Delusions

Contrary to the widespread belief that downsizing got rid of bloated supervisory ranks, David Gordon's research shows that in fact managerial ranks in U.S. corporations have been growing. Gordon maintains that stagnant wages create the need for more overseers. He asks, "If workers do not share in the fruits of the enterprise, if they are not provided with a promise of job security and steady wage growth, what incentive do they have to work as hard as their bosses like?"[19] He concludes that this state of affairs requires the stick strategy—more managers to threaten or punish workers if they don't perform.

In the past two chapters we have seen that the stick is often replaced by William H. Whyte's mild-mannered therapist. By making people "feel good" about their work, employers may have wittingly or unwittingly distracted workers from the what's-in-it-for-me question. They tried the best they could to engineer the social system of work and get people to focus on the intrinsic rewards of work. Furthermore, the "friendly corporation" often meant that managers weren't honest with employees about their performance. Sloppy managers even today give inflated assessments of employees to avoid conflict and morale problems. (This is also true of teachers.) And to some extent, these management practices succeeded. Wages stayed under control, labor union participation declined, and the remaining unions are weak. The balance of power was overwhelmingly in the employer's favor.

On the one hand, workers are overseen by warm fuzzy "coaches," while on the other, businesses are being run by the likes of Albert J. Dunlap, a.k.a. "Chainsaw Al," the CEO best known for dismissing 11,200 employees and dramatically turning around the fortunes of Scott Paper. Wall Street loved him. When Sunbeam announced that it had hired Dunlap to revive its lagging fortunes in 1996, its stock price leaped 49 percent, Dunlap had a "running scared" vision of business as war. As he put it, "The predators are out there, circling, trying to pounce and make you their next meal."[20]

In his best-selling book *Mean Business,* Dunlap's arrogance is surpassed only by his banality and self-righteousness. He proudly informs the reader that his name has become a verb in the business lexicon. Dunlap, whose other nicknames include "the Shredder" and "Rambo in Pinstripes," offers this definition of "to Dunlap": it means "someone is focusing on what that person does best and is eliminating everything that is not the best."[21] Other definitions are printed on the book jacket. They include turning a company around with lightning speed and protecting and enhancing shareholder value. These aren't what most people would think if a CEO came in and "Dunlapped" their company. They would probably think of fast brutal job cuts. Meanwhile, Dunlap tells his readers why he deserved to be paid so much money: "The company was worth $2.9 billion when I arrived and more than $9 billion when I left." "I was the biggest bargain in the corporate world."[22] Dunlap's problem, and perhaps the problem with the ideology that lean and mean is best, is that there is more to running a business than cutting the workforce. Dunlap learned this the hard way. On June 15, 1998, Sunbeam employees in Florida broke into cheers when they heard that Dunlap was removed from his job by the board of directors after several quarters of disappointing earnings and declining share price.

While few would argue with the assertion that CEOs work hard, running a successful business also requires good employees. There are no good companies without good employees. Business publications such as *Forbes* and *Fortune* have celebrated the heroic business leaders for so long that few people flinch at their larger-than-life salaries. Somehow the causal connection between the work people do in a company and their compensation has been severed. For the average worker there is little correlation between wage and effort, work and worth.

Some CEOs are like Dunlap and feel they deserve their pay; others, who are less comfortable with it, may engage in self-deception. A report on TQM compiled for the executive organization the Conference Board provides an insight into one form of self-deception. The report, published in 1993, analyzed studies of TQM programs to see if TQM really worked for companies. One part of the study, called "Reinforcing Commitment to Quality: Assessing Incentives," asked managers what they thought were the most effective incentives for building employee commitment to quality. It was based on 140 responses to a mail survey of companies from the Fortune 500 service and industrial lists. The researchers found that most senior managers believed that special celebrations and ceremonies and noncash recognition were the best incentives for nonmanagers. They also thought special ceremonies and celebrations also worked well for middle managers along with promotions tied to quality performance. But for senior managers, they responded that the best incentive was cash rewards tied to quality performance.[23] The Conference Board report didn't attempt to interpret the data, but seemed to assume that what the managers reported was true. No one thought to ask the employees what kinds of rewards motivated them.

Since the time of Elton Mayo, the managerial challenge has been, How do we get people to work more without having to pay them more? Research has shown that raising salaries doesn't necessarily make people work harder and that employees like to be appreciated and complimented on a job well done. However, we also know that the main thing that makes people unhappy at work is the feeling that they are not getting a fair deal. Is it possible that TQM works so well that employees really don't ask "What's in it for me?" anymore? That they really care only about recognition for quality and not about pay? This is highly unlikely. The survey respondents were engaged in either wishful thinking, self-deception, or rationalization.

One of the great paradoxes of employer-employee relationships is that it's just as easy to exploit someone's contentment as it is to exploit his or her misery. On the one hand, work is about human dignity, identity, self-expression, and usefulness in the world. It is more meaningful to people when they are able to regard it as more than a purely economic transaction. Training, job enrichment, and more say in the work process have, for many, made work more interesting and rewarding. Trying to make work more interesting and satisfying is a noble intention in and of itself. However, making work better so that you can convince employees to work for unfair wages is exploitation. Not all people look for meaning in work, but most look for just rewards. There is something dishonest about an organization where workers create profits for the company and get a party, while senior management receives huge bonuses and stock options. This is the winner-take-all mentality. Those at the top take the lion's share of rewards, and the gap between those at the top and those in the middle and bottom of organizations and society grows.

Is this the ultimate triumph of the past one hundred years of management? Have corporations finally found the ghost in the machine that moved employees to want to work more for less pay? To some extent the management developments of the past one hundred years have triumphed. Scientific management not only produced plentiful consumer goods cheaply, but it convinced workers to trade freedom in the workplace for freedom in the marketplace. The legacy of welfare capitalism with its paternalistic practices and company benefits is that it made employees, especially white-collar ones, comfortable on the job and loyal to their companies. Unions seemed irrelevant to employees of "field of dreams" companies.

Perhaps the greatest boon to employee motivation in recent years did not come from psychology, but from economics. Economists aren't concerned with the ghost in the machine; they have a more frightening specter: the global economy. This new ghost is unpredictable and illogical, yet it has had a strong influence on management behavior. For some managers, being competitive in the global economy is an end in itself. In this battle any worker can be a casualty and no employer has to be responsible. When Japanese banks fail, businesses in faraway places may fail and workers lose their jobs. Even caring and good-willed managers and business owners often feel helpless in its wake. Trust, loyalty, and the work ethic don't make as much sense in this capricious economic environment. The local economy could be booming, employees could be doing their best work, the company could be producing a good product, and you could still lose your job. This state of affairs creates uncertainty and fear—no job is safe, but then again, maybe it never really was. The worst part about it is that this economic picture often overrides and silences discussion about the moral commitments of employers to employees. Some business leaders feel that they are less responsible for their failures because they can blame them on things beyond their control, such as the global economy or the stock market, when in fact many business failures that result in job losses are the product of human errors. Business leaders, under pressure to produce short-term profits or overly eager to increase the value of the stock options in their compensation packages, are often too lazy or deficient in imagination to figure out ways to save jobs.

The costs of a worldview in which businesses and governments have little control over the economy can be great. As mentioned earlier, the amount of control people believe they have over the world around them influences the meaning of work in a culture. Work is important if we believe that we have the ability to control our future. The reverse is also true. As William Julius Wilson said, work gives people self-efficacy, and as William Morris observed, worthy work gives us hope. Without a belief that humans control and take responsibility for the economy, and that individual effort at work makes a difference, there is little reason to care about work.

The Work Ethic of Fear

The most compelling explanation of Arlie Russell Hochschild's paradox about why workers chose to put in long hours at the expense of their families is near the end of her book. After she had completed her interviews, the company went through a "re-engineering process," which was cheerfully called "Amerco Competes." And then the downsizing began. One of the first to go was the psychologist who ran the work-life balance program. She wasn't fired, she was "internally de-hired." Amerco, always the caring company, set up a two-month stress reduction workshop for salaried employees to help out those who weren't laid off but had to work even longer hours.

Hochschild's book got the most attention because of her discovery that some people preferred to be at work rather than at home with their families. But her own findings also suggest that some people were not taking advantage of family policies and were putting in long hours because they wouldn't admit what they knew in their hearts—that their company, like many others going through TQM and reengineering, would probably begin downsizing. Maybe they sensed all along that the company's family benefits conflicted with job security. Hochschild finds evidence for this in a line from the employee handbook: "Time spent on the job is an indication of commitment. Work more hours."[24]

While TQM and reengineering offered many organizations more efficient ways of organizing work, the extent to which teams and the other managerial facets of these programs really motivated employees is open to question. The extraordinary gains in productivity and quality and the ability of firms to "do more with less" might just as well have been spurred by the work ethic of fear than by any clever management theory. As we saw earlier, fear is the oldest way to get people to work. Explicit fear, such as knowing that we will be fired, has limited benefit because it can depress, paralyze, debilitate, or infuriate us. That's why employees rarely receive much advance notice about layoffs. But subtle fear, based on uncertainty about the future, compels many to work at a frantic pace. Worries about not falling behind in some undefined competition drives many of us to work long hours. Managers fear losing business and worry about taking vacations because they don't want to miss out on anything. Employees may eventually burn out or self-destruct, but they will put in more work, for a while. Today's company men and women work longer hours and tolerate greater pressure than Whyte's organization man. Some feel as if they are running in a race that has no finish line. Their only hope is to stay in the race.

Luther's and Calvin's work ethic pales next to this work ethic of fear. Unlike the Protestant work ethic, the work ethic of fear does not hold out hope of salvation, but only offers the opportunity to work more. The marketplace is fickle and far more demanding than any single boss.[25] Nowadays when people are laid off, employers tell them, "Sorry, it's the economy" or "We can't compete unless we move the plant overseas." Frustrated unemployed workers don't always know who to blame or who to yell at. They can't blame managers or politicians, because nobody can control the global economy. Unemployed workers often blame themselves or harbor an unfocused rage. Their lives have been turned upside down, often for the sake of making their company more competitive in some yet-to-be-defined future.[26]

Idiots Promoted to Management

Most employees have never been fooled by the mild-mannered therapist at work. They've just kept their mouths shut. General cynicism about employers has permeated the popular culture. Scott Adams's comic strip *Dilbert* is probably the best and most accurate critique of what many today think about work. It appears in 1,700 newspapers in fifty-one countries. Dilbert cartoons are clipped and posted on the walls of organizations almost everywhere that they are available. In his first book, published in 1996, Adams said that he received thousands of letters from people about his cartoons, most of which said, "That's just like my company." He decided to do an unscientific survey to find out which management practices were most annoying to employees. TQM, empowerment, and reengineering were among the usual responses, but the top vote-getter was "idiots promoted to management," which is the theme of one of his books.[27]

Adams admits that no matter how absurd he makes his cartoons, he can't keep up with the examples that are sent to him by readers. Dilbert cartoons lambaste downsizing, reengineering, quality, team building, consultants, training programs, and leadership. Readers provide him with examples of disingenuous or contradictory company programs, as with the company that initiated a random drug-testing policy at the same time it started an "individual dignity enhancement" program.

In his second book, *The Dilbert Future,* Adams speaks to the Conference Board survey in which managers said employees were most motivated by awards and ceremonies, not money. Adams says these recognition schemes offer employees things that "come out of a laser printer instead of the U.S. Treasury." He writes, "Somewhere right now I'm sure there is a manager sticking a bent paper clip into an eraser and wondering if he can pass it off as the 'Excalibur Award for Excellence.' " He goes on, "That's exactly the kind of recognition employees crave—recognition as suckers."[28]

Prime-time TV has picked up on the cynicism of workers. In 1998, in the sitcom *Two Guys, a Girl and a Pizza Place,* one of the main characters, a woman in her twenties, tells her friends how much she hates her job:

I have to put on heels, which I hate, and go out in the real world and sell chemicals, which I hate. . . .

Yeah, but you make a bazillion dollars.

Yeah, selling my soul! Look, if I close this deal today, I make a commission on 500 gallons of toxic cleaner I'm selling to some oil rig. So,

I can enjoy a weekend at the Cape while killing off all the sea life between here and Guam.[29]

Also in 1998 there was wave of sitcoms about people who had been fired and had started their own businesses, usually making less money. For example, *The Closer* was about an adman who quits the big firm to run his own business on a shoestring. Most of these shows weren't successful. Perhaps they hit a raw nerve. The sitcom answer to resentment in the corporate workplace is to work at home, not work at all, or make work an insignificant or nonexistent part of the plot. The popular shows of the 1990s, such as *Seinfeld* and *Everybody Loves Raymond*, have been about people who don't have to go to an office every day.

If Karl Marx were around today he might call for a revolution— "Workers of the world, unite! You have nothing to lose but your chains." But these workers, who work in cubicles or teams, can't and don't unite, and they *do* have something to lose, their jobs. As a result, there are no strikes or protest movements; the only signs of discord are the Dilbert cartoons that grace the walls and cubicles of offices today. Employees haven't been altogether honest with their employers about the way they feel, in part because they are afraid, in part because a growing portion of the workforce has become cynical. Cynics are much harder to work with than revolutionaries because they don't believe in anything, they don't band together into unions, and they don't protest. Instead they stage silent strikes of passive resistance and sneer as they cash their paychecks.

Workers' public silence over drastic reductions in benefits, longer hours, increased workloads, downsizing, and skyrocketing executive compensation is deafening. However, workers do talk about these things in cyberspace. The Web magazine *Disgruntled* bills itself as a "Business Magazine for People Who Work for a Living." It offers news and information about work and workers' rights, and a place for employees to vent their anger and frustration. The site opens with a quote from Ronald Reagan: "They say that work never hurt anybody, but I say hey, why take a chance."[30] Readers can send in their complaints to different departments, such as "Roasting Turkeys: The Biggest Turkey I Ever Worked For," "Just Cause: Tales of Wrongful Termination," and "Union Hall: Tales of the Good, Bad and Ugly of Being in a Union." The tone of the site is humorous and irreverent—bosses are frequently referred to as "assholes."

While complaining about work on the World Wide Web may have therapeutic benefits, it doesn't do much else to disperse the resentment and anger that come from the growing feeling that workers aren't getting a fair shake. Alecia Swasy, a psychologist at Xerox, warns that when workers do not have an independent voice, such as a union, to express their anger after downsizings, they may become destructive or litigious.[31]

Resistance

The unhappy workers who vent in cyberspace look like wimps compared to union members at UPS, Caterpillar, and General Motors who were willing to walk off the job and sacrifice their own income to improve wages and working conditions. One wonders if there is a negative correlation between company attempts to build "teams" and the ability of employees to work together to bring about change. Strikes require individuals to make a sacrifice for their own good and the good of others. But perhaps as the people at the top of the organization become more selfish, so do those at the bottom. In today's uncertain environment, employees look out for themselves and don't rock the boat. As we'll discuss later, they can always turn to shopping and other amusements to smooth over unhappy work lives.

Labor union membership has been on a steady decline since its heyday in the 1950s to 1960s. Union workers accounted for 14.1 percent of all workers in 1997 and 14.5 percent in 1996, as compared to 20.1 percent in 1983. Some of labor's defeats in the 1990s were devastating. In 1996 the number of strikes was 374, the lowest level in fifty years. By 1998 the number of strikes rose slightly, to 394.[32] One cause for the increase in strikes was that employers had continued to ask for concessions from unions on wages, work hours, and job tenure, even after the companies had profitable years.

Caterpillar workers were on strike on and off from 1991 until 1998; in 1994–1995 they stayed out for seventeen months. During that time they watched their company hire replacement workers and post profits for four straight years. When the strike was settled in 1998, the new labor contract stipulated that new hires would earn 70 percent less than current employees. Workers will receive one pay raise of 2 to 4 percent for three out of the six years of the contract, and the new contract lasts six rather than three years.[33]

In 1997, 190,000 UPS workers went on strike. Union leader Ron Carey's public comments about huge executive salaries, the broken social compact, and outsourcing spoke to most American workers. He said, "America doesn't want throwaway workers" and "People don't have part-time children or part-time mortgages."[34] The main area of contention in the strike was that only one fifth of UPS workers were full-time. The part-time workers made, on average, less than half as much as the full-time workers. The average UPS union member lost about twenty-five hundred dollars in salary and three thousand dollars in profit sharing during the strike. The union won, but the gains were a meager 3 percent raise for full-time employees and a 7 percent raise for part-timers.

There was something almost quixotic about the GM strike of 1998. The strike began on June 5 at the Flint Metal Center, an outdated and inefficient metal-stamping plant. Employees walked off the job because GM refused to modernize the plant. The automaker then infuriated its employees by sneaking into the plant during a holiday and removing the dies for the GMT800, a new sports utility vehicle, so that they could make it at another location. The upshot of the eight-week strike was that the dies were put back into the Flint Metal Center and the union agreed to let the company cut eight hundred jobs, but many of the other underlying problems were not solved.[35] After the strike was settled, the company announced that it would be building new highly automated plants. The strike put a brief stay on the downsizing of the workforce. The union's one small victory was that the company agreed to build the new GM plants in America.

Some union leaders think that now is the time for unions to rise from the ashes as they did in the 1930s.[36] Doris Crouse, field director for union mobilization in Virginia, says that the main reason that workers come to see her about union affiliation is not because of money, but out of a desire for dignity and respect. She says that she is amazed "that employers don't ensure that workers are treated fairly and with dignity and respect because those things don't cost them any money."[37]

Unions are still the only institution that equalizes the power relationship between employer and employee. The only other option open to an employee who is wronged is individual legal action, which takes time and money. But some workers really don't care about power and voice. They just want to be taken care of and treated fairly by a paternalistic employer. Many of these people wax nostalgic about "the good old days."

A Dying Breed

On December 11, 1995, the Malden Mills textile factory in Massachusetts burned down. This event might not have made national news if it had not been for what the factory owner, Aaron Feuerstein, did after the fire. Feuerstein not only distributed Christmas bonuses to his employees, but for the next three months, while the factory was being repaired, he continued to pay them their full salaries. In the midst of daily accounts of downsizing, the story of Malden Mills rivaled the Jimmy Stewart classic *It's a Wonderful Life* as the warm-and-fuzzy Christmas story of 1995. Feuerstein still honored the basic social contract between employer and employee, "If you pay people a fair amount of money, and give them good benefits to take care of their families, they will produce for you."[38] Feuerstein was an instant hero, overwhelmed by letters, cash contributions for his workers, and public accolades from President Clinton and other prominent people. The irony is that there are still scores of small and midsize private or family-owned businesses run by people like Feuerstein.

The White Furniture Company in Mebane, North Carolina, was one such business earlier in the century. Dave and Will White founded the company in 1881, and it became a respected maker of fine reproductions. On December 21, 1923, their factory burned down and the White brothers, like Feuerstein, gave out Christmas bonuses and promised to hire everyone back when the factory was rebuilt. According to family legend, when the factory reopened, Will made sure that all of the employees were back. One employee was missing because he had gone to Virginia to find work. Will tracked the man down and wired him money so that he could come back to work.[39]

We can get nostalgic for "the good old days" when companies were run by paternalistic owners like Feuerstein and White. Often we think the past was better because we miss something that we've lost. The downside of paternalism is that employees sometimes *are* treated like children, which as we saw earlier is an ongoing complaint about work. Also, paternalism is only as good as the person running the company.

While men like Feuerstein and the White family should be admired for their commitment to employees, we also know they are a dying breed. The White company struggled through the 1970s in bad financial shape. Then it merged with the larger Hickory Manufacturing Corporation in 1985 after an ugly proxy fight in which members of the

White family were split on whether to sell the business. By May 1993, the family business, now part of a corporate conglomerate, closed, leaving its 203 employees unemployed. As Bill Bamberger and Cathy N. Davidson point out in their moving photo chronicle of White Furniture, *Closing,* there is an increasing disparity between the realities of the postindustrial economy and the old-fashioned virtues of loyalty and the work ethic.[40] Employers still want loyal employees who work hard, but they can't promise them loyalty in return.

Harry and Mary

Employees from a division of a Fortune 500 company met for a business ethics seminar in 1997. They were divided into small groups and asked to discuss ethical problems that they had encountered at work. The groups then had to pick out the best case study to present to the other groups. Their company was downsizing and implementing a quality program at the time. After hearing a wide array of business cases, the last group came up and somewhat apologetically said that their case was different from the rest. They called their case "Harry and Mary." Harry and Mary both did the same job and both received virtually the same performance appraisals for the high quality of their work. Harry isn't married and doesn't have many interests outside of work, so he often works ten to fourteen hours a day. Mary is married, has three children, and is active in her church. She works a regular eight-hour day. The groups' ethical problem was that the company kept telling them that the quality of their work was what was most important, but they didn't believe it. What they wanted to know was, If management had to choose between Harry and Mary, which one would they pick to stay?

This question raises some fundamental ones about work and life today. If the old social contract of corporate America has been ground to a pulp by the "demands of the global economy" and the need to be "lean and mean," then where does that leave people like Mary? She has a choice between putting in more time at work with no guarantee of reward for it, or working nine to five and continuing to spend time on the other things in her life. To do the latter may mean risking her job. More and more people find themselves in this bind. Such choices require reflection on what is important and how one wants to live his or her life. The last part of this book looks at work in terms of broader questions about how we want to live.

PART THREE

WORK AND LIFE

10.

Time

One of the great ironies of modern life is that we live longer but we seem to have less time, because we have more things to do. In her book *The Overworked American,* economist Juliet Schor describes how work hours have been increasing over the past twenty years while leisure and vacation time have decreased. According to her estimates, the average employed person in America worked 163 hours more in 1987 than in 1969. Women average 305 more hours of work than they did in 1969. The amount of free time fell nearly 40 percent since 1973, from twenty-six hours a week to slightly under seventeen.[1]

We are familiar with the litany of problems related to time and work. Many families cannot live comfortably or have the lifestyle they want on one income, so both parents work and spend less time with their children. The ones who could get by with working less often get caught in the trap of consumer desire and debt. Some people work more because they want more; some work more because they are afraid of losing what they have. As we have seen, downsizing often forces workers to put in longer hours, and few complain to their bosses, because they fear losing their jobs. Others work more because they make so little. The lucky ones work more simply because they love their work. On the underside are those without work, or without enough work. In the 1890s the poorest 10 percent of men worked two hours per day more than the richest 10 percent. By 1991 the richest 10 percent of workers were working a half hour more per day than the poorest 10 percent.[2] The overemployed, the underemployed, and the unemployed all struggle with time. Time, like necessity and freedom, is intimately connected to the meaning of work. In this chapter we will step back and reflect on the meaning of time and how it has shaped the way we experience work and life.

The Meaning of Time

The meaning of time helps shape how we think about our lives. Plutarch identified Cronus, the father of the ancient Greek gods, with Chronos, the personification of time. The god Cronus was both cruel and kind. He castrated his father with a sickle and went on to rule over a golden age when people did not have to work. Chronos is usually depicted carrying a sickle. In the classical era the sickle represented the harvest and death. In the Middle Ages the image of Father Time carries a scythe. The iconography of time depicts time as something that reaps good things and sows death. In the Middle Ages the Church said that time belonged to God. Usury was forbidden because usurers charged interest based on time and it was forbidden to sell that which belonged to God. Sloth was a sin because God, having given us the gift of time, wanted us to use it well. These older views of time remind us that we wedge work and everything we do in our lives, into a space between birth and death.

The Enlightenment pushed the dark side of time into the background. Our modern ancestors replaced the scythe, symbol of death, with the clock, symbol of optimism, order, and progress.[3] Time, a component of the work ethic, is synonymous with money and action. The old analog clock represents an optimistic view of time that is going somewhere for some good reason. We can see where we have been and where we are going. The contemporary digital clock depicts time as a series of events that are either before or after each other; it moves only forward and doesn't let you know where you've been. Time is a sequence of ordered events that simply accumulate.[4]

These two views of time depict different views of work. In the first, work is a quest or a project with a goal—it has some point to it, beyond making a living. In the second view of time work is performed to make a living or taken on a day-by-day basis, but it has no direction or particular point to it. The traditional affiliation of death with time offers a broad perspective on what work might mean in the course of a lifetime. The Enlightenment picture makes us think about work in terms of progress in our lives. In contrast, the economic view focuses on the immediate future, or work as a day-by-day event, and what work buys. We don't "pass" time; we have to be thrifty with it. The economic notion of time dominates the way people experience life at work and sometimes at home. We do things with time—we spend time, waste time, save time, sell time, make time, and sometimes do time. Most of all, we live under the shadow of the idea that time is money.

Perceptions of Time

Before the clock, time was measured by the cycles of the sun and seasons. Up to the beginning of this century, people believed that clocks were the objective measures of time. A watch measured every event, and synchronized watches worn by different people would agree on the time interval between two events. This is the practical notion of time that most people still carry with them. However, when scientists noticed that the speed of light appeared the same to every observer, no matter how fast the observer might be moving, they had to abandon the idea that there was a unique absolute time. Instead, according to relativity theory, observers would have different measures of time as recorded by a clock that they carried. Different observers wearing different watches would not necessarily agree. This is a more personal notion of time, relative to the observer who measures it.[5]

Chronobiologists, who examine time rhythms in living organisms, suggest that body temperature and metabolic rate affect an individual's perception of time. For example, children have lower body temperatures, so for them time moves slowly. This observation explains what is behind the dreaded refrain of children during long car trips: "Are we there yet? When are we going to get there?" Aging people have higher body temperatures and perceive time as moving quickly, hence, for them, "It seems like just yesterday."[6]

Events and change tie us to time. If the whole world and everything in it, including the clocks, stopped, then we could not measure time. If the clocks worked, then some events would be taking place, namely the movement of the parts in the clock, or the vibration of an atom in an atomic clock. Today, clock time measures events. In the past, events measured time. For example, in Madagascar a half hour was measured by the time it took to cook rice. A moment was the time it took to fry a locust. In Chile it took one Ave Maria to cook an egg, and an earthquake could last two Credos. According to *The Oxford English Dictionary*, "pater noster wyle" marked a segment of time. *The New English Dictionary* gives us "pissing while" as a form of arbitrary time measure.[7] Agrarian societies chart time by natural events, and many cultures used religious events to mark the passing of time.

Different cultures experience time in different ways. The sociologist Emile Durkheim observed that we get our ideas of space and time from our culture and the cultural ideas of space and time dictate our culture.[8] This seems circular but is not necessarily a vicious circle, because the concept of time is open to revision. Cultures change and adapt their concepts of time, just as they can revise and change their notion of work. Every society has its own social time. Social time determines a general path of life—when you do what. It tells you when to eat, when you should go to school, and when you are old enough to drink, drive, get married, or retire. The social meaning of Sunday, for example, is so ingrained in our culture that mental patients who are given good care during the week tend to take time off from their erratic behavior on Sundays. It is noteworthy that 75 percent of men who suffer sudden death heart attacks do so on Monday morning. Do they live *for* or *through* the weekends?[9] Is dying on Monday an act of consideration for the weekends of doctors, friends, and families? Or is it a purely physiological phenomenon? Or a commentary on how people feel about work?

Culture also defines the time that we spend in various interactions with others. The practice of taking turns is a culturally determined form of interaction time. Interaction time also determines how long we talk to each other given the role that we play in various situations. When someone you don't know well passes you in the hall at work and says "How are you?," you know that the question requires a short answer—or none. Times vary in different parts of the United States. People who move from the Northeast to the South notice that interaction time in the office is longer. The question "How are you?" might well be met with a discourse on the person's pickup truck. If someone in the North gave a full reply, people would consider the person unsophisticated; in the South it would be rude not to allow time for a longer reply. And when we ask "How are you?" in the role of a parent or a spouse, we usually expect longer answers.

In addition to social time, we have self time and organization time. Self time is the time that you use for things like writing your grocery list, personal grooming, relaxing, and so on. Organization time is more highly structured than interaction time and self time. It usually goes by the clock. If you are having a conversation with a coworker at lunch, you are subject to interaction time and it would be rude to interrupt the conversation for a self time activity like making your grocery list. However, it is not considered rude to interrupt the conversation because of organization time, namely, the lunch hour is over. Organization time is far more rigid than interaction time and self time.

Sometimes social time, interaction time, self time, and organization time conflict. Young people want to get married before they graduate from high school; a colleague keeps you in a conversation so long that you miss the train; your boss keeps you so busy that you are unable to eat lunch. One result of these conflicts is that we have to wait. In a clock-oriented society where time is money and consumerism focuses on immediate gratification of desires, waiting is one of the most stressful and difficult parts of life. (It's why people sometimes want to *kill* time.) Teaching children to wait is an important and difficult part of parenting.[10] The ability to wait is a necessary skill in a world where organization time often takes precedence over self time and interaction time.

Speed

Since time is money in our culture, we design tasks and events to pass quickly and minimize waiting. The shop tries to deliver the pizza in thirty minutes or you get it free. Video games challenge players to kill little creatures at an increasingly frantic pace. Yet doing things faster does not give us more free time. Planes, cars, and computers are fast, but we go more places and do more things with them. The faster we work, the faster our time fills with new work. The faster we go, the less time we have. The greater the focus on speed, the less patience people have with each other. On the one hand, a fast-paced life causes stress and people complain that they never have any free time. On the other hand, speed can be exciting. In his recent study of the geography of time, Robert Levine measured such factors as the pace that people walked and talked in various cities and towns. He found that people who lived in fast-paced cities like Boston and New York rated their lives as happier and better than people who lived in towns and cities with a slower pace of life.[11]

We measure computer memory in nanoseconds—equal to one billionth of a second. Anyone who works with two computers of different speeds knows the frustration of the slower one. People who live with computer workers sometimes complain that disputes over time are a major source of friction. Service workers complain that clients take too long to say what they want. Children who work with computers sometimes protest that their teachers are too slow. Some prefer to learn from a computer because reading about things takes too long.[12] It is easy to lose track of time when you work on a computer, because computer time is devoid of most of the physical, social, and conceptual markers we otherwise use. It doesn't get tired, bored, or distracted by other thoughts.

Our perception of time also includes the spatial notions of nearness and distance. Temporal panic occurs when a work deadline draws near and you get another assignment with a deadline close to the first. Time seems to approach faster than your ability to finish the first project. As Alvin Toffler pointed out in *Future Shock,* whole cultures can experience temporal panic in times of rapid social change.[13] Just when people are beginning to deal with one state of affairs, they have to deal with another.

We constantly hear how quickly things change today, but this rate and degree of change is not unprecedented. Imagine what it would have been like to live through the years 1850 to 1903. In your lifetime you would see the invention of lightbulbs, phonographs, telephones, radios, automobiles, subways, diesel engines, refrigerators, and airplanes.[14] These inventions affected the average person's daily life in far more fundamental ways than today's cutting-edge advances in computer technology and biotechnology.

The pace of time is related to the number of things we have to do. Not only do we spend more time working, but we are more mobile, we have more places to go, more things to buy, and more recreational activities available to amuse us. The more activities we try to fit into a space of time, the faster time seems to go. We may or may not have less time today, but it is certainly true that we *feel* as if we have less time because we have more to do.

Clock Discipline

Work requires cooperation, but modern work also requires synchronization. Working by the clock does not come naturally to people. Employers once struggled to get people to work according to the clock. In his well-known essay on time and work discipline, historian E. P. Thompson characterized preindustrial labor as alternating bouts of intense labor and idleness wherever people controlled their working lives. Skilled craftsmen slept late and then worked later. Routine life was not common. For example, as late as the early seventeenth century, the working-class people of England seldom ate meals at regular times.[15] Life in preindustrial days was a bit like the life of a college student—irregular eating and sleeping, intermingled with intense drinking, partying, and all-night work sessions. Thompson and other historians chronicled the struggle of getting workers to put in a full day and a steady workweek. To the modern observer, preindustrial attitudes toward time seem comical and childish because we are habituated to the demands of organization time. Employers and tourists notice the same behavior in workers in some developing countries. The preindustrial worker isn't lazy; he or she doesn't regard time as money and doesn't see the point of working more than is necessary. Leisure is more valuable than money.

The challenge of getting people to work regular hours was particularly great with regard to skilled workers who wanted to maintain the stance that they were free independent contractors selling what they made to the employer rather than selling their time. Male and female workers in seventeenth- and eighteenth-century Europe refused to work on the first day of the week. They called the self-imposed holiday St. Monday. Men spent Mondays drinking, hanging out on street corners, fighting, or betting on dog or cock fights and tavern games—Sunday was for their families and Monday for their friends. Women also did their share of drinking, but they usually spent their Mondays doing household chores.[16] Vestiges of St. Monday were still apparent in the 1970s. In his best-selling novel *Wheels,* Arthur Hailey tells us that auto insiders never bought cars that were made on a Monday, because after the weekend employees either called in sick or came in tired. Workers on Mondays tended to produce cars with a less reliable performance record than cars made on other days.[17]

Resistance to working by the clock led to a debate over contracted work and wage labor in eighteenth-century England. Employers believed that the only way they could force people to work regular hours was by paying them low wages so that they would have to put in more time to stay alive. In the early 1900s Henry Ford took a much different tack. Rather than using low wages to improve work discipline, he increased pay and shortened the workweek. He realized that the best way to turn people into steady workers was to pay them enough to make them avid consumers and give them enough time off to shop—both were good for business.

Craftsmen and craftswomen supported the St. Monday tradition because they worked only to get what they needed; they chose leisure over discretionary income. Also, workers did not make a sharp distinction between when they worked and when they played. They didn't need planned company coffee breaks to build camaraderie. Workers sometimes got up and left in the middle of a workday to have a few drinks and a long lunch. Consider the following description of workers given by Englishman John Hughton in 1681.

> When the framework knitters or makers of silk stockings had a great price for their work, they have been observed seldom to work on Mondays and Tuesdays but to spend most of their time at the alehouse or nine-pins. . . . The weavers 'tis common with them to be drunk on Monday, have a headache on Tuesday, and their tools out of order on Wednesday.[18]

In the 1770s English social reformers emphasized the importance of teaching the value of time in school. For example, William Temple worried that pauper children were "losing their time" and suggested sending them to school two hours a day and the workhouses for the rest of the time. He said, "We hope that the rising generation will be so habituated to constant employment that it would at length prove agreeable and entertaining to them."[19] In America, Ben Franklin endorsed time thrift and wrote in his autobiography that he never took St. Monday when he worked as a printer's apprentice. Religious groups preached that time was a precious commodity—their sermons carried an awareness of death. Conformity to work time came from preachers, schools, consumerism, and the belief that rational use of time would lead to moral improvement and progress.

New technology such as the steam engine also required regular work hours. People developed an internal notion of time that is the mark of workers in industrialized countries. They don't just sell their skills, they sell their time, and in doing so they sell their freedom to do what they want to do during that time. The early craftsmen were reluctant to relinquish this freedom to come and go when they wanted. Self-employed craftsmen sold their skill and service directly to the customer. They got what they gave. No one else profited from their time.

The chronically unemployed are a bit like the early industrial workers. They do not possess an internal sense of work time (or perhaps they have lost it). Hence they often fail to hold a job because they are always late, they can't keep time obligations, or they have a hard time fitting into organizational time patterns. It does seem that without some training, discipline, and practice, people do not naturally work by the clock.

Historians and sociologists explain the transition to modern consciousness of clock time in a number of ways. For example, workers may have preferred a more regular life to a life of overwork, underwork, wageless leisure, or debt-ridden toil. They may have demanded a reduced but regular workday as compensation for the loss of autonomy that they suffered at work. As Gary Cross points out, while the decline of independence and self-management was regrettable, "Time had a social meaning outside of work in new (and sometimes perhaps even more satisfying) patterns of family life."[20] Timed work in a place outside the home, he writes, made workers embrace a clear segmentation between work and life as a way to protect the interests of the family.

Time and Task

Today, time measures and structures tasks, rather than tasks measuring and structuring time. Task-oriented communities and occupations such as farming do not have as sharp a split between work and leisure as time-oriented communities and occupations. In the first case the workday is built around a series of tasks, whereas in the second case the workday is built around working a designated number of hours. One standard criticism of technology is that it serves to de-skill workers by taking over the tasks that they do.[21] Technology may de-skill crafts and professions, but the shift from task orientation to a time/money orientation of crafts and professions demoralizes them and strips them of their integrity.

Crafts and professions tend to be task-oriented, unless the practitioners are employed by institutions that are time-oriented. For example, an independent cabinetmaker makes furniture for his customers. He may promise his customers that pieces will be finished at a certain time, but the time spent making the furniture will "depend on how long it takes." He may spend fourteen hours one day and six another. If the cabinetmaker works in a furniture factory, he has to put in eight hours a day, whether the cabinet is finished or not, and he'll expect overtime pay if he works longer. But if he has to produce a certain number of cabinets in a day, the quota, not the clock, defines his day.[22]

The practice of law has shifted from task orientation toward a time orientation in large law firms. The major task of a lawyer is to prepare and present cases for clients. However, large law firms sometimes put excessive emphasis on the number of hours billed to the client and the monetary value of the labor. As discussed earlier, professionals are supposed to be concerned with task, not time and money. Large law firms have in a sense industrialized or Taylorized law, by not only making it a time-sensitive job, but by breaking down tasks, such as case preparation, into smaller components done by cheaper labor—associates, paralegals, assistants, interns, secretaries, and others.

Similarly, a doctor has patients to see and a surgeon has operations to perform. The number of hours one works doesn't determine the job. The problems that patients present and the doctor's ability to solve them define the job. However, these days, if a doctor works in an emergency room or for an HMO, time also structures her job. She will have to be there between certain hours, even if there are no patients. However, we would think it highly unprofessional for a doctor to take the time structure too seriously. If a disaster occurs at the end of her shift and patients flood the emergency room, we expect the doctor to help out, not punch out. This kind of professionalism is important because it links the performance of specific tasks to the civic spirit of a common good, not the clock.[23]

The defining moral aspect of what it means to be a professional is dedication to the task, not the clock. When the institutions that employ professionals put intense time/money pressures on them, they can undercut the integrity of their work. Businesses make a sharp class distinction between the hourly worker and the salaried worker; even though most salaried workers work a nine-to-five schedule, many tend to work longer hours without being paid for overtime. Managers and clocks monitor the hourly worker. Salaried workers sometimes get paid more and are treated as if they are professionals. Like the professional or the craftsperson, they may be asked to stay longer to get the job done. Still, unlike the self-employed professional, they usually cannot go home before the end of the workday simply because a job is finished.

The Freedom to Go Home

Some people prefer to have a certain task or quota of work for the day (as long as the task and quota are reasonable). This model of work can be very satisfying because it makes work finite. You can step back at the end of the day and say it's done, or I'm finished, and then go home. When time is the marker of work, work can seem endless. Store clerks and service employees who work by the clock sometimes complain that the worst days are the slow ones when you watch the clock until it says you can go home.

Wishful thinking on the part of employers holds that the more hours people work, the more they produce. This isn't always true. For example, at Warner Gear, management defined the workday as "maximum utilization of the worker," which meant 7.1 hours at their machines. The union wanted to define a full workday as the time it took to produce 121.25 percent over the base incentive rate of production. One shop leader argued that most employees worked their hardest in the first four hours. He said we should get paid for what we do. "The guys in the factory will police themselves—if someone on the line goofs off, we make sure that he doesn't get his incentive pay."[24]

One of the issues disputed in the 1998 General Motors strike was the "pegged rate." Pegged rates allow workers to collect their full pay as soon as they reach their quota for the day. The practice was started in the 1940s, when the auto industry was at its peak. At the parts-stamping factory where the GM strike started, Steven M. White's job is to pull a thirty-pound, six-foot-long steel rail rod onto a conveyor belt, lower it onto a brace, and weld the bumper bracket on its side. If all goes well, White can reach his quota by one-thirty or two, with a half hour taken for lunch. For working six and a half or seven hours, White gets a full eight hours of pay at nineteen dollars per hour. He is not allowed to leave the factory until he has spent eight hours there, but he can take a break after he has reached his quota. Donald Hackworth, group vice president for North American car operations, said the company spent thirty-three million dollars in overtime because people like White were allowed to quit early. That overtime contributed to a fifty-million-dollar loss for the factory. The obvious answer would be to raise the quota, but then some workers could not meet it in eight hours. Sabrina Johnson operates a robot that welds steel bars in the cradles for GM's midsize cars. She says it is very difficult to finish work early. However, she believes that the pegged rates give workers an incentive to work harder.[25]

Pegged wages present a paradox about time and work that goes back to the problem of the stint. If White had to work eight hours, he might produce the same amount as he did in six. Without the incentive of free time or increased pay, there is no reason to work faster and do more. The real problem is that once employers see what workers can produce in five hours, they can't help but want them to produce more by staying seven, or they up the quota or piece rate to get more. This makes perfect economic sense, but for some people longer workdays yield diminishing returns. After a hundred years of research on work fatigue and motivation, we still aren't very clear on how much a person can produce in a particular day, especially in nonphysical labor. Frederick Winslow Taylor and his time-motion studies were able to describe to us what "Schmitt" did, but we know little about what Schmitt thought. Could he have lifted more? We don't know what he did when no one was watching.

As much as employers want to believe that the more time people spend at work, the more they produce, it isn't always true. The ability to go home when the job is done is a powerful motivator because it gives people a sense of control over their time and work. Perhaps what is most unsatisfying about modern work is that people frequently are paid not for what they produce, but for their time. As we have seen, the promise of free time certainly motivates people to work faster and probably works as well as, if not better than, monetary incentives. In the Bolivar case, free time exerted such a strong pull that employees acted irresponsibly, cutting corners and sometimes cheating so they could leave early.

Over the years, some companies discovered that shortening work hours can increase efficiency and morale. In 1930 the Kellogg Company switched from an eight-hour to six-hour workday to cope with the Depression through job sharing. They found that with a shorter day productivity increased and they did not need to bring in extra workers. Under the eight-hour day, employees packed an average of eighty-three cases of cereal in an hour. Under the six-hour day, employees packed ninety-three cases. Morale increased, and the unit price of production decreased to the point that the company could pay the same amount of money for six hours as they did for eight.[26] Here again we might question whether productivity went up because of the shorter hours, because people feared losing their jobs, or because they were grateful to Kellogg for keeping them employed.

The struggle of our preindustrial ancestors against clocked time and the present status of people who work jobs structured by time and task suggest three things about work and time. First, maybe task orientation is more natural and satisfying than time orientation of work. Second, perhaps many of us would be happier working in intense spurts, followed by longer periods of free time. But third, given the clock regimentation of our culture, many people might be totally lost without the regulating structure of the nine-to-five workday.

Flexible Time

Flextime programs give employees some control over their work hours. They include a variety of arrangements, depending on the business. Some schemes allow people to set their starting and quitting times each day. For example an accounts receivable clerk with children might work from seven to three so she can be home when school is out. A young single clerk may like to party at night and work from ten to six. Other flextime programs offer compressed workweek options that allow a person to work ten hours a day for four days instead of eight hours a day for five. Some flextime programs let people work long hours one week and bank them for future time off. According to the Society for Human Resource Management, 46 percent of firms have flexible starting times and 23 percent permit compressed workweeks.[27] Managers sometimes complain about flexible work schedules because they are complicated to manage. Nonetheless, productivity and job satisfaction of federal workers shot up after the government implemented flexible work schedules in 1985.

Flextime programs are, in some ways, the most radical management innovation of this century. Unlike many of the management schemes that we have looked at, flextime is designed to improve employee satisfaction and morale by helping employees fit work into their lives. For the past one hundred years, most management initiatives have been geared toward helping people fit their lives into work. Even the benevolent family programs such as day care are there so that employees' outside obligations don't get in the way of their work obligations. While flextime is a drop in the bucket, it offers some opportunity to shape work around one's life.

Another way that people arrange work around their lives is through part-time work. Part-time work has gotten a well-deserved bad reputation in recent years, first because many employers are getting rid of full-time employees and replacing them with cheaper and easily disposable part-time employees, and second, because many people who have part-time jobs don't have benefits and are stuck in poorly paid dead-end jobs. However, many people prefer to work part-time. Economist Alec Levenson studied figures gathered by the Bureau of Labor Statistics since 1964. His analysis suggests that four out of five Americans who work part-time, less than thirty-five hours a week, do so because they do not want full-time work.[28] They want work to fit around their family commitments.

Why Home Seems Like Work

Most of us don't have free choice over the time we work. We arrange our lives around work, and sometimes the structures of work creep into our lives outside of work. The task versus time orientation of work explains why we experience the work we do at home differently from the work we do at the office. We don't say, "I have to put in six hours of work today." Instead we say, "I have to do the laundry, clean, mow the lawn, cook dinner," etc. These tasks may take four, six, or eight hours. Some people enjoy puttering around the house. Puttering is engaging at random in a series of tasks, usually fixing, arranging, or making things. We freely engage in puttering and we do so without a sense of time or urgency.

Talking and playing with children is usually not a time-restricted or time-constricted activity. We don't say, "Whoops, I was supposed to spend four hours playing with my child, but I only spent three" or "I mistakenly spent five." However, the advent of divorce and two-career families has added time constraints to these interactions. When a court says that a father may visit his child on Wednesdays and Saturdays from noon to five, what was once a spontaneous interaction turns into something constrained by blocks of time.

In autonomy, task structure, and rhythm, the traditional home-maker's work has more in common with the structure of the craftsper-son and professional than with that of the "empowered" workers in some large organizations. In the minds of many, people who work in the home don't have the same social status as other workers because they don't work regular hours for pay. This is ironic, since they usually have more freedom and autonomy than some highly paid professionals. The task structure of housework and child care give those who work in the home an event-centered notion of time. The only problem with this is that it can isolate a person and put him or her out of sync with the world outside the home. Consider the excuse that a mother wrote explaining her daughter's absence: "Please excuse Jennifer for missing school yesterday. We forgot to get the Sunday paper off the porch, and when we found it on Monday we thought it was Sunday."[29]

People often complain that because of work they don't have enough time for housework, personal chores, and their children. Once time pressure is added to these tasks we begin to experience home life much the same way that we experience work for pay. Families try to cope by creating lists and schedules. Time-pressed parents sometimes organize their children's activities into "play dates," after-school lessons, and "quality time." Sometimes children respond like angry workers. They stage noisy or violent demonstrations, they go on strike, or more often than not they demand more perks and benefits, such as Barbie dolls, video games, and vacations at Walt Disney World. In school, they sometimes expect a reward for the amount of time spent working on an assignment, not the quality of the result. When work takes up all of a person's time or consumes the person, home may cease to be a refuge from work and become another workplace. As Arlie Russell Hochschild discovered in her study, some people prefer the office workplace to the one at home.

Two-career families tend to put an extra burden on women, who still do most of the work at home. The fact that women are often too exhausted to take care of their home and family has had a strange effect on some women's fantasies. Feminist author Naomi Wolf points out that women's expectations for their professional and home life have doubled rather than eased. As a result of this, magazines have emerged that speak to their fantasy of being great workers at home. Wolf observes that publications such as *Victoria, Martha Stewart Living,* and a variety of gardening magazines allow the harried service worker, whose three kids are at home with a baby-sitter, to imagine that she will someday have time to embroider a sampler, spend three hours making everything in a meal from scratch, or cultivate bonsai plants.[30] It is not so much that she really wants to do these things as it is she would like to have the luxury of time to do them *and* the feeling that she is doing her job outside of work well.

Another odd effect of the time burden is that more and more people regard daily grinds, such as cooking, as hobbies or crafts done in one's free time. The "craft" of cooking is now separate from the daily routine. A whole industry called the "home-meal replacement market" has sprung up to take care of the daily meals of time-pressed workers. For example, if you live in San Ramon, California, you can stop at the Chevron station off Route 680, fill up your tank, and bring home a three-cheese pasta and fresh panini for dinner.[31] In Virginia, Ukrop's Fresh Express offers a complete, freshly prepared dinner in a bag to go. Fast food has been with us for a long time, and so have gourmet take-outs. But now people want to eat on their own plates the kind of food that they might have cooked if they had the time. This is why shops such as Boston Market offer simpler fare, such as meat loaf and mashed potatoes. Maybe this is nostalgia, maybe it's guilt, and maybe it's just a passing fad. After all, not everyone likes to cook or is a good cook.

The more the time demands of work dominate our lives, the more all activities feel like work. The clock and the schedule rob our social life of spontaneity. It is becoming rare for people to drop in at a friend's house unannounced. We assume that our friends are busy at home and don't want to be disturbed. When you constantly feel pressed for time, home entertaining feels like work rather than an enjoyable leisure activity. Everyone is engaged in important work at all times or is working at relaxing. What everyone probably isn't doing is sleeping. According to neurophysiologist Stanley Coren, "thanks to our high-tech, clock driven life style," we get an estimated five hundred hours less sleep per year than we physically need.[32]

Evolutionary psychologists John Tooby and Leda Cosmides observed that the popularity of the TV comedy show *Cheers,* set in a barroom, reflected a "visceral yearning for the world of our ancestors—a place where life brought regular random encounters with friends, not just occasional, carefully scheduled lunches with them."[33] In his study of blue-collar workers in America, labor historian David Halle writes that the blue-collar worker lives for leisure, not work. According to Halle, the fact that the blue-collar worker's social life is often separate from work allows him or her to have more spontaneous leisure.[34] For the professional or white-collar worker, whose work might be more rewarding, work sometimes interferes with leisure and hence makes it necessary to schedule leisure time.

The Flexible Workplace

Being "at work" usually means being in a particular place at a particular time. Like the time of work, the place of work adds a finite boundary to the job. Industrialization not only changed work by regimenting it according to the clock, but it also took work out of the home or small workshop, drawing a line between home life and work life. Lately, computers, e-mail, fax machines, cellular phones, and beepers free us from the walls of the workplace. It is now possible for some to do their jobs wearing pajamas in their beds or a bathing suit at the beach. Beepers allow us to get "important" phone calls in the grocery store or amusement park. Similarly, the car phone and car fax keep us connected while we are commuting or stuck in traffic. Soon we might even have an Internet connection in our car. In 1998 Microsoft introduced a prototype of a flat-panel video display that can be bolted to the dashboard, allowing drivers to see how fast they are going *and* get their e-mail (perhaps doubling the chance of getting into a crash). These inventions liberate us and give us flexibility and mobility. They offer us the wonderful feeling of working for ourselves on our own time and in our own territory. But sometimes this feeling is an illusion.

The technology that allows workers to be away from their desks in the workplace may also serve to spread out or increase the amount of time people work. Industrial thinking said the worker produced during the hours that you had him or her in the building. Now an employer can electronically tether employees to work no matter where they are. They can work at home, on their way to work, at their kid's ball game, and while on vacation. Flexibility regarding location also gives flexibility to work time. For example, some law firms have twenty-four-hour word-processing units, which allow people to work at any hour. Many celebrate these developments. It is nicer to work at the beach than in the office, and sometimes you get more work done at home.

However, we also have to consider the possible trade-offs. The new technology has given us more freedom, but it potentially makes us twenty-four-hours-a-day, 365-days-a-year employees. In a series of court cases, employees tried to get overtime compensation for being on call. In one case, a biomedical repairman had to be on call 365 days a year. While off duty, he had to stay sober, carry a pager, and be able to arrive at work within twenty minutes. He was a prisoner to his job. An appeals court found that the conditions of being on call still left the repairman free to enjoy other pursuits and hence he did not deserve back pay. The same court ruled that an ambulance dispatcher, who was required to be at home between five p.m. and eight a.m. every day, should not get overtime pay because she was free to "entertain guests, sleep, watch television, do laundry, and baby-sit."[35] A consequence of removing boundaries of time and location from work is removing the wall between work life and home life, between organization time and self time.

An increasing number of companies aren't content to simply let people work at home, they are moving toward imposing structure and supervision on work in the home. In 1998 Merrill Lynch set up a "telecommuting lab," which all employees who want to telecommute must take. Most of the employees eligible to work at home perform clerical back-office functions for the firm. The first day in the lab consists of technical instruction. After that, employees are left to do their work in the lab, which has a large window that overlooks office buildings and woods. At the end of two weeks, trainers decide who is ready to telecommute. Then someone from the company goes to the employee's home and inspects the work area to make sure that the employee has all the necessary electronic equipment, phone line, software, and an ergonomically correct office chair. Employees also have to submit a schedule for formal starting and stopping times, lunch breaks, and specified times to check e-mail. If they have children, they have to provide proof to the company that they have child care during work hours.[36] The setting is different, but the structure of work is basically the same.

Telecommuting for the clerical employee is different from that of a professional. No one inspects a college professor's home to see if he or she has the right kind of chair. Nor are professionals expected to submit a schedule for what they do when they work at home. For them, the proof is often in the product. If they write at home one expects to see publications. As we saw earlier, professional work usually has a task rather than a time orientation.

Telecommuting opens up a new set of possibilities for work, but like all innovations it has potential problems. The professional risks constantly being at work no matter the time or place. For the nonprofessional who does sales calls or information processing, working at home may be better than working from a cubicle, but the same structures of work and supervision exist at home. Sociologist Jon Johnson believes that virtual workplaces will drive some managers crazy because they "no longer have arbitrary control, and that means so much to organization men."[37] But now some have figured out how to exert their control off-site as well. Just as computers can set us free, they can also monitor work more tenaciously than Big Brother. Johnson also believes that some employees who work in the office may become jealous because they think those who work at home are slacking off all day. Another obvious problem is that employees don't have the informal "water cooler" experiences that are important in building personal relationships with coworkers.

The flexible workplace can be a solution to the time problems families face, or it can be the root of their problems. We have gone from moving our homes into the organization to moving the organization into our homes. It again raises the question of whether life should be part of work or work part of life. Where do you go at the end of the day when you work at home?

The Importance of Being Busy

Our culture has tended to bestow an elevated status on people who work all the time. Acknowledging that someone is very busy is one way that we show deference and respect. We determine much about a person's status by the amount of time that he or she has. Consider the often uttered sentence, "I know that you are busy, but . . ." Sometimes it's almost embarrassing to admit that you aren't busy or that you have plenty of time. After all, important people have little time, less impor-tant people more time, right? Some people believe that they are so im-portant that they either don't use their vacation time or are quick to cancel vacations when something comes up at work. (As mentioned earlier, this behavior may also be due to fear.) This state of affairs is the antithesis of the leisure class that Thorstein Veblen described. For Veblen, people demonstrated their status through conspicuous leisure; today, people do it by conspicuous work. Lawrence Shames argues that interesting work is such a luxury that people are greedy for it. He writes that they put in sixteen-hour days in part because they don't want to share the work with others. They are greedy for the illusion of indispensability, the drama of sitting at the table.[38]

Some organizations take pride in the fact that their employees work eighty-hour weeks. Medical residents go through a rite of passage by working hundred-hour weeks. Then there are those who rebel against the idea of working all the time but realize the importance of "face time," or the appearance of being at work after hours. Face time is a symbolic ritual in which employees show up to do image-making work rather than real work. By doing face time the employee signals that he or she is not only hardworking but ambitious, enthusiastic, and a team player. One young lawyer found a way around the problem of being at work after hours. Every Saturday he would drive to his office and park his conspicuous old beat-up car in the parking lot. He would jog home and then jog back and pick up his car later in the day. Instead of doing face time he did car time.

Wanting Something More

Time is given to us for free, but then we sell it, spend it, buy it, invest it, save it, and kill it. The question in many people's minds is, Should we use so much of it up on the job rather than doing other things? In her 1963 classic *The Feminine Mystique* Betty Friedan wrote about "the problem that has no name," which she described as a voice inside women that was saying "I want something more than my husband, my children, and my home." Today many time-pressed men and women are expressing a similar concern. Work has crept in and dominated their lives. For some, it seemed to promise so much, in terms of money, status, belongingness, and self-esteem, but as it takes a bigger bite out of people's time, they too begin to wish for "something more" besides work.

In his book *Fire in the Belly,* Sam Keen explains the problem this way: the difference between the sexes erodes when people let work and consumption define them. He argues that when work dominates people they become neutralized, degendered, and subservient to the rules of the market. According to Keen, organizations that push people to work excessive hours destroy the fullness of manhood and womanhood.[39] Albert Camus once said that without work "all life goes rotten." But without free time life can go rotten too.

This leaves us with a related set of questions about time and work. How is work related to free time and leisure? And how does our desire to buy things affect how we spend our time?

11.

Leisure and Consumption

Leisure is a special experience. It consists of activities that are freely chosen and good in themselves. Listening to music for pure enjoyment is one such pursuit. Aristotle believed that leisure was necessary for human happiness. Most people today think that we conduct business so that we can make money and buy things. And some trade time for leisure so that they can buy more things. Aristotle said we conduct business (or are "unleisurely") so that we can have leisure.[1] Leisure brings out what is best and most distinctive about being human—our abilities to think, feel, reflect, create, and learn. We need leisure to develop wisdom.

The word for leisure in Greek is *skolé*; in Latin it is *otium*. In both languages the word for work is simply the negation of the word for leisure; *ascholia* and *negotium* both mean "not leisure."[2] This is also true in Spanish. Today *negocio,* the word for business, means "no leisure." Greek, Latin, and Spanish words compare work to leisure as if to say that leisure is the center of life. The English word *leisure* comes from the Latin *licere,* which means "to be permitted." Our language compares leisure to work as if to say that work is the norm of life and leisure is when we are "permitted" to stop working. The British essayist and self-confessed workaholic G. K. Chesterton wrote there are three parts to leisure: "The first is being allowed to do something. The second is being allowed to do anything and the third (and perhaps most rare and precious) is being allowed to do nothing."[3]

In his book *Of Time, Work, and Leisure,* sociologist Sebastian de Grazia observed that although work can ennoble us, wear us down, or make us rich, it is leisure that perfects us as human beings. Writing in 1962, de Grazia applied Aristotle's notion of leisure to the twentieth century. He wrote, "Leisure and free time live in two different worlds. . . ." Free time refers to a special way of calculating a special kind of time. Leisure refers to a state of being, a condition of man."[4] It is a frame of mind or attitude of imaginative people who love ideas. Until World War I, educated Virginians defined a Yankee as a person who didn't understand how to use his leisure.[5] For de Grazia, leisure is a special intellectual state that few people are capable of having. It is more than simply organized activities, amusements, relaxation, and free time.

The idea that leisure is something that only a few people attain leaves us to wonder: Is leisure elitist, or do people like Aristotle and de Grazia take an elitist view of leisure? After all, who are they to make judgments on what is and is not leisure? Besides eating, sleeping, procreating, and getting ready for work, how we use our free time is a highly personal matter. Class, taste, income, education, and personal preference certainly influence what we choose to do. Just as there is a pecking order in work there is also one outside of it. Golfers look down on bowlers, tennis players look down on golfers, opera lovers sneer at soap opera fans, *New York Times* readers condescend to *National Enquirer* readers, Bloomingdale's shoppers scorn Wal-Mart shoppers. The prosperous and better-educated think (and have always thought) that their leisure pursuits are more enriching and self-fulfilling than those of the poor and the working class. But there are larger questions behind de Grazia's and Aristotle's discussions of leisure that get to the heart of how people experience life. Before we move to these questions, however, we need to look at the relationship of work to the way we spend our free time.

Work and Amusements

The Reformation, with its emphasis on work, did its best to make Sunday a boring day. Luther got rid of the saints and their holidays. The Protestants associated work with virtue and hence leisure with vice. In the Middle Ages holidays were times for music, dancing, and drinking, but later, in Protestant countries, they became days for silence and meditation. In the 1640s the Puritans, who dominated the British Parliament, banned all Christmas festivities and enjoyments, including plum pudding and mince pie. In our own times, starting in the 1980s all workers began to lose holidays and paid vacation time, and some managers began acting like Scrooge on Christmas. In 1986, when Christmas fell on a Thursday, 46 percent of employers gave workers Friday off. In 1997, when Christmas fell on a Thursday, only 36 percent did. Holidays are more than days off; they are supposed to be public celebrations. But the public can't celebrate together if most people are working.

According to de Grazia, businesspeople liked the idea of making Sunday a dismal bore because that would make work more desirable.[6] If leisure were too rewarding and too much fun, people wouldn't want to go back to work. But the Protestants and employers were probably more concerned about amusements than leisure. *The Oxford English Dictionary* defines an amusement as a pleasurable occupation that distracts or diverts attention from something. Interestingly, it comes from the word *muse,* which in this context means to be "affected with astonishment" or to be put into a "stupid stare."[7]

In the industrial era the English took legal measures to repress popular amusements in order to develop conduct suitable for work discipline. The Poor Law Amendment Act of 1834 wiped out the infrastructure of working-class entertainment. By restricting people to their parishes, the law effectively got rid of traveling balladeers, entertainers, and itinerant salesmen. The 1835 Highways Act forbade all street "nuisances," including soccer players, street entertainers, and traders. In the same year the Cruelty to Animals Act outlawed activities such as cockfights, but allowed fox hunting and other aristocratic pursuits. Working-class amusements moved off the streets and into pubs, which began providing various forms of entertainment to their customers. America never took such harsh legal measures except during the Prohibition years. Supporters of Prohibition argued that a shorter workweek would surely lead to more drinking.

At the turn of the century, employers opposed giving Saturday off because they claimed that their employees would only get into trouble. For example, in the early 1900s a Massachusetts firm required workers who were unwilling to attend church to stay indoors and "improve their time" by reading, writing, or performing other valuable duties. Mill owners of the time forbade drinking and gambling and justified the twelve-hour day and six-day week as means of keeping workers from vicious amusements.[8] This was not a totally unfounded fear. As mentioned earlier, workers in the early industrial days of England often used their leisure time to drink, fight, and bet on animal contests, such as cockfights.

In early twentieth-century America, millions of workingmen spent their free time in bars and union clubs. There were more than ten thousand saloons in New York in 1900. In *Cheap Amusements,* Kathy Peiss estimates that workingmen in New York spent about 10 percent of their weekly income on personal expenses, the bulk of which were for beer and liquor, tobacco, and movie and theater tickets. An extensive study of workingmen's leisure found that married men spent half of their free time with their families. Workingmen felt that their work gave them a "right" to amusements after work—"I worked for someone else all day and now I deserve to have someone or something work to entertain me."[9]

Married women did not start going out for entertainment in great numbers until after the invention of the nickelodeon in 1905. When young women found job opportunities outside domestic labor, they flocked to work in industry, department stores, and restaurants. Having grown up seeing their mothers work from dawn to dusk and observing domestic servants work twelve-to-fourteen-hour days, they too felt they had a "right" to outside entertainment. Workingwomen who loved to party were called "rowdy girls" in the Victorian era. They relished the freedom of going out with their friends, dancing, and socializing in mixed company. A manager from Macy's complained that young girls went out dancing on weeknights and came in exhausted for work the next day.[10] Women also integrated amusements into their work. Female factory workers practiced the latest dance steps outside the factory during their breaks. Female cigar rollers insisted on having someone read the newspaper to them while they worked. Women became very protective of their work hours and filed grievances when asked to work overtime or when detained after closing time. Women workers were largely responsible for getting the workweek shortened for all workers. The more women worked by the clock outside the home the more they too felt entitled to a good time—something to distract them or take them away from work. Life became more segmented into bouts of uninterrupted work and bouts of amusement.

Not only did employers worry about the effects of workers' leisure on job performance, they had misgivings about what might happen when employees socialized together outside work. Union halls were just one form of association. Groupings of nonunion workers were also a threat because they gave employees ample time to bond and discuss working conditions and complaints, providing a fertile field for union organization.

In 1914 Henry Ford established a sociological department in his company. The department's mission was to supervise workers' lives so that they would be thrifty, industrious producers. They urged employees not to smoke and drink.[11] Today's reformers who want to control sex and violence on TV, cigarettes, drugs, and alcohol face an uphill battle. If people like to engage in these activities during their free time, they will until they find—or the market offers them—alternatives they like more.

Television

Mass entertainment caters to passive leisure. One might even argue that television serves as a form of social control. The quality of "mass leisure" or amusements cannot vary too much from work, because if they did, the worker would have a difficult time adjusting to the worlds of work and leisure. Mass amusements provide relief from work without making the return to work unbearable.[12] Again, if this sounds like leisure snobbery, consider this: How many people would want to work less so that they could watch more television? While it is true that some people might like to see their soap operas every day and others might wish they could have a day off to watch a World Series game, one rarely hears someone say, "Gee, I'd really like to have more time off to watch television." People wish for time off to build wood-strip canoes, travel, or spend time with their families, but *not* to watch more televi-

sion (even if that's what they actually would do with time off)
lies the major difference between amusement and this more ele
idea of leisure. Mass entertainment we can pick up or drop at any ti
without longing or regret. It is enjoyable, but has no lingering meaning
for most people. While many enjoy TV or miss it because they are used
to having it on all the time, most people do not long for it.

Witold Rybczynski notes in *Waiting for the Weekend* that television
is "voracious." Most Americans watch about three hours of television
per day, or twenty-one hours per week. Rybczynski tells us that the
only other pastime in history that engaged people for that many hours
was reading, during the eighteenth century. He believes that one reason
why people spend more time watching television than reading is that
reading requires a short regular daily habit, whereas television can be
watched at irregular intervals. Also, you have to remember or reread
old parts of a book in order to remember the plot. With television, little
mental effort is required from the viewer, and it is not necessary to remember the plot. Not only do continuing TV shows review the plot of
the series, they also show previews of what is going to happen next in
the show. Rybczynski remarks that there is generally so little mental involvement in TV watching that it should really be called TV *staring*.[13]
This makes it the perfect "amusement" or diversion from work—
because it really is capable of putting us into a "stupid stare."

In contrast to amusement, leisure activities entail the same kind of
sustainable involvement and satisfaction that people find in meaningful
work. Leisure is usually an activity that requires reflection, learning, or
the development of skill. Rybczynski argues that the weekend is not a
place to escape work, but a place to create meaningful work and compensate for the lack of personal rewards on the job. But as we have
seen, some people are either too tired or too busy for such leisure.
Many want amusements that help them escape from work. There is
nothing wrong with amusements like watching television, but there
may be something wrong with work that so zaps us of our strength and
resources that that's either all we feel like doing or all we can think of
doing.

How Work Shapes Leisure

...here was no such thing as human nature. Instead, people become what they are through what they do. Work not only creates the material world but it molds people from beings guided by animal instincts into conscious, self-directed, goal-oriented beings. When work is dull and mindless, it stifles the development of a person. Marx writes that such a person is only human in his animal functions (eating, sleeping, and procreating) and is an animal in his human functions (work and free time).[14]

As we saw earlier in the Bolivar and Marienthal cases, work or lack of work can influence leisure in either a positive or a negative way. Research by sociologists confirms this view. Stanley Parker tells us that work shapes our free time because work is always in the back of our minds. When work is dull, tiresome, or stressful people are sometimes unable to do anything satisfying in their leisure. According to Parker, most sociological studies support the idea that people's leisure mirrors certain aspects of their work. These studies go back a long way. One from the early 1900s found that the workers who had the most menial and lowest-paid jobs spent the greatest amount of time in saloons, washing the workday away with beer.[15] Sometimes those with exciting jobs demand exciting leisure and those with boring jobs settle for passive leisure. For example, a study in the late 1970s compared work and leisure across various occupational groups. It found that air traffic controllers, who had stressful and demanding jobs, expressed a greater preference for challenging leisure activities than did civil servants. A six-year longitudinal study of Swedish workers discovered that those whose jobs had become more passive took on more passive leisure, while those whose jobs had become more active took on more active leisure.[16]

Some amusements resemble aspects of work. Parker uses the game of bingo as one such example. It is played in a large hall and the players sit at tables that are organized in rows. There is a caller and a "supervisor."[17] Players mark off the letters and numbers called. They "work" through their card, and if all goes well they get paid. The supervisor designates certain periods for refreshments. There is no skill or personal challenge in the game. Playing bingo is similar to routine work. The activities themselves require little if any skill and have no intrinsic interest, and one cannot get better at them through practice (despite the fact that some gamblers believe that their "skill" improves over time). The excitement of bingo is the hope of a big payoff at the end. Bingo also allows for socializing, but that too is somewhat limited by the structure of the game.

Once leisure was regarded as a time for the amateur. The word *amateur* comes from the Latin *amator,* lover: *The Oxford English Dictionary* defines an amateur as "one who loves or is fond of something" or has a taste for something. The amateur cultivates a pastime because it is interesting and intrinsically rewarding and not for external rewards like money and fame. However, some prefer to take a professional approach to their leisure activities. This attitude may include buying expensive equipment, like the latest high-tech running shoes or experimental tennis racquets. With a *très* serious attitude and the best equipment, people "work" at their tennis game, take lessons, keep charts on their scores and times, and so on. Their leisure assumes the serious, no-nonsense attitude of work. This may be a continuation of one's attitude toward work or a longing for something not present at work, such as the desire to learn or get better at something. When such weekend warriors copy the dress or style of the professional, their leisure activity becomes a simulation of the pro's work. Often, what they lack in skill they make up for in equipment. For some, buying the equipment for a sport or hobby is as much fun as—if not more fun than—using it.

The content of leisure and work may also overlap in a positive way, especially when people like their work. Then we find the stockbroker who likes to gamble, the art teacher who likes to paint, the academic who enjoys lounging in a hammock reading journals. Some of us enjoy leisure activities that compensate for creativity, skills, or social interactions that we don't exercise or take part in at work.[18] Examples of this abound: the office manager who paints with watercolors, the hospital administrator who does woodworking, the police officer who participates in a local theater group. Personality is also a factor in how people act at work and during leisure. The meticulous librarian collects stamps, the gregarious mailman heads up the community center basketball team. It takes a certain talent in life to separate work from leisure. Many get so overwhelmed by the physical and psychological strain of making a living that they are unable to pursue engaging leisure. For them, separation of work from life might be healthier than integration of work with life.

Trading Leisure for Consumption

In 1970 economist Steffan Linder published *The Harried Leisure Class*. In it he argued that in affluent societies, when people have to choose between more free time and more spending, most choose more spending. That is why he believed that an increase in income is not necessarily an increase in prosperity. In 1986, for example, Americans spent more than thirteen billion dollars on sports clothing, which meant that they traded 1.3 billion hours of potential leisure time for leisure clothing.[19] Spending money takes time—time to make the money, time to shop, and time to enjoy the things the money buys, such as cabin cruisers, package tours, and the like. Americans not only have less vacation time than Europeans, but they spend three to four times as many hours shopping as Europeans do.[20]

Consumption ties a tighter knot between work and free time than any of the schemes of reformers, employers, or governments. William H. Whyte was right to be concerned about the organization man's shallow roots in the community and deep roots in the organization. What he didn't calculate was the way that consumerism and credit reinforce the grip of work on people. Consumption creates a *need* to work even when the desire to work is weak. However, it can also make work feel more burdensome. The market tempts people with more leisure options than they can afford or have time to enjoy. We wish we didn't have to work so that we could enjoy what the market has to offer us in terms of toys, vacations, and other amusements—all of which cost money.

Even teenagers trade their leisure for consumption. In the past, teens often had to work to help their families or pay for college. Some still do, but now a growing number of middle-class teens work to buy luxury items for themselves. As we have seen, generations of Americans have encouraged young people to work, in the belief that it keeps them out of trouble and develops discipline. In a 1986 study, researchers Ellen Greenberger and Laurence Steinberg came to a radically different conclusion about work and teenagers. They found that teens often get into more trouble when they work too much than they do during free time. This is because they suffer the stress of work and school and they have the money to buy drugs and alcohol. But most interestingly, Greenberger and Steinberg also suggest that too much work not only interferes with teens' schoolwork but can cause an "adjusted blandness" at a time when they should be curious, imaginative, and combative.[21] This "adjusted blandness" is exemplified by the routine "have a nice day" patter of counter workers in fast-food restaurants. Greenberger and Steinberg think that this is unhealthy.

At first their argument seems to go against the Protestant work ethic. But Greenberger and Steinberg maintain that instead of fostering respect for work, teenage employment often leads to increased cynicism about the ability of work to provide any personal satisfaction beyond a paycheck, since teens often work in menial jobs. They ask us to consider the image of a sixteen-year-old boy, who comes home from a long afternoon of work in a fast-food restaurant, downs a few beers, and thinks to himself, "People who work harder at their jobs than they have to are a little bit crazy."[22] Work is "bogus"—you do the minimum necessary to get paid.

Other researchers believe that the social meaning of work determines whether work is good or bad for teens. In 1993 J. Schulenberg and J. G. Bachman found that teens suffered when they worked *only* for the money, for long periods of time, at boring jobs that were unconnected to future work. A study conducted by H. W. Marsh in 1991 indicated that when teens were working to save money for college, their grades improved, even when the teens had boring jobs. When teens worked to buy extras such as cars and CD players for themselves, their grades went down, regardless of the job.[23] During the Depression era, similar studies showed the beneficial value of any kind of work for young people who contributed to the support of their families at a time of crisis. The young people gained self-confidence and a sense of efficacy from helping to care for their families.

These studies on teens offer an insight into how the meaning of work changes when teens conform to the demands of the workplace in order to conform to the desires elicited in the marketplace. Sometimes the reasons *why* we work are more important than the work we actually do. The experience of working to support a family or go to college may well be more satisfying than working for clothing and CD players, because the goals themselves are more lasting and meaningful. Nonetheless, many would still argue that it is better for young people to earn money to buy what they want than to have it given to them.

When teens substitute consumer goods for leisure, they get caught up in the work-and-spend pattern of their parents and something is lost. If they give up their free time so that they can make money to buy things, they don't have the leisure to discover what they like to do. They don't have the time to discover what activities they find intrinsically good. Far from fearing it (as parents and others in authority do), there is something to be said for doing nothing and hanging out with one's friends. While there may be the potential for trouble, there is also the potential to learn how to enjoy life on one's own terms and not those of the consumer market.

Critics of Consumerism

Of course, critics of consumerism and materialist values are legion. Somewhere in every major world religion is a warning about the dangers of the unfettered desire for material objects. We noted earlier that most of the seven deadly sins concern desire for material things. Nonetheless, many economists and businesspeople are cheered by the fact that consumer demand is insatiable. In *Social Limits to Growth,* Fred Hirsch wrote that the satisfaction that people derive from goods and services doesn't depend on their own consumption, but on the consumption of others, or "keeping up with the Joneses," which makes desire limitless.[24] Juliet Schor's recent book *The Overspent American* picks up where Hirsch left off in his 1976 work. She argues that in the past our neighbors ("the Joneses") set the standard for what we wanted and thought we should buy. Today, she says, people often don't know their neighbors, and they compare what they own and want to own against the standards set by a wider range of people, such as those at work, on TV, in advertisements, and elsewhere. When we kept up with the Joneses, we kept up with people who had similar incomes. When we try to keep up with people at work or in the news, we may be trying to keep up with people who make many times more than we do.[25] This draws one into a seamless cycle of spending, debt, and longer working hours. Schor tells us that people who had been sucked into this cycle, "increasingly looked to consumption to give satisfaction, even meaning to their lives."[26]

Earlier we discussed David Riesman's observation, made in the 1950s, that Americans were becoming more other-directed. The other-directed person not only seeks affirmation from people but is driven by the material incentives of the market and the psychological incentives offered by employers. Riesman was right. It is ironic that we live in a free society that offers us choices, yet in spite of this, or perhaps because of this, much of our behavior is still determined by what others think we need and should want.

For Schor, consumption is largely connected to status. Social commentator Barbara Ehrenreich takes another tack. She believes that consumption is a form of compensation. She says that many middle-class people are disappointed with work and have jobs that give them no pleasure. In her book *Fear of Falling,* Ehrenreich argues that the middle class, unlike the working class, grew up expecting to have work that had intrinsic value. It wasn't that such jobs were scarce, but that they failed to pay enough to support the lifestyle that some people want. As a result of this, Ehrenreich tells us, "The would-be regional planner turned corporate lawyer, the would-be social worker turned banker, must compensate for abandoned dreams with spending."[27] They bury themselves in increasing consumer demands and the pleasure that buying things brings them. Work, leisure, and consumerism lock us into a vicious circle. We work more to afford the things we want to buy, then we buy things and use our free time to compensate in some way for our hard work.

The "Customer" Is King!

People all over the world enjoy Coca-Cola, Big Macs, blue jeans, and VCRs. Consumer expenditures and replacement purchases rose during seventy of the eighty-four years between 1900 and 1984 as consumers continually switched to newer goods. From this fact, economist Stanley Lebergott argues that buying newer goods is a more "worthwhile experience" than sticking with the old.[28] But why is buying something new more "worthwhile"? Sometimes newer products carry more prestige, work better, are more attractive, or have features that better suit our needs. However, this still doesn't explain why the act of buying something is a "worthwhile" or worth-our-time experience. Is the joy of buying something on a par with the joy of owning it? Not always. Schor tells us that people with "compulsive buying" disorder shop all the time, but easily lose interest in what they buy when they bring it home.

In her book *Consuming Passions,* Judith Williamson tells us that the marketplace consumes our passions and disarms them so that they are no longer threatening to the existing social order.[29] Shopping is a hunt in which we attempt to get the best price and the best value. It makes us feel creative and in control as we buy the sweater we saw in Saks Fifth Avenue at a half-price sale at Lord & Taylor. Buying things cheers us up when we're down. A Saturday in the mall stimulates the senses with the sounds of people, the smells of food, and the abundant array of goods. In a consumer society, the desire for consumption is at least as important as consumption itself.

Money conceals many things, including how you earned it. As citizens we may be abused by the IRS, as parents we may be ignored by our children, as spouses we may be unappreciated, and as workers we may be powerless, but as customers we are sovereign. In the marketplace it doesn't matter who you are as long as you have cash, checks, or plastic. Almost anyone can decide, deliberate, express opinions, and make judgments about goods and services. Best of all, sales "associates" are paid to listen to customers and treat them with respect (despite numerous exceptions). The British used to say, "Americans give service without politeness and the British give politeness without service." Nowadays, especially under the influence of the "quality" movement in business, consumers demand and often get both. If they don't, they can call for the employee's superior, yell, scream, and carry on in ways that would be unacceptable at home or at work. As customers we can have the feeling of being the boss. It's no wonder that the word *customer* has caught on in many new contexts. Organizations promise to treat their employees like customers because the customer is supposed to be "king" (or queen). Similarly, government agencies now refer to the people they serve as "customers" in the hope that civil servants will give "customers" better service than they gave citizens. Not only is it fun to buy things, but we expect to be treated with respect when we do it as "valued customers."

Consumerism picks up where the work ethic left off—or never took hold. Organizations no longer need to rely on people having a moral commitment to work. Shopping malls, debt, and the advertising industry whip everyone, even moody teenagers, into obedient workers and customers. If we have indeed traded freedom in the workplace for freedom in the marketplace, then one way to regain control is to restrict our freedom in the marketplace. Living below our means may not be as much fun as living above them, but it does allow more flexibility in deciding where we work and how much we work. Debt and desire can tether us to a job that we hate and devour the time that we might spend doing something we like.

Intrinsic Rewards

The strongest defining feature of leisure is that it is intrinsically rewarding: we do something for the sake of doing it and because *we* like it. For those who have meaningful work, there is little qualitative difference between work and leisure. As mentioned in chapter 1, some leisure activities would be less pleasurable if we had to do them for pay. A person who enjoys sewing might easily learn to hate it working as a professional seamstress. Sewing for your friends and family is different from sewing for the public. Freedom to start or stop doing something is a major element of leisure. So, for some, being paid to sew would take the fun out of it. For others being paid to sew might be their idea of meaningful work. The reason why leisure is important for everyone is that life would be barren if we could not spend time doing things just simply because we enjoyed them or found them rewarding. While some people dream of getting paid to do something that is intrinsically rewarding, researchers have found that paying people to do things that they would do without pay actually decreases their enjoyment of the activity.

In a field experiment, researchers Mark R. Lepper and David R. Greene observed nursery school children and determined what appeared to be each child's favorite play activity. They then rewarded the children every time they engaged in this activity. In a short time the children began to show less interest in the activity.[30] Psychologist Edward Deci had performed similar experiments on adult subjects, who were asked to do enjoyable puzzles. They too appeared to find the task less interesting when they received external or extrinsic rewards for it.[31] Deci called this the "overjustification effect." In other words, when you pay people to do something that they already find rewarding, they feel they are getting more than they should for doing it. To balance things out, people devalue the intrinsic reward and/or meaning of the task and focus more on the pay.

Even if it is not the case that we compensate for external rewards, Deci's experiment does tell us something about those unique and personal human experiences that we seek for no other purpose than personal gratification.

A simple story from Jewish folklore makes the same point as the research on intrinsic motivation. It goes like this: A Jewish tailor moved into a town in the American South. When the Ku Klux Klan heard about it they incited a group of local children to go and yell insulting names in front of his shop every day. On the first day that the children showed up, the tailor came out of his shop and said, "I will pay you each a quarter for every bad name you shout at me." They were delighted. The next day when the children showed up the tailor said, "I will pay you ten cents for every bad name that you call me." Many of the children complained, but grudgingly agreed. On the third day the tailor gave the children a nickel, and the day after he gave a penny. When the children came on the fifth day, the tailor said, "I am not going to pay you anymore." Whereupon the children grudgingly responded, "If you won't pay us, then we won't come and yell at you anymore."[32]

By making the children's taunting into a business transaction, the wise tailor undercut their mean-spirited enjoyment. Once the children were paid to do what they liked, they no longer wanted to do it for fun as they had earlier. They felt they *deserved* to be paid.

Unless you block out the world around you (as many people do), it's difficult to enjoy leisure in a work- and consumer-oriented society that sometimes seems to be falling apart. Leisure is free, self-determined, reflective, and gratifying. It is what you really want to do, when you want to do it. Leisure doesn't cost money, it can be hanging out with friends or family, reading a novel, or just daydreaming. It is a time in which we do those things that are valuable to us and worth doing. Because leisure is a time when we are free, it is also a time when we are most ourselves. Without leisure we might lose track of who we are. Without leisure we may find it more difficult to make sense of our lives.

12.

The Search for Something More

The way we think about work, leisure, and the way we live depends on how we see the big picture of life. On a day-to-day basis most of us deal with decisions about our lives ad hoc, sometimes losing sight of what is important to us. We know that work can make life miserable or rewarding. In the first chapter we talked about the trade-offs that one sometimes makes between meaningful work, leisure time, pay, and security. Some people, but not all, might choose meaningful work, especially if they didn't have to sacrifice too much income or free time for such a job. But what is "meaningful work"? For some, meaningful work is interesting and satisfying; for others it is work that contributes to society. Still others want work that gives meaning to their lives. To explore the nature of meaningful work and the desire for meaningful work, we must first confront the mother of all philosophic questions: What is the meaning of life?

The meaning of life is an unwieldy question. Next to it, the meaning of work seems more manageable. As we have seen, for the past decades management gurus have touted the view that managers "make meaning." In popular management books, business leaders have talked about how they create meaningful work for their employees. We, and even they, would consider it presumptuous if they said that they created meaningful lives. Questions about the meaning of work and the meaning of life entail an analysis of why we are here, what we should be doing, and what makes us happy, and the meanings discovered by individuals and manufactured by the culture. So the more pertinent question is not, What is meaningful work? but rather, Is it possible for organizations to provide meaningful work? Most important, on a personal level, What is the relationship between meaningful work, a meaningful life, and happiness?

Short Takes on the Meaning of Life

Some people think the meaning-of-life question is silly because there is no universal answer to it. Consider the ubiquitous story about a man who gives up his job, his family, and his wealth in a quest for the meaning of life. He treks to various corners of the earth. Finally, emotionally broken and physically weak, he reaches the place of a famous guru in the Himalayas. He falls to his knees, and says,

> Oh wise one, I have traveled far and given up everything in my quest. I am near death. I beseech you, please tell me the meaning of life.
>
> The guru pauses, looks out into the distance and says, "Life is a river."
>
> The man stands up, looks at him, and says, "Do you mean to say that I have sacrificed everything and all you can tell me is that life is a river? That's the stupidest thing I've ever heard!"
>
> The guru shrugs his shoulders and says, "You mean it *isn't*?"

The story is either funny, sad, or dumb, depending on the listener. The joke reflects a worry that life is absurd. Events are absurd when the pretentiousness and solemnity of the situation conflict with the reality of it. We all take our lives pretty seriously and don't want to believe that the universe is laughing at us.

Intellectuals delight in delivering one-liners on the great question. In *The Meaning of Life,* philosopher Hugh S. Moorhead collected statements on the meaning of life from 250 writers and scholars. Moorhead sent each author a copy of his or her book and asked each to inscribe the flyleaf with thoughts on the question, "What is the meaning or purpose of life?" The answers ranged from a plain "I don't know" to quotes from other authors to detailed accounts. Ved Mehta said that he didn't know, but that he knew it when he saw it in others.[1] Fellow author Bel Kaufman quoted Horace Walpole, "Life is a comedy to those who think and a tragedy for those who feel."[2] The great logician W. V. Quine quipped, "Life is what the least of us make the most of us feel the least of us make the most of."[3] And humorist Andy Rooney wrote, "To Hugh Moorhead, who searches for the meaning of life while I'm out looking for a good loaf of French bread."[4] Novelist James A. Michener gave a terse, practical account:

> . . . The main purpose of life is: 1) to have a job in whose purpose you can believe; 2) to have friends whose immediate purposes you can trust; 3) to have some spot on the earth to which you can return as home; 4) to be at the same time a citizen of a larger world.[5]

Other contributors said that life was what you made it or touched on themes of love and work. Novelist Leon Uris said that the value of life was a "beloved partner," while philosopher Karl Popper said that the meaning of life was to help others and make people happy. Theologian Hans Küng said that the meaning of life can only come from following Jesus. Freudian psychologist Lucy Freeman said the meaning of life was to be able to love and do work that you enjoy.

Out of the 250 quotes there is only one reference to children providing meaning. Arthur Miller asks, "Life's purpose? Can it be to create something alive?"[6] Even his comment is ambiguous, because Miller could be referring to his plays. The absence of children or the creation of life is odd because people often report a closeness to the mysteries and meaning of life when they give birth or watch children being born. Maybe respondents don't mention children because that answer is too obvious or because only one sixth of the respondents were women, and the men came from the generations in which men smoked cigarettes in the waiting room while their wives had babies.

The answers in Moorhead's book focus on themes such as creativity, love, God, work, and the freedom to determine meaning. Since all the respondents were writers or scholars, their reverence for work is not for all paid work, but for *their* creative work. In a scene in his novel *The Book of Laughter and Forgetting,* Milan Kundera pokes fun at people who write to give their lives meaning. A Paris taxi driver tells his passenger that he is writing a book about his life. When the passenger asks if he is writing the book for his children, the taxi driver says, "My kids don't give a damn." He says he is writing a book because "it will do many people a lot of good." Kundera calls this man a "graphomaniac," or someone obsessed with writing books for strangers. He says graphomania afflicts people who live in societies where there is prosperity and leisure to write, where people feel isolated, and where there is an absence of social change in the internal development of the nation.[7] When people feel alone and cut off from friends and family, they seek meaning in their own lives by telling strangers about their lives. The act of creation leaves something of the person behind in the world—"I create, therefore I am." This is one reason why artists consider their work meaningful.

Nowadays everyone wants to get into the act of writing about his or her life. Think of all the autobiographies and memoirs by major and minor celebrities. Those who write best-selling autobiographies—Donald Trump, for example—have not only created business empires but have, in effect, made a "business" out of their lives. Not only do some people feel a need to tell strangers about their lives (and to make money doing it), but other people like reading about the lives of strangers. It's like getting to know someone without having to give up any part of yourself. Those with or without artistic talent can also express their deepest ideas and feelings to strangers in self-help groups or therapy. The therapist, however, offers a different cut on the meaning-of-life question.

The Therapeutic Approach

Sigmund Freud thought that the meaning-of-life question was a sign of mental illness. In a letter to Marie Bonaparte he wrote: "The moment a man questions the meaning and value of life, he is sick. . . . By asking this question, one is merely admitting to a store of unsatisfied libido to which something else must have happened, a kind of fermentation leading to sadness and depression."[8]

The meaning-of-life question is depressing when posed in a negative way, such as, "Life has no meaning, so why should I go on living?" For example, the accomplished pessimist Arthur Schopenhauer believed that life was a great disappointment. He wrote, "the world in all its ends [is] bankrupt, and life is a business that does not cover its expenses."[9] Fortunately, depressed and pessimistic people are not the only ones who ask questions about life. At one time or another most of us question the meaning of our lives. After all, as Socrates said, the unexamined life is not worth living.

Psychotherapist and concentration camp survivor Viktor E. Frankl developed a therapy around the meaning-of-life question. Logotherapy (its name is derived from the Greek word for meaning, *logos*) rests on the assumption that the desire for meaning is the primary force in humans. Logotherapy confronts and reorients the patient toward life's meaning. Frankl believed values, not pleasure and pain, move people. Human beings are distinctive because they are responsible creatures willing to live and die for ideals. Each person has to arrive at a personal answer. However, we don't find the meaning of life solely within ourselves. We find the meaning of life in the world and discover it by transcending or getting out of ourselves. Frankl says that while the meaning of life changes and is different for different people, they can find it by doing a good deed (good works), experiencing a value, and lastly by suffering.[10] Frankl criticizes the American view of mental hygiene that considers suffering and unhappiness signs of maladjustment. This, he says, leads to great unhappiness over being unhappy. According to Frankl, suffering ennobles rather than degrades a person. He notes how people now go to therapists when in the past they would have gone to a priest, minister, or rabbi—or simply endured. People also turn to popular self-help books and support groups when they feel empty and question life's meaning. A handful of enterprising philosophers in New York and Amsterdam have set up shop and, for an hourly fee, will discuss with any and all takers the great philosophic questions about life. Perhaps this trend illustrates how inept we have become at engaging in dialogue about life with friends whom we trust.

In *Habits of the Heart,* Robert Bellah and others point out that we live in a therapeutic society. Therapy, they argue, stresses personal autonomy and presupposes institutional conformity. It also serves as a model for the interactions that we have as customers and service workers and also generally as employers and employees. Bellah et al. believe that the contractual relationship between the client and the therapist mirrors the contractual situation of the bureaucratic world, which has become a model for all human relations.[11] The client pays the therapist to listen. The therapist listens, but does not pass judgment. Even the language of some therapists mirrors business thought. Consider the way M. Scott Peck talks about self-discipline in his best-selling book *The Road Less Traveled:* "Delaying gratification is the process of scheduling the pain and pleasure of life in such a way as to enhance the pleasure by meeting and experiencing the pain first and getting it over with. It is the only decent way to live."[12] This might just as easily be a statement about capitalism and the work ethic as about how to live. He tells us that pain is a good investment, making us capable of reaping happiness profits.

For those who are grappling with a philosophic, not an emotional, problem, the therapeutic and pop psychology avenues fail because they focus either on alleviating the symptoms of the question (such as depression or discontent) or on providing packaged answers. As Bellah points out, the therapist's knowledge is psychological, clinical, and often amoral. Frankl says that he does not make moral judgments, while Peck goes to the other extreme and offers advice on how to live. Many seem to like Peck's approach. *The Road Less Traveled* has sold over five million copies.

Bellah et al. challenge the individualistic approach of therapy and the idea that self-fulfillment and growth are endless processes that go on in private. He and his colleagues think the therapeutic approach emphasizes adapting people to society, not engaging them in a public dialogue about what society should be like. In short, they argue that private therapy encourages either enthusiastic or skeptical adaptation to work, rather than active public participation in shaping the values and goals of the workplace.[13]

When it comes to the meaning-of-life question, readers who turn to pop literature want someone to inspire them and give them an answer. Those who turn to therapy want someone to listen, not engage in a value-laden dialogue. Often they just want to feel better about their lives. Lastly there are those who want the question resolved, and they frequently turn to religion.

The Religious Answer

In "My Confession," Leo Tolstoy questions why he should live and sets out to find the answer. Tolstoy tells us that he thought all humanity knew about the meaning of life but he didn't. He found that the rational knowledge of wise people did not give meaning to life. Humanity had an irrational understanding of life's meaning. Tolstoy describes how he went to live among the peasants and discovered that their strong and genuine religious faith "gave them a meaning and real possibility of life."[14] While to the modern reader Tolstoy romanticizes the peasants' lives, through their lives he sees the vanity and pampered appetites of his own life. The mystical and irrational elements of religious faith that created hope and meaning for the peasants greatly moved Tolstoy.

All religions answer the meaning-of-life question for those who have the faith to be comfortable with mystery. In Christianity, the true believer is a pilgrim and life a journey to eternal salvation. The meaning of all things good and evil is part of a God's plan. God gives life meaning and brings about a long-term good for those who love him. Faith both answers and eliminates the meaning-of-life question. Everyone's life has the goal of immortality. We are all participants in reaching that goal. When people's lives become stressed out and chaotic and there seems to be no worldly answer to their problems, faith offers hope and consolation. It restores order and calm to life.[15] For true believers, faith makes life worthwhile and sometimes provides some of the same benefits of therapy.

Theologian Reinhold Niebuhr describes Christianity and Judaism as dialogues with God. When people feel that their lives are fragmentary and don't make sense in their society or in the broader view of human history, then they feel a need for another dimension to the self. Niebuhr believes that when we ask the meaning of life, we are unsatisfied with the rational "meanings" around us. According to Niebuhr, the self takes part in and creates various historical dramas known to have meaning.[16] The meanings of these events are too simple, and they leave people who seek a deeper meaning unsatisfied. The meaning-of-life question expresses a desire for spirituality and faith. Biblical faith rests on the ability of people to commit themselves freely. It is a leap of faith, not a logical conclusion of the mind. Religions supply people with assurances that their lives are not arbitrary and subjective.

The themes of faith and hope in religious writings add importantly to the meaning-of-life question. Both religious and nonreligious notions of faith and hope are the underpinnings of all morality, and morality is part of meaning. You cannot have ethics without faith in the idea that it is always best to do the right thing, if not in the short run, in the long run. We also need faith to trust people and care for them.

Morality requires us to be hopeful that the future will be good or at least better in some way because of our actions and sacrifices. We may not have a good answer for the meaning of life, but we do know that when people are in despair and have lost all hope, life appears to have no meaning. Similarly, it's safe to say that when people possess religious or nonreligious faith and hope they feel that life has meaning.

While the religious answer to the meaning-of-life question offers hope, the philosophic approach to the question usually yields more questions.

The Philosophic Question

Surprisingly few contemporary philosophers tackle the meaning-of-life question. When they do, their answers, perhaps unavoidably, are usually not as concrete as the answers given by theologians or psychologists. Philosophers often provide us with insight into the nature of the question itself. E. D. Klemke breaks the question down into three parts, which differ only in scope. The first question is about why the universe exists and what its purpose is. The second is, Why do humans exist and what is their purpose? It is the third rendition that interests most inquirers: Why do I exist and for what purpose? If there is a purpose, how do I find it? If there isn't, how can my life have significance or value?[17]

Some philosophers dismiss the meaning-of-life question because asking it implies that there is one answer. Others think it is a nonsense question because there is no answer. Richard M. Hare believes that just because we can't answer the meaning-of-life question doesn't mean that life has no meaning.[18] All the things that we value have meaning to us, but those things often change over time.

We can also question whether the meaning of life is a real problem or one that only exists when someone raises it. For example, we might ask, can a person lead a meaningful or meaningless life and not know it? If so, to what extent does it matter at all? Imagine a woman who is bored with her life of charity work and only continues doing it because she has nothing else to do. An admirer writes a biography of the woman extolling her virtues and the value of her life and work. When the woman reads the book, does she discover the meaning of her life?[19] It seems improbable. Perhaps the meaning-of-life issue is not a judgment about whether we lead a worthy or valuable life, but instead is about the way we go at life: how we use our energy and resources to do what we think is important to us—actions that help us understand who we are.[20] If that is the case, then the bored charity worker does not lead a meaningful life. She seems to have missed the point of what she does and why she does it. In this sense, meaning is a personal perception.

Another way to treat the question is to convert it to a question about the mark you make on the world. Did you leave the world better than you found it? Robert Nozick translates this into a query about the value of a life. Using the language of economics, he says that an immoral life is less valuable than a moral one. Being moral doesn't always serve one's immediate interests, but in the end an immoral person pays the price of having a less valuable existence. For Nozick there are "opportunity costs" to leading a valuable life, but a valuable life leaves something behind.[21] Meaning is not strictly a personal matter. It depends on how well people connect with things outside themselves that are valuable. So according to Nozick, the woman who spends her life doing charity work leads a valuable life, even if she doesn't think so.

Yet as philosopher L. J. Russell points out, if the meaning of life only consists of its consequences, then you end up with a paradox from *Alice's Adventures in Wonderland:* "Jam tomorrow, and jam yesterday, but never jam today." You leave the world better for your children, they do the same for theirs—but no one ever gets to eat the jam.[22] The meaning of life is a balance between living for the present and for the future. Russell and a number of other philosophers argue that the meaning of life is about how we should live, but Russell asserts that the hardest part of living is living for today.

Like Nozick, Aldous Huxley thought a meaningful life is more than just a matter of finding something, it's a process. He wrote that life is not a crossword puzzle or a search for the Holy Grail; each answer is a working hypothesis, one that we use to experiment with reality. You have to look at what other people know about life and not only look inward. We don't create the meaning and value in our lives. We discover it. The best answers are the ones that allow a person to live his or her life to the full. Some people are not well suited for the world and that is why they fail to find meaning in their lives. For Huxley, the nature of such discovery is not like finding something that is passively waiting for us. Values and meaning are there, but they are "lit up" by the focus and attitudes that people bring to life.[23] In other words, only certain kinds of explorers find meaning—because of what they bring to the search. Everyone is capable of finding meaning and value in the world, but few are able to animate and "light up" those meanings alone.

Philosopher Kurt Baier argues that it doesn't even make sense to say that there is a purpose or function to our lives. For example, if you asked a waitress, "What is your purpose or function?" she would probably say to wait on tables, but then if you asked again, "Yes, but what is your real purpose," she might take offense because you are asking, "What are you here for?" Individuals may serve a function on the job, but their lives don't have functions like knives or machines. Some will say, "The purpose of my life is to find the cure for cancer" or "to stamp out world hunger." The inference here is that the purpose of their work is the purpose of their life. However, this may not be the case for most people. The waitress probably doesn't think the purpose of her life is the same as the purpose of her work.

Baier makes the point that the lack of purpose in a person's life does not detract from his or her living a meaningful life. This is particularly good news for those who do not see their work as their life. Baier thinks people should live a *worthy* life, one that makes others happy and thus contributes to the world. He says a fundamental part of morality is recognizing that others have a right to lead worthwhile lives. Morality does not necessarily make your life worthwhile—but it helps to make others' lives worthwhile.[24] In theory, if everyone respected everyone else's right to a worthwhile life, then we would all lead worthwhile lives.

We might also ask, Is a meaningful life a happy life? In the case of the charity worker, we might say that objectively, in terms of her influence on others, her life had meaning, but subjectively it didn't and she wasn't happy. So in a sense a meaningful life may not be a happy life. Then we must ask, Is a life full of happiness a meaningful one? The answer to this depends on how one characterizes a happy life.

Happiness

Aristotle says happiness is the purpose of life. It is our final goal and end of life because we seek happiness for no other reason than to have happiness. According to Aristotle, three things contribute to a happy life: practical wisdom, excellence, and pleasure. Learning about the world is an important part of leading a happy life. This doesn't mean that everyone has to become an academic, but rather that Aristotle recognized learning at all levels, and developing a talent or skill is a rewarding part of living. Aristotle offers a moral and intellectual account of excellence. By taking some liberties with Aristotle, we can use both of his explanations to put together a picture of work conducive to a happy life. Excellence in work consists of creating a good product, the skill and expertise and high standards used in making the product, and a worker who is morally excellent, or virtuous.[25]

Lastly, Aristotle says pleasure—but not just any pleasure—is important to happiness. For him, only noble and moral pleasures lead to genuine happiness. Most important, Aristotle tells us that pleasure arises only from action.[26] Happiness comes only to the active person. That is why Aristotle's ideal life of leisure is not an idle life, but a socially, physically, and mentally active one. Humans are most happy when they *do* things. Locking someone up, alone in an empty jail cell, is one of the worst tortures known. We not only take away the prisoner's freedom, but we deprive him or her of human action and interaction. Survivors of prisoner of war camps often claim that their ability to create physical and mental activity is what kept them sane and alive.

Aristotle believed that happiness is an assessment of life as a whole. It is more than the sum of the happy parts—you don't have to be happy all the time. A happy life will also include some pain and sorrow. For Aristotle, one of the most important components of a happy life is self-sufficiency, which is the ability to take care of ourselves, and freedom from want. He did not think that happiness necessarily comes from getting what you want in life, because sometimes we either don't know what we want or are not happy when we get what we want. Both happiness and meaning are tied to morality. If you want to be happy, you should be a moral person and want things that are morally worth wanting.[27]

The universal demand for happiness and the widespread unhappiness in our culture are the products of a culture that is oriented to work, according to Hannah Arendt. In such a society we achieve happiness only through work, which is a process of exhaustion and rejuvenation. We put in a hard day's work and then listen to music or have a beer "to relax" and hence prepare for the next day's work. Arendt argues that in the past, "neither the craftsman nor the man of action ever demanded to be 'happy' or thought that men could be happy."[28] Today's workers think they should be happy, just as they expect to be amused.

Psychologist Mihaly Csikszentmihalyi's research on happiness seems to back up Arendt's idea that work shapes the way we think of happiness. Csikszentmihalyi studied happiness by looking at the characteristics of particular happy moments. He believed that by understanding the dynamics of these happy times, we can better understand how to lead a happy life. He observed that on rare occasions people report having peak or optimal experiences, which he calls "flow." During these times, he says, people harmoniously order their consciousness. They pursue an activity for its own sake and become totally absorbed in a task. Csikszentmihalyi found that peak experiences occurred while people did finite tasks that required concentration and had clear goals, immediate feedback, and deep involvement to the point of forgetting life's problems. These tasks also allowed the worker to exercise complete control to the point of not worrying about not having control. When engaged in certain types of tasks, people reported losing a sense of time and a sense of themselves. However, after they finished the task, they felt good.

Csikszentmihalyi discovered that people experienced flow for about half of the time that they were at work and only 18 percent of the time during leisure. This meant that when they reported being in flow at work they were feeling creative, strong, active, concentrated, and motivated.[29] During leisure, half of the people reported feeling passive, weak, dull, and dissatisfied. Csikszentmihalyi also found that a majority of his respondents reported that when they were at work, they preferred to do something else, but this was not true during leisure. In other words, their desire to be at work was low, even though they reported having higher-quality experiences at work, whereas they preferred leisure even though they reported a lower quality of experience. Did work provide the structure for happiness or happiness the structure for work? These may be chicken-and-egg questions, where both are true because we can't tell which came first.

Csikszentmihalyi offers three explanations for this apparent important contradiction. First, he says our culture tells us that work is an infringement on personal freedom, and this prevents us from paying attention to peak experiences at work. In other words, people are happy, but their attitudes and values about work prevent them from acknowledging it. This doesn't seem likely, given the strong affirmation that our culture gives to work. His second explanation is that peak experiences at work consist of someone else's goals, not ours. This might really mean that when you experience flow you forget that you are working for someone, and the sense of freedom makes you feel more as you would if engaged in a leisure activity. Lastly, Csikszentmihalyi says that formal jobs build in the qualities of peak experience, such as goals, feedback, and so on, and not all leisure activities have this quality. Yet many of them do. People can experience flow while playing the piano or playing Ping-Pong, running, building a model airplane, or reading a good novel. Most people have had the kind of experience that Csikszentmihalyi describes and would agree that it is a happy moment, but we wouldn't want to leap to the conclusion that the only or most likely place to find happy moments is at work.

The real insight stemming from Csikszentmihalyi's research is that people in our culture increasingly lack the capacity to engage in activities outside of work that offer these moments of happiness. For many, life consists mostly of exhaustion from work and then rejuvenation for work. Their lives are like the Danaïdes' leaky water jars—they pour bits of happiness in, but the jar itself will never be full. This is why Aristotle emphasizes that happiness is life as a whole and not a series of fleeting events.

Hungry Spirits at Work

A certain longing for "something more" crept into the business literature at the close of the twentieth century—perhaps because people were working longer hours in a hectic and erratic business environment. Business books with words like *spirit* or *soul* in the title started appearing. Some were religious, others were about spirituality without religion, and others about new forms of pop therapy.

Michael Novak's *Business as a Calling: Work and the Examined Life* explains why business is meaningful work and why business is a noble profession. Combining the Protestant notion of a calling with the Catholic ideal of good works, Novak tells us that business builds praiseworthy forms of community and is a calling in which people are tested and accomplish something. "Business," he writes, "is the best real hope of the poor."[30] Peppered with some Horatio Alger–type stories, and tips on how to be a virtuous businessperson, his book draws the traditional Protestant connection between success in business and God's favor. Novak cites a study of church attendance by elites from areas such as the news media, business, congressional offices, labor unions, the military, and religious organizations. The study found that groups with the highest proportion of weekly church attendance—after religious professionals—were the military at 49 percent and then business at 35 percent. Labor union leaders, at 31 percent, came close to business, but then after that congressional aides scored 17 percent, news media leaders 9 percent, and TV and movie producers, 4 percent. A Conference Board survey of senior executives at Fortune 500 companies claims that 65 percent said that they worshiped at churches or synagogues regularly.[31]

Just as there are no atheists in foxholes, there are apparently few in business, according to Novak. He says both business and the military depend on fate, and hence both have a need for belief in divine providence. He then goes on to assert that professions of the "adversary culture," which he defines as "those who think themselves superior, such as the media," seem to diminish practitioners' religious energies and deplete their religious curiosity.[32] Novak concludes that since America is a very religious culture, businesspeople are closer than the media to the average American, who is religious. There is much to disagree with in Novak's argument, but for our purposes, his point about occupations is provocative.

It makes sense that someone who works to change the world might find the meaning of life in his or her calling. For example, reporters who cover wars and famines or uncover corruption and pollution may find inherent meaning in their work. The work they do may give meaning to their lives in a more direct way than the businessperson's work does. (After all, sometimes the only poverty a businessperson alleviates is his or her own.) But church attendance doesn't mean that the businessperson is closer to heaven than the reporter; if anything it might mean that the businessperson needs that "something more" that religion often provides. Lower church attendance may also mean that the reporter's schedule doesn't accommodate regular religious services. Curiously, Novak's observation also makes one wonder if the high level of religious belief among businesspeople makes it easier for them to acquiesce to the actions of a capricious and all powerful market. Is the ability to trust in divine providence and the market related to the ability to trust in the invisible hand of the market?

Unlike Novak's rosy account of business as a calling, Charles Handy's book *The Hungry Spirit* is a lament about the spiritual emptiness of business. Handy says we are confused by the consequences of capitalism, which improved our material well-being "but divides rich from poor, consumes so much of the energies of those who work in it, and does not, it seems, always lead to a more contented world."[33] Capitalism delivers the means of life, but not its ends. Handy's prescription for finding meaning in life and work is that we engage in "proper selfishness," which is the search for ourselves through others. At work and in business, he tells us, people should seek a purpose that is bigger than themselves.

Handy asks, "What are we doing to ourselves?" He cites data on American workers that show 42 percent of workers feel "used up" at the end of a day and 69 percent would like to lead a more relaxed life. Only 21 percent of young people think they have a chance of living the good life, compared with 41 percent twenty years ago. After much handwringing, Handy's real prescription is that we cultivate the human spirit and become kinder, gentler, and more responsible. He still likes capitalism, but believes that the brutality of markets has to be buffered by human intervention.

Jay Conger offers a cogent analysis of this "longing for something more" in his collection *Spirit at Work*. In the past, communities such as extended families, churches, temples, and civic groups offered support and gave us a place to contribute and establish connections. Today, divorce has broken up families, people don't know their neighbors, and many no longer have the time for or interest in community work. Hence, says Conger, the workplace is the essential area of life for us, and people consciously or unconsciously bring their needs for community and spirituality to work. But spirituality does not necessarily mean religion. "The growing hunger for community offers new doorways for spirituality to enter and enrich our workplace."[34] Conger refers to religion professor Wade C. Roof's secular definition of spirituality: "In its truest sense, spirituality gives expression to the being that is in us; it has to do with feelings, with power that comes from within, with knowing our deepest selves and what is sacred to us."[35] This is another way of defining what we have been calling the ghost in the machine.

Conger is on target when he talks about people bringing their spiritual needs to the office. In some companies, employees now pray and study religion at work. For example, at Boeing in California workers can go to Torah, Koran, or Bible study classes. A Muslim employee, Levent Akbarut, told a *New York Times* reporter, "Before I had to spend two and a half hours a day to go to the mosque and pray. "Now we schedule it like any other business meeting."[36] Don Kline, from the Fellowship of Companies for Christ International, estimates that there are up to ten thousand Christian study classes in the workplace. Rabbi Yehuda Krinsky, a spokesman for the Chabad Lubavich, the oldest group of rabbis who give classes in the workplace, estimates that their group has conducted about 60 study classes in New York City and about 720 around the country.

What Does It All Mean?

While this interest in religion and spirituality at work is admirable, it is also problematic. Novak may be right that business leaders have a need to believe in divine providence. In a tumultuous economic environment, employees may have this need too. Conger may also be right that people have spiritual and community needs that are not met outside of work. However, he also wonders if management theories over the years—human relations, Japanese management, quality of worklife, teamwork, vision, empowerment—have been used to tap into spiritual needs. Perhaps herein lies the key to this longing for something more. As discussed earlier, all of these management programs have been searching for "the ghost in the machine," or a person's inner motivation, goodwill, and energy. One might call this the human spirit. But whether you call it a ghost or a spirit or internal motivation, for most of this century employers have tried to get at *it* and harness *it* to improve the productivity in their organizations. First scientific management tried to capture the body, then human relations tried to capture the heart, and now some consultants want to tap into the soul.

From management's perspective, the spiritual approach picks up where the psychological approach left off. In the 1950s management theorists cultivated workers' "need" for belongingness. In the 1990s they are cashing in on their needs for spirituality and meaning. The nonreligious spiritual approach is most interesting. It offers a combination of religion "lite" and therapy "lite." This approach attempts to satisfy what some want from religion without the work of faith and what some want from therapy without the work of changing. But the biggest problem is that behind this desire for spirituality often lurk serious ethical problems about how employers and employees treat each other. In the end, spirituality at work does what pop psychology and management fads have always done: it attempts to make people *feel* good and adapt, not address the serious problems of power, conflict, and autonomy that make people feel bad in the first place.

Richard Leider, the author of *The Power of Purpose: Creating Meaning in Your Life and Work,* confirms this view. With record low unemployment in 1998 employers are doing what they can to keep employees happy. Leider says, "Many companies are wondering, "How do we attract and renew and bring out the energy and talents in our people?"[37] Consultants such as Terrence Deal, coauthor of a book discussed earlier, *Corporate Cultures,* has picked up on this longing for more. In *Leading with Soul,* Lee Bolman and Deal contend that managers or business leaders need heart, hope, and faith rooted in soul and spirit "for today's sterile bureaucracies to become tomorrow's communities of meaning, and for our society to rediscover its ethical and spiritual center."[38] If the organization is going to supply spiritual and religious needs, it will need to develop "holy" men and women to manage them. Management training programs are unlikely to do this and, as mentioned earlier, few business schools are up to the task.

Many employees are dissatisfied, overworked, and worried, and are wondering about their lives. While it is nice and perhaps comforting for some employees to have religious meetings at work, the worst thing that we can do is relegate religion to the workplace. As we have seen, ever since the 1950s work has claimed more and more of employees' lives. First the organization man moved to suburbia and then into the corporation. Now he can even pray at work. Even the care of the soul is subject to a competitive marketplace. When churches, mosques, and temples can't compete with the demands of the workplace they move into it. Businesses merge, restructure, reengineer, and die. The economy is on a roller-coaster ride. Of all the institutions in society, why would we let one of the more precarious ones supply our social, spiritual, and psychological needs? It doesn't makes sense to put such a large portion of our lives into the unsteady hands of employers. Most people have come to realize this, but they still do it. The problem is, To what community of prayer will the Boeing employee turn when he is downsized?

Prayer meetings at work are not the solution to employees' needs for something more. They are a symptom of the problem. The real problem is that their work zaps them of the energy, the time, and perhaps even the will to take part in meaningful activities and communities outside of work. If employers want to fill this need for something more, the answer is not in a prayer meeting or a seminar on finding your soul. They need to rethink the structure of the workplace and give employees more time and flexibility to lead good lives outside of work without fear of losing promotions, bonuses, or jobs. But employers are not the only ones to blame. Many employees have gotten lazy and willingly let their employers take responsibility for parts of their lives.

Meaningful Work

We have been looking at various perspectives on the meaning of life, happiness, and the desire for something more, or spirituality. These perspectives help us answer the key questions "Can organizations provide meaningful work?" and "What is meaningful work?" Certainly people can and do find interesting and engaging jobs in organizations. But as shown, if the desire for meaningful work relates to the broader question of meaning in a person's life, then there is no reason to believe that employers have any great insights to offer. While special individuals may have insights into the meaning of life, managers, who must be responsive to the bottom line, are unlikely sources for such insights.

Fortunately, our lives consist of all sorts of activities that we consider work but that fall outside the economic definition of work for pay, these include volunteering, hobbies, and learning new things. Life would be empty if we could not engage in activities that were good in themselves and not driven by necessity. When we redefine meaningful work to be work that has meaning in our lives, then our survey of answers to the meaning-of-life question helps us understand meaningful work. Different things will be valuable to different people at different times. As we saw in the beginning of the book, the priority that we give to meaningful work, leisure, consumption, and security often changes over a lifetime. Like the meaning-of-life question, meaningful work has subjective and objective features to it. One man's meaningful work may be one woman's meaningless work. The social meanings and moral values of work vary over time for cultures and individuals.

Humans are seekers of meaning. We not only make sense of the world, we assign significance to it. Organizations don't create meaningful work, they are simply places where one might find it. People employed in what the company or society deems meaningful work may not find the work meaningful because they are personally unable to "light up" the meanings around them. Such was the case of the charity worker mentioned earlier. Individuals or organizations can try to create meanings, but if those meanings are illusions created with smoke and mirrors, they produce nothing but cynicism. We talked earlier about a company that called people who worked individually a "team." Renaming things does not always change their meaning. To find meaning, people first have to grasp the truth or reality of a situation. The objective element of meaningful work consists of the moral conditions of the job itself. All employees must be treated with dignity and respect. (All too many workers over the years have complained because they were not "treated like adults.") From this principle come others such as honesty, fairness, and justice. To seek meaning, one has to feel like a human being.

The subjective elements consist of the outlooks and attitudes that people bring with them into the workplace. Our ability to find and "light up" meaning comes from personality, life experiences, and the things we value. The best way to understand the idea of lighting up meanings is to look at what it means not to exercise this ability. Earlier we discussed the sin of sloth, or acedia. While the early Christians talked about it in spiritual terms, in secular terms sloth is apathy, lack of care, lack of joy, and a certain laziness, not about work per se, but about active engagement in life. You can work long hours today, but still be slothful.

Aristotle makes a slightly different point about how humans engage in life. He says that a slave lacks the ability to decide and deliberate, but gains it back when set free. But he also tells us that some people are slaves by nature, meaning that they are happy to let others deliberate and decide for them. They are similar to Riesman's other-directed people. Hence, the things that keep us from finding meaning are failure to actively engage in life and a certain laziness or lack of caring that allows us to let others make our decisions and tell us what things mean.

It would be wrong, in fact morally dangerous, to assume that meaningful work is purely subjective. Meaningful work, like a meaningful life, is morally worthy work undertaken in a morally worthy organization. Work has meaning *because* there is some good in it. The most meaningful jobs are those in which people directly help others or create products that make life better for people. Work makes life better if it helps others; alleviates suffering; eliminates difficult, dangerous, or tedious toil; makes someone healthier and happier; or aesthetically or intellectually enriches people and improves the environment in which we live. All work that is worthy does at least one of these things in some small or large way. Still, not all people will find worthy work personally meaningful to them.

On a day-to-day basis most jobs can't fill the tall order of making the world better, but particular incidents at work have meaning because you make a valuable contribution or you are able to genuinely help someone in need or you come up with a creative solution to a difficult problem. These meaningful acts are distinctive because people do them with a good will and not for the sake of a paycheck. They are inherently rewarding and often occur unexpectedly. Such moments fill valuable lives. A life abundant with small acts of kindness is not necessarily a happy life, but it does have meaning because it leaves behind something that mattered to others. And is apt to be happier than a life that lacks such moments.

Meaningful work is something that we have to find on our own. We may not be able to define it, but we know it when we see it. While some occupations, such as religious service, appear to be inherently meaningful they still are meaningful only if the person who engages in them finds them so. Meaningful work is not always a bed of roses. It sometimes involves pain, drudgery, and stress. Those who have it may still come home from work frustrated or tired. However, having meaningful work energizes one's life as a whole. That is the most distinctive thing about it. In this respect the experience of meaningful work and the elevated notion of leisure that we have been discussing are almost indistinguishable from each other. These kinds of activities are important parts of happy lives, and those who don't have them at work may still have them in leisure. It is the way that we experience them that matters, not the specific activities. Meaningful work can include anything from brain surgery to trash collection. As we saw in the last chapter, you don't need to have a fancy hobby to have leisure; reading a book or playing with your children count too.

Lastly, we look at the role of hope and faith in meaningful work. Under the Protestant ethic work had meaning because people believed that all work, no matter how dirty and rotten, had dignity since it was the work that God gave us along with hope for eternal salvation. A calling was meaningful work because it was work done for a purpose determined by God. The problem with this assumption is that not all jobs are created equal. It takes tremendous faith to overcome the demoralizing impact of a tedious dead-end job that offers no hope of a better life. Unemployment not only destroys hope, but it destroys the faith that we had in organizations and the social and economic system. Not everyone wants meaningful work. Many people just want to be treated with respect and to earn a decent living. In the long run, goodwill cannot be psychologically engineered, but it tends to flourish among people who are treated with dignity. Organizations do not have a moral obligation to provide meaningful work; however, they do have an obligation to provide work and compensation that leave employees with the energy, autonomy, will, and income to pursue meaning at work and a meaningful life outside of work.

Epilogue

Honest Work

Neither famine nor disaster ever haunt men who do true justice;
but lightheartedly they tend the fields which are all their care.

—HESIOD

Hesiod had no illusions about work—lightheartedly or not, tending the fields was still the backbreaking work of tending the fields. However, work seemed better when honest workers received a just reward for their labor. Justice, Hesiod argued, is at the heart of a good life, and when life is good, work is better. Today we often assume the reverse; if work is good, then life will be better. Whether life makes work better or work makes life better depends in part on which is more important. For some, work is simply the means of making a living; for others, it is that and an end in itself.

This book traces the meaning of work from curse to calling—and beyond. Twentieth-century management theories shaped the meaning of work and the expectations about it. History has shown that there was no golden age of work. Besides providing the necessities of life, work can also provide great misery or great joy. The misery of work is frequently caused by others, whereas the joy we usually find on our own. That is why, when people dream of their ideal jobs, they often dream of working for themselves.

Critical analysis of the history of work helps us reflect on the following questions: First, has work gotten better? More important, what does "better" mean? Clearly wage labor is better than slavery. For most people, work is less physical, dirty, and dangerous than it was for the slave, the peasant, the indentured laborer, and the early industrial worker. But "better" should also include the moral relationship between employers and employees. Is there more fairness in the workplace? Are individuals treated better? Or, as we asked in the last part of the book, Has work improved our lives? Again this depends on what "better" means. While work may improve the material conditions of life, does it improve the quality of our lives? Do our jobs make us better persons?

I have criticized modern management for focusing more on trying to make one *feel* good than on creating a just workplace. One result of the psychological approach to management and the innovations of welfare capitalism in the twentieth century was the eventual decline of unions, which were supposed to ensure justice at work. Another result of modern management techniques was that they reshaped the social significance of work so that work slowly took over a larger slice of our lives. Lastly, while employees were busy having their "hot buttons" pushed, hanging from ropes in Outward Bound programs, and building teams and task forces, wages remained stagnant, while behind boardroom doors corporate executives patted themselves on the back with bonuses, stock options, and platinum parachutes. In the past thirty years the incomes of the rich have gone up, while middle-income wages barely kept pace with inflation and the real wages of low-income workers fell.[1] One look at the wage gap between executives (successful and otherwise) and the average worker, and work doesn't seem very fair.

Today employers know they can't promise much to employees, especially when they must promise so much to stockholders. They know they can't get trust and commitment with smoke and mirrors. Nonetheless, most still try. As shown, their inflated rhetoric sometimes creates cynicism or feelings of betrayal in employees. In some organizations, employees are "empowered," but no one seems to be in control. When an economic downturn occurs, business leaders, like stealth bomber pilots, drop their load of pink slips—and watch the value of their stock options soar. Then they put their hands in their pockets and whistle at the sky. "Redundancies," they insist, are the result of stiff competition, the market, Wall Street, foreign labor markets, or the workers themselves. This stance allows management to shun responsibility and maintain power over employees without accountability to them. Workers, however, are held accountable not only for their own mistakes but for the mistakes and "bad luck" of management or the economy. Empowered, so-called, on the job, they are powerless over their employment itself. They may work long hours, produce high-quality products, and still lose their jobs. When workers get laid off, they shake their fists at the same sky as if some primitive god of fate governs them. Or worse, they take it personally and blame themselves.

We may lament the passing of the paternalistic corporation that once provided some community, security, and material well-being, but today's economic environment allows for no going back. And as we have seen, some elements of the former era are not worth revisiting. The downsizings of the 1990s were a wake-up call. The social compact—You do your job well and you stay employed—is dead, at least for the time being. Jobs were lost and lives were ruined, but one message came through loud and clear: Employment insecurity is the new way of life, even during times of low unemployment. Many workers have begun to rethink their commitment to employers, because their employers have changed their commitment to them. The extra sacrifices of missed family birthdays because of long hours at the office no longer make sense, and maybe never did. As the old saying goes, people on their deathbeds rarely wish that they had spent more time at the office.

So what can work promise and what *can* it deliver? From the perspective of business, the first step toward honest work is to abandon management practices that amount to psychological manipulation or empty propaganda. Neither is efficacious anymore (if they ever really were), especially with young people who have been brought up on *Dilbert,* talk-show psychology, leftover 1960s rebellion, contemporary politics, and advertising. Managers often fret that young workers lack commitment and view employment as short-term. This short view is not because workers in their twenties, say, are lazy or morally decadent. It is because they are realists. They have watched as the middle-aged men in suits lost their jobs. They know the economy is, while seemingly robust, always precarious. A "get it while you can" attitude makes perfect sense in this environment. Twenty-somethings often tell us they want to work for ten or fifteen years, make their fortunes, and quit. Unlike their middle-aged elders who look at them oddly or dub them "slackers," they are not mourning some lost age of work; they are simply trying to construct a strategy for leading a good life. Whether this strategy is feasible for most people is questionable.

If businesses believe they reap greater benefits from a lean, mean, and easily disposable workforce, they also have to understand the costs. There are no quick fixes for the loss of trust and goodwill. Hiring, firing, and training people are expensive propositions. We also don't know what a nomadic workforce will do to communities and families that are already fragile. Some workers find the variety and challenge of job-hopping exciting; others hate the uncertainty. The irony is that if job security is really rare, smart employers will have to start offering security provisions as a means of luring top talent into their organizations. A few already have.

Corporations say they try to help employees balance work and family by providing perks ranging from on-site day care to personal shoppers during the holidays.[2] Such programs work on the assumption that if you make people's lives easier, they will work better. While the programs are well-meaning, employees run the risk of working in "Pullman Towns." Similarly, prayer meetings belong in the community, not in the workplace, even if employees say they want them. In an environment where employment is precarious, it is important for people to be connected to activities and organizations unrelated to work. In this way they build more stability into their lives. If they lose or change their jobs, they'll have other friends, communities, and interests to support them. Even employee benefits like health insurance are good things but can have unintended consequences. Some people find themselves chained to jobs they hate because they can't afford to lose coverage. Or if they lose their jobs, they are unable to pay for life-saving medicines or medical treatments. They depend on their jobs not only to subsist, but to keep themselves or a loved one *alive*. Corporate day care may be a good deal for parents, but when the parents those their jobs, the children's lives are disrupted as well. This is why, in a world where job security is increasingly fragile, we need to move away from entrusting important elements of our welfare and social life to employers. The problem with a Pullman Town is that it can be attractive, convenient, paternalistic, and well-ordered. But we end up living with greater dependency on the fate of our employers. In today's volatile work world this doesn't make sense. Moreover, when other aspects of our lives become circumscribed in the workplace, we lose our perspective on both work *and* life.

Honest work rests on the assumption that the best way to keep promises is to make promises you can keep. One bogus promise that some employers make is that although they can't promise job security, they can promise training for "employability." While it is true that experience in one job can help one get another, it is misleading to think that an employer knows how to train a person for all the skills that will be needed in the future. Much of what students learn in business and technical schools is already obsolete by the time they enter the workforce.

If the old social compact is dead, what might a new one look like? If an organization can't promise job security, it can at least promise to share information. Here most managers would balk—"We can't tell employees about layoffs in advance, it would ruin morale." Yet if you ask anyone who has worked in a company that is downsizing, he or she will tell you that the rumor mill carries stories of layoffs long before they are announced. In the information age it is increasingly difficult to keep secrets. While management can't share all information, they should share as much as possible information that affects the lives of employees. Management can give employees some information so that the employees can plan their future. Honest work means telling painful truths and preparing others for them. Basically, it's "treating workers like adults."

The old social compact was either paternalistic, therapeutic, or a little of both. Under this unwritten, unspoken contract the company's primary moral commitment was to care—"You do your job well and we'll take care of you." If the company cared for employees, employees usually cared for the company. Sociologist Richard Sennett asserts that the corrosion of character is inevitable in the current unstable employment environment. He writes that the scarcity of long-term commitment disorients and loosens bonds of trust, and divorces will from behavior.[3] But he assumes that long-term relationships are the only avenues to commitment and that long-term employment with one firm is the key to character development. However, while work itself is important for character, there is no reason to believe that changing employers frequently will harm one's character. Serial employment does not necessarily have the same impact as chronic unemployment. People can still gain a sense of self-efficacy, discipline, integrity, and pride from the work they do and from the fact of employment itself.

Mutual respect may be one way to forge short-term bonds of commitment. One of the most tangible ways to show respect for others and to earn their respect is by telling them the truth.[4] We don't always enjoy hearing the truth or like the bearer of truth, but we grow to trust those who tell it to us. Keeping employees informed offers a minimal level of moral decency and is perhaps the best avenue to building trust. If both employers and workers are subject to the whims of the market, shared information help to level the playing field and allows both to look after their own interests.

Respect, trust, and honesty work two ways. Employees also have to deliver on their promises. But workers sometimes engage in their own untruths. There have always been people who are lazy and think employers owe them a living. Others deceive themselves with inflated ideas about the value of their talents and contributions. These lies are often fed by managers who are too lazy or self-interested to give them honest assessments of their work performance. The most common lies told in the workplace (and for that matter in the classroom) are about performance. It's easier and less time-consuming to tell people that they are above average than to tell them they are below it and why. When you respect someone, you not only feel that you owe the person the truth, but that he or she is capable of handling the truth. The truth will help the person to become better. Obviously most employees and students are not above-average, but they have a better chance of really becoming above-average if you tell them how they can improve.

In the introduction I said that we needed to examine the traditional work ethic and see how it fares. Under this ethic, integrity is contingent on how a person works, not where he or she works or for how long. In the past, people tended to chart their career paths though one organization, and a strong work ethic often got them ahead. (Sure, sometimes they got ahead because of office politics.) Today they may have to chart their own careers through many organizations. Those who are most successful will still be the ones who work well and hard. The old work ethic has been around for a long time and is not likely to die off completely in the future. One's personal integrity will still depend on how one works, even if work takes on new forms, in new locations, and for multiple employers.

Lastly, management theorists and employers have to discard the idea that employees must devote their lives to work to do a good job. No, TQM does not have to be "a way of life." If anything, those who lead good, full lives outside of work are just as likely or more likely to do a good job. But jobs should be designed so that they are not overly tedious or demeaning. And what we do at work shouldn't inhibit our ability to pursue a good life outside of it. Technology that allows one to work away from the office is a positive step toward integrating work with life, as long as it doesn't result in a person's always being on call or at work. Some innovations, such as flexible work hours, telecommuting, and job sharing, are positive.

One reason why I have been critical of modern work goes beyond injustice in the workplace, management manipulation, or economic insecurity. When I look at the historical big picture, I am perplexed at the domination of life by paid employment at a time when life itself should be getting easier. We live in extraordinary times, in which a majority of people in postindustrial societies have an unprecedented array of choices about how they live, where they live and work, and what they buy. Machines *are* our slaves, and the basic necessities of life are, for the majority of people, relatively easy to obtain. This is an era when life should be filled with all sorts of rewarding activities. Yet many find themselves caught up not only in long hours of work but in debt, and suffering from stress, loneliness, and crumbling families. Why? In part because we always want more, in part because we don't realize that we have choices.

We now face the problem of rising expectations, rising frustrations, and numerous choices and rewards. We think we are entitled to have everything, or, in the phrase that some feminists have recently abandoned, to having it all—a great job, a large income, plenty of leisure, and security.[5] With so many desires and so many choices, some can't or don't choose how they want to live. Instead they let advertisers, employers, or the opinions of others choose for them. Yet if we are willing to make some trade-offs between an interesting or prestigious job, consumption, leisure, and security, we can gain control and possibly improve the quality of our lives. Of all these trade-offs, containing our desire to consume may be the most difficult, but also the most liberating. The seductive array of things that we can buy ties us to our jobs and often deprives us of our time.

Maybe work dominates many lives today because we have not fully developed a talent for making so many decisions. As Aristotle suggests, we have not learned how to use our freedom. Perhaps now, more than ever, young people need to take Aristotle's advice and study the liberal arts so that they can learn how to make life choices. We have let work dominate us because it organizes our lives and it has obvious built-in rewards. But one can only marvel at the possibilities for work and life once those who "long for something more" figure out what that "something" is and choose to pursue it.

The broader question is, Do we know what kind of life we want and are we willing to give up something for it? Or, to put it another way, Is the life we have now worth what we are giving up for it? Meaningful work is rare, but is out there to be found either in a paid job or in our free time, if we really want it. Not everyone wants it, finds it, or considers the same things meaningful. A work-dominated life is fine if it is a conscious choice and makes one happy. But if it doesn't, then we should start thinking of how to fit work into our lives instead of fitting our lives into our work.

This book offers no blanket prescriptions about how to live—some may chose to balance work and leisure, others may choose to work virtually all the time, and still others may choose not to work at all. All it offers is a critical picture of work, a starting point to think about the place of work in our lives given the new employment realities. The foundation of a life that works ultimately begins with a clear picture of what work is and what we want to do with our limited time on earth.

Notes

Chapter 1. Why Work?

1. See William Julius Wilson, *When Work Disappears: The World of the New Urban Poor* (New York: Alfred A. Knopf, 1996), p. 11.
2. Ibid., p. 52.
3. Ibid., p. 75.
4. Marie Jahoda, Paul F. Lazarsfeld, and Hans Zeisel, *Marienthal: Sociography of an Unemployed Community* (Chicago: Aldine-Atherton, 1971), cited in Wilson (1996).
5. Paul Corrigan, "The Trouble with Unemployment Is That You Never Get a Day Off," *Freedom and Constraint: The Paradoxes of Leisure: Ten Years of the Leisure Studies Association,* ed. Fred Coalter (New York: Routledge, 1989), p. 192.
6. Aristotle, *Politics,* in *The Complete Works of Aristotle: The Revised Oxford Translation,* trans. Benjamin Jowett, ed. Jonathan Barnes (Princeton: Princeton University Press, 1984), vol. 2, p. 2117.
7. Ibid., pp. 2014–2016.
8. Ibid., pp. 2121–2128.
9. *The Compact Oxford English Dictionary,* new ed. (Oxford: Clarendon Press, 1991).
10. Elizabeth Perle McKenna, *When Work Doesn't Work Anymore: Women, Work, and Identity* (New York: Delacorte Press, 1997), p. 14.
11. Jean-Jacques Rousseau, *The Social Contract and Discourses* (London, Penguin Books, 1973), p. 104.
12. Georg Wilhelm Friedrich Hegel, *The Philosophy of Right,* trans. T. M. Knox (Oxford: Clarendon Press, 1952), p. 129.
13. Karl Marx, *Grundrisse: Foundations of the Critique of Political Economy,* trans. Martin Nicolaus (New York: Vintage Books, 1973), pp. 325–326.
14. Quoted in Marshall Sahlins, *Stone Age Economics* (Chicago: Aldine-Atherton, 1972), p. 28.
15. Ibid., p. 20.
16. Ibid., p. 27.
17. Ebenezer Cobham Brewer, *Brewers Dictionary of Phrase and Fable,* rev. Ivor H. Evans (1870; New York: Harper & Row, 1989).
18. *Aesop's Fables,* trans. G. F. Townsend (New York: McLoughlin, 1924), p. 16.

19. Lloyd W. Daly, *Aesop without Morals* (New York: T. Yoseloff, 1961), p. 163.
20. Ibid., p. 251.
21. James Northcote, *Fables, Original and Selected: Second Series* (London: John Murray, 1833), p. 11.
22. Isaac Watts, "Against Idleness and Mischief," in *Horae Lyrica and Divine Songs* (Boston: Little, Brown, 1854), p. 320.
23. This program was part of the PBS *Ethics in America* series, 1987.
24. John Maynard Keynes, *The General Theory of Employment, Interest, and Money* (New York: Harcourt, Brace & World, 1936), p. 359.
25. Bernard Mandeville, *The Fable of the Bees,* 3rd ed. vol. 1 (London, 1724), cited in Alasdair Clayre, *Work and Play* (London: Weidenfeld & Nicolson, 1974), pp. 107–108.
26. Ibid., p. 109.
27. For a great discussion of how private vices became public virtues, see Albert O. Hirschman, *The Passions and the Interests: Political Arguments for Capitalism before Its Triumph* (Princeton: Princeton University Press, 1977).
28. Keynes (1936), p. 358.
29. Thomas J. Stanley and William D. Danko, *The Millionaire Next Door: The Surprising Secrets of America's Wealthy* (Atlanta, Ga.: Longstreet Press, 1997), p. 45.
30. Ibid., p. 37.
31. Eric Hoffer, *Between the Devil and the Dragon: The Best Essays and Aphorisms of Eric Hoffer* (New York: Harper & Row, 1982), p. 109.
32. Bernard Suits, *The Grasshopper: Games, Life, and Utopia* (Toronto: University of Toronto Press, 1978), p. 166.
33. For a somewhat different discussion of these values, see Lawrence Hayworth, *Decadence and Objectivity* (Toronto: University of Toronto Press, 1977), ch. 4.
34. *Work in America: Report of a Special Task Force to the Secretary of Health, Education, and Welfare* (Cambridge, Mass.: MIT Press, 1973), p. 10.
35. Michael Ryan, "Why?" *Parade,* September 21, 1997, p. 16.
36. "Securities Firm Chief to Be Priest," *New York Times,* November 20, 1997.
37. Amy Feldman, "It's Back to the Street for Priest," New York *Daily News,* April 20, 1999.
38. Leslie Eaton, "Is There Life after Wall Street?" *New York Times,* January 29, 1998.
39. Ibid.
40. Reed Ableson, "When Was Turns to Why," *New York Times,* November 11, 1997.
41. Jane Gross, "Women and Their Work: How Life Inundates Art," *New York Times,* August 23, 1998, Business section.
42. McKenna (1997), p. 114.

Chapter 2. What Is Work?

1. Bertrand Russell, *In Praise of Idleness and Other Essays* (1935; New York: Barnes & Noble, 1962), p. 11.
2. Hermann von Helmholtz, "The Conservation of Force: A Physical Memoir," in *Hermann von Helmholtz,* ed. Russell Kahl (Middletown, Conn.: Wesleyan University Press, 1971).
3. Russell (1935; 1962), p. 11.
4. Ludwig Wittgenstein, *Philosophical Investigations,* trans. G.E.M. Anscombe (New York: Macmillan, 1953), sec. 198.
5. Ibid., 1953, sec. 67.
6. Vicki Hearne, *Adam's Task: Calling Animals by Name* (New York: Alfred A. Knopf, 1986; Vintage Books, 1987), pp. 167–170.
7. Studs Terkel, *Working: People Talk about What They Do All Day and How They Feel about What They Do* (New York: Pantheon Books, 1974), p. xxiv.
8. Edwin McDowell, "Little Travel Agency That Could; Rosenblath's Key to Growth Is Corporate Business," *New York Times,* October 16, 1997
9. Karl Marx, *Grundrisse: Foundations of the Critique of Political Economy,* trans. Martin Nicolaus (New York: Vintage Books, 1973), p. 611.
10. Richard Burke, "Work and Play," *Ethics* 82 (October 1981), pp. 33–47.
11. Quoted in Patricia Kitchen, "Labor Day for Wishful Thinking," *Newsday,* August 31, 1997.
12. Elliott Kulick and Dick Wilson, *Thailand's Turn* (New York: St. Martin's Press, 1992), p. 69.
13. James O'Reilly and Larry Habegger, *Travelers' Tales Thailand* (San Francisco: Travelers' Tales, 1993), pp. 53–54.

14. Lee Braude, *Work and Workers: A Sociological Analysis* (New York: Praeger Publishers, 1975), p. 17.

15. Yves Simon, *Work, Society, and Culture* (New York: Fordham University Press, 1971), p. 22.

16. *The Oxford English Dictionary* (Oxford: Clarendon Press, corrected reissue, 1933).

17. *The Random House Dictionary of the English Language,* 2nd ed. (New York: Random House, 1987).

18. *Webster's New Unabridged Dictionary,* 2nd ed. (New York: Simon & Schuster, 1983).

19. Seyyed Hossein Nasr, "Islamic Work Ethics," in *Occasional Papers of the Council of Scholars,* no. 4 (Washington, D.C.: Library of Congress, 1984).

20. Hannah Arendt, *The Human Condition* (Chicago: University of Chicago Press, 1958), p. 7.

21. Georg Wilhelm Friedrich Hegel, *Reason in History: A General Introduction to the Philosophy of History,* trans. Robert S. Hartman (New York: Liberal Arts, 1953), p. 9.

22. Raymond Williams, *Keywords* (New York: Oxford University Press, 1985), p. 176.

23. Adam Smith, *The Wealth of Nations* (1776; Baltimore: Penguin Books, 1982), p. 430.

24. *The Compact Oxford English Dictionary,* new ed. (Oxford: Clarendon Press, 1991).

25. Ibid.

26. Friedrich Engels, in *Collected Works of Karl Marx and Friedrich Engels,* vol. 18 (New York: International Publishers, 1981), p. 198.

27. *Webster's* (1983).

28. Lucian Febre, "Travaille: L'Évolution d'un mot et d'une idée," *Journal de psychologique normale et pathologique* 41:1 (1948).

29. Adriano Tilgher, *Work: What It Has Meant to Men Through the Ages,* trans. Dorothy Canfield Fisher (1930; New York: Harcourt, Brace & World, 1958), p. 3.

30. Braude (1975), p. 5.

31. Titus Lucretius Carus, *The De Reum Natura,* trans. R. Humphries (Bloomington: Indiana University Press, 1974), p. 25.

32. Homer, *Odyssey,* book 11.

33. Albert Camus, *The Myth of Sisyphus and Other Essays,* trans. Justin O'Brien (New York: Vintage Books, 1955), p. 88.

34. Genesis 3:17.

35. *The Compact Oxford English Dictionary* (1991).

36. Robert K. Barnhart, ed., *The Barnhart Dictionary of Etymology* (New York: W. W. Wilson, 1988).

37. Ernest Klein, *A Comprehensive Etymological Dictionary of the English Language,* vol. 1 (Amsterdam: Elsevier, 1966).

38. *The Compact Oxford English Dictionary* (1991).

39. Ibid.

40. Ibid.

41. William Bridges, "Leading the De-Jobbed Organization," in *The Leader of the Future: New Visions, Strategies, and Practices for the Next Era,* ed. Frances Hesselbein, Marshall Goldsmith, and Richard Beckhard (San Francisco: Jossey-Bass, 1996), pp. 11–18.

42. Williams (1985), pp. 336–337.

Chapter 3. From Curse to Calling

1. Adriano Tilgher, *Work: What It Has Meant to Men through the Ages,* trans. Dorothy Canfield Fisher (New York: Harcourt, Brace & World, 1958), p. 3.

2. Ibid., p. 40.

3. Hesiod, *Theogeny, and Works and Days,* trans. M. L. West (Oxford: Oxford University Press, 1988), p. 37.

4. Tilgher (1958), p. 3.

5. See Hannah Arendt, *The Human Condition* (Chicago: University of Chicago Press, 1958), p. 80.

6. Aristotle, *Politics,* in *The Complete Works of Aristotle: The Revised Oxford Translation,* trans. Benjamin Jowett, ed. Jonathan Barnes (Princeton: Princeton University Press, 1984), vol. 2, pp. 1995–1997.

7. Ibid., p. 1996.

8. In G. S. Kirk, J. E. Raven, and M. Schofield, *The Presocratic Philosophers,* 2nd ed. (Cambridge: Cambridge University Press, 1983), p. 195.

9. Tilgher (1958), pp. 5–7.

10. Quoted in E. J. Dijksterhuis, *Archimedes,* trans. C. Dikshoorn (Princeton: Princeton University Press, 1987), p. 13.
11. Richard Abbott Gard, *Buddhism* (New York: Braziller, 1961), p. 133.
12. Robert Flaceliere, *Daily Life in Greece at the Time of Pericles,* trans. Peter Green (New York: Macmillan, 1965), p. 131.
13. Thomas George Tucker, *Life in Ancient Athens* (London: Macmillan, 1929), p. 122.
14. Aristotle, *Politics* (1984), p. 2028.
15. Plutarch, *Life of Marcellus,* trans. John Dryden and Arthur Hugh Clough (New York: Modern Library, 1934), p. 14.
16. Irene M. Franck and David Brownstone, *Artists and Artisans* (New York: Facts on File, 1987), p. 191.
17. Molière satirizes the gentleman doctor in his play *Le Malade imaginaire* (The Imaginary Invalid), written in 1673.
18. From Rolf B. White, *The Last Word on Management* (Secaucus, N.J.: Lyle Stuart, 1987), p. 103.
19. Matthew 6:26.
20. Matthew 6:28.
21. Mark 10:25.
22. 2 Thessalonians 3:6–12.
23. See Jaroslav Pelikan, "Commandment or Curse? The Paradox of Work in the Judeo-Christian Tradition," Occasional Papers of the Council of Scholars, no. 4 (Washington, D.C.: Library of Congress, 1984), p. 13.
24. Quoted in Siegfried Wenzel, *The Sin of Sloth: Acedia in Medieval Thought and Literature* (Chapel Hill: University of North Carolina Press, 1967), p. 5.
25. St. Thomas Aquinas, *On Evil,* trans. Jean Oesterle (Notre Dame, Ind.: University of Notre Dame Press, 1995), p. 369.
26. Ibid., p. 368.
27. John Cardinal Newman, quoted in Dennis Clark, *Work and the Human Spirit* (New York: Sheed & Ward, 1967), p. 24.
28. Jacques Le Goff, *Time, Work, and Culture in the Middle Ages,* trans. Arthur Goldhammer (Chicago: University of Chicago Press, 1980), p. 89.
29. Ibid., p. 118.
30. Ibid., p. 119.
31. See Jacques Le Goff, *The Birth of Purgatory,* trans. Arthur Goldhammer (Chicago: University of Chicago Press, 1984).
32. John F. New, *Renaissance and Reformation* (New York: John Wiley, 1969), p. 123.
33. Quoted in Le Goff (1980), p. 66.
34. Ibid., pp. 66–67.
35. See Johan Huizinga, *The Waning of the Middle Ages* (New York: St. Martin's Press, 1924), pp. 44–45.
36. Robert Ergang, *The Renaissance* (Princeton: Van Nostrand, 1967), p. 86.
37. Huizinga (1924), p. 44.
38. Quoted in Tilgher (1958), p. 43.
39. See Ian Todd and Michael Wheeler, *Utopia* (New York: Harmony Books, 1978), p. 32.
40. Ibid., p. 43.
41. Keith Thomas, on "Work and Leisure in Pre-industrial Society," *Past & Present* 29 (1964), pp. 50–62.
42. New (1969), p. 116.
43. Ralph Davis, *The Rise of the Atlantic Economies* (Ithaca, N.Y.: Cornell University Press, 1973) p. 18.
44. See Paul Bernstein, *American Work Values: Their Origin and Development* (Albany: State University of New York Press, 1997), p. 43.
45. John A. Garraty, *Unemployment in History: Economic Thought and Public Policy* (New York: Harper & Row, 1978), pp. 27–28.
46. Luther, quoted in Pelikan.
47. Max Weber, *The Protestant Ethic and the Spirit of Capitalism,* trans. Talcott Parsons (1930; New York: Scribner's, 1958), p. 104.
48. Ibid., p. 194.
49. "Apology of the Augsburg Confession," 27:37, in *The Book of Concord: The Confessions of the Evangelical Lutheran Church,* trans. and ed. Theodore G. Tappert in collaboration with Jaroslav Pelikan et al. (Philadelphia: Fortress Press, 1959), p. 275.
50. Max Weber (1958), p. 41.

Chapter 4. Romantic Visions

1. Daniel Defoe, *The Adventures of Robinson Crusoe* (1719; New York: W. W. Norton, 1975), p. 5.
2. Ruth Danon, *Work in the English Novel* (Totowa, N.J.: Little, Brown, 1985).
3. Defoe (1719; 1975), p. 30.
4. Ibid., p. 55.
5. Max Weber, *The Protestant Ethic and the Spirit of Capitalism,* trans. Talcott Parsons (1930; New York: Scribner's, 1958), p. 52.
6. Ibid., p. 182.
7. See Richard M. Huber, *The American Idea of Success* (New York: McGraw-Hill, 1971), p. 20.
8. Ibid., pp. 24–25.
9. Quoted in Daniel T. Rogers, *The Work Ethic in Industrial America, 1850–1920* (Chicago: University of Chicago Press, 1978), p. 131.
10. Ibid., 139.
11. See Alan Trachtenberg, introduction to *Ragged Dick,* by Horatio Alger Jr. (New York: Signet Classic, 1990), p. xviii.
12. Quoted in Huber (1971), p. 53.
13. B. C. Forbes, "Fact and Comment," *Forbes* 60 (October 1, 1947), p. 10.
14. B. C. Forbes, quoted in Huber (1971), p. 216.
15. Russell Herman Conwell, quoted in Huber (1971), p. 61.
16. James A. Garfield, quoted in Huber (1971), p. 40.
17. Quoted in Rogers (1978), pp. 5–6.
18. Karl Marx, *The German Ideology,* quoted in *Karl Marx: Selected Writings,* ed. David McLellan (Oxford: Oxford University Press, 1977), p. 169.
19. Quoted in E. P. Thompson, *William Morris: Romantic to Revolutionary,* rev. ed. (London: Merlin Press, 1977), p. 309.
20. Ibid., p. 100.
21. William Morris, *Useful Work versus Useless Toil* (London: Socialist League Office, 1985), Socialist Platform no. 2 (first published 1885), p. 21.
22. Ibid., p. 38.
23. Irene M. Franke and David M. Brownstone, *Artists and Artisans* (New York: Facts on File, 1987), p. vii.
24. Luigio Brentano, *Medieval Craft Guilds,* ed. Edwin R. A. Seligman (London: Trubner and Co., 1870), p. 9.
25. Talcott Parsons, "Professions," in *Encyclopedia of the Social Sciences,* ed. Edwin R. A. Seligman (New York: Macmillan, 1942), p. 537.
26. Talcott Parsons, *Essays in Sociological Theory, Pure and Applied* (Glencoe, Ill.: Free Press, 1949), p. 187.
27. Lawrence Hayworth, *Decadence and Objectivity* (Toronto: University of Toronto Press, 1977), p. 110.
28. Elliott Krause, *Death of the Guilds: Professions, States, and the Advance of Capitalism, 1930 to the Present* (New Haven: Yale University Press, 1996).

Chapter 5. Work and Freedom

1. David Ewing, "Civil Liberties in the Corporation," *New York State Bar Journal 50* (April 1978) pp. 188–191.
2. Jean-Jacques Rousseau, "A Discourse on a Subject Proposed by the Academy of Dijon: What is the Origin of Inequality Among Men, And Is It Authorized by Natural Law?" in *The Social Contract and Discourses,* trans. G.D.H. Cole (New York: E. P. Dutton, 1950).
3. Aristotle, *Politics,* in *The Complete Works of Aristotle: The Revised Oxford Translation,* trans. Benjamin Jowett, ed. Jonathan Barnes (Princeton: Princeton University Press, 1984), vol. 2, p. 1991.
4. Ibid., pp. 1999 and 1986.
5. Ibid., p. 2032.
6. Aristotle, *Economics,* in *Complete Works* (1984), vol. 2, p. 2132.
7. Ian Fisher, "Selling Sudan's Slaves into Freedom," *New York Times,* April 25, 1999.
8. "By Any Other Name," *Economist,* January 6, 1990, p. 42.
9. From the Anti-Slavery Society study "A Pattern of Slavery: India's Carpet Boys" (London: 1990).
10. Michael Specter, "Traffickers' New Cargo: Naive Slavic Women an Easy Cargo," *New York Times,* January, 11, 1998.

11. Ibid.
12. John Spencer Bassett, *Slavery in the State of North Carolina* (Baltimore: Johns Hopkins University Press, 1899), pp. 23–24.
13. Anthony Bimba, *The History of the American Working Class* (1927; Westport, Conn.: Greenwood Press, 1968), p. 13.
14. John van der Zee, *Bound Over: Indentured Servitude and the American Conscience* (New York: Simon & Schuster, 1985), p. 38.
15. Ibid., p. 253.
16. Abbot Emerson Smith, *Colonists in Bondage: White Servitude and Convict Labor in America, 1607–1776* (Gloucester, Mass.: Peter Smith, 1965), ch. 1.
17. Ibid., p. 38.
18. Van der Zee (1985), p. 30.
19. "The Profits of Sin," *Economist,* August 12, 1995, p. 23.
20. Bimba (1927; 1968), p. 22.
21. Van der Zee (1985), p. 30.
22. Friedrich Engels, "The Condition of the Working Class in England," in *Collected Works of Karl Marx and Friedrich Engels,* vol. 4 (New York: International Publishers, 1975), p. 468.
23. Eugene Genovese, *The Political Economy of Slavery: Slavery in the Economy and Society of the Slave South* (New York: Pantheon Books, 1966), p. 199.
24. Ibid.
25. Van der Zee (1985), p. 34.
26. John Locke, *Two Treatises on Government* (Cambridge: Cambridge University Press, 1970), p. 187.
27. Ibid., p. 188.
28. Ibid., p. 189.
29. "Monkey Business," *Economist,* December 13, 1997, p. 57.
30. Paul Fussell, *Class* (New York: Summit Books, 1993, Ballantine Books, 1984), p. 43.
31. W. J. Rorabaugh, *The Craft Apprentice: From Franklin to the Machine Age in America* (New York: Oxford University Press, 1986), p. 51.
32. Ibid., p. 27.

Chapter 6. Taming the Worker

1. David Montgomery, *Workers' Control in America* (Cambridge: Cambridge University Press, 1979), p. 9.
2. Anthony Bimba, *The History of the American Working Class* (1927; Westport, Conn.: Greenwood Publishers, 1968), p. 173.
3. Ibid., p. 167.
4. Montgomery (1979), pp. 11–13.
5. Robert Kanigel, *The One Best Way: Frederick Winslow Taylor and the Enigma of Efficiency* (New York: Viking Penguin, 1997), pp. 99–100.
6. William M. Leiserson, *Adjusting Immigrant and Industry* (New York: Harper & Brothers, 1924), p. 105.
7. Frederick Winslow Taylor, *The Principles of Scientific Management* (1911, New York: W. W. Norton, 1967), pp. 44–46.
8. Kanigel (1997), p. 209.
9. Ibid., p. 561.
10. Taylor (1911; 1967), p. 7.
11. Kanigel (1997), p. 12.
12. David Brody, *Workers in Industrial America: Essays on the Twentieth-Century Struggle* (New York: Oxford University Press, 1980), p. 134.
13. Hugh G. J. Aitken, *Scientific Management in Action: Taylorism at Watertown Arsenal* (Princeton: Princeton University Press, 1985), p. 150.
14. Brody (1980), p. 13.
15. Quoted in Thomas R. Brooks, *Toil and Trouble: A History of American Labor,* 2nd ed. (New York: Delacorte Press, 1971), p. 153.
16. Quoted in Brody (1980), p. 54.
17. Ibid., p. 54.
18. Brooks (1971), p. 130.
19. Ibid., p. 147.

20. Ibid., p. 148.
21. Quoted in Brody (1980), p. 77.
22. Paul Bernstein, *American Work Values: Their Origins and Development* (Albany: State University of New York Press, 1997), p. 196.
23. See Kanigel (1997), p. 17.
24. Fritz Roethlisberger, *Management and Morale* (Cambridge, Mass.: Harvard University Press, 1941), pp. 9–10.
25. Ibid., pp. 14–15.
26. See Abraham Zaleznik's forward to *The Humanist Temper: The Life and Work of Elton Mayo,* by Richard C. S. Trahair (New Brunswick, N.J.: Transaction Books, 1984), p. 8.
27. Elton Mayo, *The Social Problems of an Industrial Civilization* (Boston: Graduate School of Business Administration, Harvard University; London: Routledge & Kegan Paul, 1949), pp. 68–69.
28. Ibid., pp. 69–70.
29. Ibid., p. 64.
30. Roethlisberger (1941), p. 19.
31. Mary B. Gilson, *American Journal of Sociology* 46 (1940), pp. 98–101.
32. Ibid., pp. 90–91.
33. Quoted in Trahair (1984), p. 266.
34. Quoted in Trahair (1984), p. 267.
35. Thomas A. Kochan, Harry C. Katz, and Robert R. B. McKersie, *The Transformation of American Industrial Relations* (New York: Basic Books, 1986), p. 216.

Chapter 7. How Did Work Get So Confusing?

1. Andrea Gabor, "Hard Work and Common Sense," *Los Angeles Times Book Review,* February 8, 1998, p. 5.
2. Peter Drucker, *The Concept of the Corporation* (New York: John Day, 1946), p. 157.
3. Ibid., p. 158.
4. Peter Drucker, *The End of Economic Man* (New York: John Day, 1939), pp. 78–80.
5. Peter Drucker (1946), p. 134.
6. See Morton Keller, "The Making of the Modern Corporation," *Wilson Quarterly* (autumn 1997), pp. 58–69.
7. C. Wright Mills, *White Collar: The American, Middle Classes* (New York: Oxford University Press, 1951), p. xvii.
8. Ibid., p. xi.
9. Ibid., p. 233.
10. David Reisman, *The Lonely Crowd* (New Haven: Yale University Press, 1950), pp. 14–21.
11. William H. Whyte, *The Organization Man* (New York: Simon & Schuster, 1956), pp. 6–7.
12. Ibid., p. 80.
13. Ibid., p. 32.
14. Ibid., p. 51.
15. Ibid., p. 54.
16. "Escape from the Cult of Personality Tests," *Fortune Magazine,* March 16, 1998, p. 80.
17. Guillermo J. Grenier, *Inhuman Relations: Quality Circles and Anti-Unionism in American Industry* (Philadelphia: Temple University Press, 1988), pp. 25–26.
18. William H. Whyte (1956), p. 179.
19. Joseph E. McGrath, *Groups, Interaction, and Performance* (Englewood Cliffs, N.J.: Prentice Hall, 1984), p. 23.
20. Two books that make this argument are John H. Goldthorp et al., *The Affluent Worker* (Cambridge: Cambridge University Press, 1968) and John Kenneth Galbraith, *The Affluent Society* (Boston: Houghton Mifflin, 1958).
21. David C. McClelland, *The Achieving Society* (Princeton, N.J.: Van Nostrand, 1961).
22. *Work in America: Report of a Special Task Force to the Secretary of Health, Education, and Welfare* (Cambridge, Mass.: MIT Press, 1973), p. 31.
23. Frederick Herzberg, *Work and the Nature of Man* (New York: T. Y. Crowell, 1966).
24. *Work in America,* p. 13.
25. Ibid., p. xvii.
26. Ibid.; these quotes are taken from the back jacket of the book.
27. Studs Terkel, *Working* (New York: Pantheon Books, 1974), p. xi.

28. Barnaby J. Feder, "The Little Project that Couldn't," *New York Times,* February 21, 1998.
29. Robyn Meredith, "Saturn Union Votes to Retain Its Cooperative Company Pact," *New York Times,* March 11, 1998.
30. For a good discussion of these issues, see Nancy Chodorow, *The Reproduction of Mothering: Psychoanalysis and the Sociology of Gender* (Berkeley: University of California Press, 1978).
31. Bruce E. Felton, "When Rage Is All the Rage," *New York Times,* March 15, 1998.
32. Arlie Russell Hochschild, *The Managed Heart: The Commercialization of Human Feeling* (Berkeley: University of California Press, 1983), p. 186.

Chapter 8. The Promising Workplace

1. Joanne B. Ciulla, "Why is Business Talking about Ethics?: Reflections on Foreign Conversations," *California Management Review* (Fall 1991), pp. 67–86.
2. Kenneth E. Goodpaster, "The Beliefs of Borg-Warner," Harvard Business School case 9-383-091 (President and Fellows of Harvard College, 1983).
3. Patrick E. Murphy, *Eighty Exemplary Ethics Statements* (Notre Dame, Ind.: University of Notre Dame Press, 1998), p. 27.
4. Thomas J. Peters and Robert H. Waterman Jr., *In Search of Excellence: Lessons from America's Best-Run Companies* (New York: Harper & Row, Warner Books, 1984), p. 105.
5. Deal and Kennedy.
6. Terrence E. Deal and Allan A. Kennedy, *Corporate Cultures: The Rites and Rules of Corporate Life* (Reading, Mass.: Addison-Wesley, 1982), p. 16.
7. Robert Levering, Milton Moskowitz, and Michael Katz, *The 100 Best Companies to Work for in America* (Reading, Mass.: Addison-Wesley, 1984).
8. Deal and Kennedy, p. 16.
9. Robert Howard, *Brave New Workplace* (New York: Viking, 1985), pp. 95–96.
10. Ibid., p. 120.
11. Judith Martin, *Common Courtesy* (New York: Atheneum, 1985), p. 67.
12. *Telephony,* June 22, 1987, p. 15.
13. Annetta Miller and Pamela Abramson, "Corporate Mind Control," *Newsweek,* May 4, 1987.
14. Ibid.
15. Sanford Bingham, "Kroning at Pacific Bell," *Management* (July 1987), p. 14.
16. Scott Adams, *The Dilbert Principle* (New York: HarperBusiness, 1996), back flap of the book jacket.
17. Ibid., p. 283.
18. *Venture* (March 1987), p. 54; and see Susan J. Wells, "Try Chatting at the Water Cooler," *New York Times,* May 10, 1998, Business section.
19. Monty Roberts, *The Man Who Listens to Horses* (New York: Random House, 1997), p. xii.
20. John Micklethwait and Adrian Wooldridge, *The Witch Doctors: Making Sense of the Management Gurus* (New York: Times Business Books, 1996), p. 15.
21. Ibid., p. 14.
22. Ibid., p. 15.
23. Ibid., p. 17.
24. See Adam Bryant, "All for One, One for All, and Every Man for Himself," *New York Times,* February 22, 1998, Business section.
25. Ibid.
26. Jon Katzenbach, "The Myth of the Top Management Team," *Harvard Business Review* (November/December 1997), p. 84.
27. Kimball Fisher, *Leading Self-Directed Work Teams: A Guide to Developing New Team Leadership Skills* (New York: McGraw-Hill, 1993), pp. 105–109.
28. Scott Adams, Dilbert calendar, September 21, 1998.
29. Joanne B. Ciulla, under the supervision of Kenneth E. Goodpaster, "Building Trust at Warner Gear," Harvard Business School case 0-386-0011 (President and Fellows of Harvard College, 1985), p. 11.
30. See Richard S. Johnson, *TQM: Leadership for the Quality Transformation* (Milwaukee, Wis.: ASQC Quality Press, 1993), p. 1.
31. Greg Bounds et al., *Beyond Total Quality Management: Toward the Emerging Paradigm* (New York: McGraw-Hill, 1994), p. 4.
32. J. Rampy and H. Roberts, "Perspectives on Total Quality" (Proceedings of Total Quality Forum IV, Cincinnati, Ohio, November, 1992).

33. See Randall S. Schuler and Drew L. Harris, *Managing Quality: The Primer for Middle Management* (Reading, Mass.: Addison-Wesley, 1992), p. 25.

34. Ibid., p. 21. Unlike many other management theorists, Juran does have a sense of history. His edited collection, *A History of Managing Quality* (Milwaukee, Wis.: ASQC Quality Press, 1995), is a series of essays on the history of quality in ancient China, Greece, India, and other countries.

35. Warren H. Schmidt and Jerome P. Finnigan, *TQManager* (San Francisco: Jossey-Bass, 1993), p. 31.

36. Richard J. Pierce, ed., *Leadership, Perspective, and Restructuring for Total Quality: An Essential Instrument to Improve Market Share and Productivity* (Milwaukee, Wis.: ASQC Quality Press, 1991), p. 11.

37. Schuler and Harris (1992), p. 160.

38. R. T. Mowday, "Equity Theory Predictions of Behavior in Organizations," in *Motivation and Work Behavior,* comp. Richard M. Steers and Lyman W. Porter (New York: McGraw-Hill, 1987.

39. Schuler and Harris (1992), p. 161.

40. Ibid., p. 161.

41. Pierce (1991), p. 13.

42. See B. Serlen, "W. Edward Deming: The Man Who Made Japan Famous—For Quality," *NYU Business* (Fall/Winter 1988), pp. 16–20, quoted in Schuler and Harris (1992), p. 24.

43. See Chris Argyris, Robert Putnam, and Diana McLain Smith, *Action Science: Concepts, Methods, and Skills for Research and Intervention* (San Francisco: Jossey-Bass, 1985).

44. Kathleen D. Ryan and Daniel K. Oestreich, *Driving Fear Out of the Workplace: Creating the High-Trust, High-Performance Organization* (San Francisco: Jossey-Bass, 1991), p. 31.

45. Quoted in Johnson (1993), p. 2.

46. Michael Hammer and James Champy, *Reengineering the Corporation: A Manifesto for Business Revolution* (New York: HarperBusiness, 1993), pp. 38–39.

47. Ibid., p. 65.

48. Michael Hammer, *Beyond Reengineering* (New York: HarperBusiness, 1995), p. 114.

49. Ibid., p. 48.

50. Arlie Russell Hochschild, *Time Bind: When Work Becomes Home and Home Becomes Work* (New York: Metropolitan Books, 1997), p. 17.

Chapter 9. Betrayal

1. *New York Times Special Report: The Downsizing of America* (New York: Times Books, 1996), pp. 19–21.

2. Ibid., p. 3.

3. Alberta Lindsey, "At 42, What Now?" *Richmond Times-Dispatch,* May 30, 1998.

4. Ibid., p. 6.

5. See Deborah L. Jacobs, "Laid Off? Dismissed? To Sue or Not to Sue," *New York Times,* February 8, 1998, Business section.

6. John Micklethwait and Adrian Wooldridge, *The Witch Doctors: Making Sense of Management Gurus* (New York: Times Business Books, 1996), p. 4.

7. *New York Times Special Report: Downsizing in America,* p. 41.

8. Robert C. Solomon, "Ethical Leadership, Emotions and Trust: Beyond Charisma," in *Ethics, The Heart of Leadership,* ed. Joanne B. Ciulla (Westport, Conn.: Praeger, 1998), p. 8.

9. Francis Fukuyama, *Trust: The Social Virtues and the Creation of Prosperity* (New York: Free Press, 1995), p. 27.

10. *New York Times Special Report: Downsizing in America,* p. 45.

11. "The Death of the Hired Man," in *The Poetry of Robert Frost,* ed. Edward C. Lathem (New York: Holt, Rinehart & Winston, 1979), p. 38.

12. Jim Robbins, "A Broken Pact and a $97 Million Payday," *New York Times,* April 19, 1998, Business section.

13. David Gordon, *Fat and Mean: The Corporate Squeeze of Working Americans and the Myth of Managerial "Downsizing"* (New York: Free Press, 1996), p. 20.

14. James K. Galbraith, *Created Unequal: The Crisis in American Pay* (New York: Free Press, 1998).

15. Robert H. Frank and Philip J. Cook, *The Winner-Take-All Society* (New York: Free Press, 1996).

16. See Adam Bryant, "Flying High on the Option Express," *New York Times,* April 5, 1998, Business section.

17. "Overworked and Overpaid: The American Manager," *Economist,* January 30, 1999, p. 55.

18. Quoted in Bryant (1998).
19. Gordon (1996), p. 5.
20. Albert J. Dunlap, *Mean Business: How I Save Bad Companies and Make Good Companies Great* (New York: Times Business, 1996), p. ix.
21. Ibid., p. 31.
22. Ibid., p. 177.
23. Alexander Hiam, "Does Quality Work? A Review of Relevant Studies," Conference Board Report 1043 (New York, 1993), p. 18.
24. Arlie Russell Hochschild, *Time Bind: When Work Becomes Home and Home Becomes Work* (New York: Metropolitan Books, 1997), p. 19.
25. Anthony Sampson, *Company Man: The Rise and Fall of Corporate Life* (New York: Times Business, 1995), p. 260.
26. See Maureen West "Honest Work and Honest Talk," *Phoenix Gazette,* November 3, 1995.
27. Scott Adams, *The Dilbert Principle* (New York: HarperBusiness, 1996), p. 12.
28. Scott Adams, *The Dilbert Future* (New York: HarperBusiness, 1997), p. 125.
29. David Zurawik, "Prime-Time Ploy: Dialing for Downsized, Disaffected," *Richmond Times-Dispatch,* March 21, 1998.
30. www.disgruntled.com, August 4, 1998.
31. Alecia Swasy, *Changing Focus: Kodak and the Battle to Save a Great American Company* (New York: Times Business, 1997).
32. Steven Greenhouse, "Labor Unions, Growing Bolder, No Longer Shun Big-Scale Strikes," *New York Times,* September 7, 1998.
33. Aaron Bernstein, "Why Workers Still Hold a Weak Hand," *Business Week,* March 12, 1998, p. 98.
34. Jeffrey A. Sonnenfeld, "In the Dignity Department, U.P.S. Wins," *New York Times,* August 24, 1997.
35. "Can GM and the Union Take Each Other on Trust?" *Economist,* August 1, 1998, p. 53.
36. Robert H. Zieger, *American Workers, American Unions, 1920–1985* (Baltimore: Johns Hopkins University Press, 1986), p. 27.
37. See Greg Edwards, "The New Norma Raes," *Richmond Times-Dispatch,* September 1, 1997.
38. See Jon Auerbach and John Milne, "Methuen's Unstoppable Hero," *Boston Globe,* December 15, 1995.
39. Bill Bamberger and Cathy N. Davidson, *Closing: The Life and Death of an American Factory* (New York: W. W. Norton, 1998), p. 28.
40. Ibid., p. 19.

Chapter 10. Time

1. Juliet B. Schor, *The Overworked American: The Unexpected Decline of Leisure* (New York: Basic Books, 1991), p. 29.
2. Dora L. Costa, National Economic Research Working Paper no. 6504, 1999.
3. Samuel L. Macey, *Patriarchs of Time: Dualism in Saturn-Cronus, Father Time, the Watchmaker God, and Father Christmas* (Athens: University of Georgia Press, 1987).
4. This distinction comes from the Cambridge idealist John McTaggart's A-series and B-series characterization of time. See John McTaggart, *Philosophical Studies* (London: E. Arnold, 1984).
5. See Stephen Hawking, *A Brief History of Time: From the Big Bang to Black Holes* (New York: Bantam Books, 1988), p. 143.
6. Jeremy Rifkin, *Time Wars* (New York: Touchstone/Simon & Schuster, 1987), p. 49.
7. E. P. Thompson, "Time, Work-Discipline, and Industrial Capitalism," *Past and Present* 88 (1967), p. 58.
8. Emile Durkheim, *The Elementary Forms of Religious Life* (London: Allen & Unwin, 1915), pp. 9–11.
9. J. David Lewis and Andrew J. Weigert, "The Structures and Meanings of Social Time," *Social Forces* 60, no. 2 (December 1981), p. 440.
10. Ibid., pp. 444–449.
11. Robert Levine, *A Geography of Time* (New York: Basic Books, 1997).
12. Rifkin (1987), pp. 25–35.
13. Alvin Toffler, *Future Shock* (New York: Random House, 1970; Bantam Books, 1971).
14. Steve Lohr, "The Future Came Faster in the Old Days," *New York Times,* October 5, 1997, Week in Review, p. 1.

15. Thompson (1967), p. 73.
16. Douglas A. Reid, "The Decline of St. Monday," *Past and Present* 71 (1976), p. 79–80.
17. Arthur Hailey, *Wheels* (Garden City, N.Y.: Doubleday, 1971).
18. Thompson (1967), p. 72.
19. Ibid., p. 84.
20. Gary Cross, "Worktime and Industrialization" in *Worktime and Industrialization: An International History,* ed. Gary Cross (Philadelphia: Temple University Press, 1988) p. 10.
21. For this argument see Harry Braverman, *Labor and Monopoly Capital: The Degradation of Work in the Twentieth Century* (New York: Monthly Review Press, 1975).
22. Alasdair Clayre, *Work and Play: Ideas and Experience of Work and Leisure* (London: Weidenfeld and Nicolson, 1974), pp. 214–215.
23. William M. Sullivan, *Work and Integrity* (New York: Harper Business, 1995), p. 10.
24. Joanne B. Ciulla, under the supervision of Kenneth E. Goodpaster, "Building Trust at Warner Gear," Harvard Business School case 0-386-0011 (President and Fellows of Harvard College, 1985), p. 12.
25. Keith Bradsher, "Disputed Hourly Pay Rule at the Heart of G.M. Strike," *New York Times,* July 7, 1998, Business section.
26. Juliet B. Schor, *The Overworked American* (New York: Basic Books, 1991), pp. 154–155.
27. Ann Reilly Dowd, "You Swear That Your Time Is Worth More Than Money," *Money* (May 1997), p. 25.
28. "No Part Time Job Explosion," *Economist,* August 16, 1997, p. 23.
29. See "Perceptions of Time," *Quarterly Review of Doublespeak* (July 1995), reprinted in *Chemical Engineering News,* August 14, 1995, p. 48.
30. Naomi Wolf, "Why Mom's in a State of Unrest," New York *Daily News,* May 11, 1997.
31. Stacy Perman, "The Joy of Not Cooking," *Time,* June 1, 1998, p. 66.
32. Quoted in Jane E. Brody, "Facing Up to the Realities of Sleep Deprivation," *New York Times,* March 3, 1998.
33. Robert Wright, "The Evolution of Despair," *Time,* August 28, 1995, p. 53.
34. David Halle, *America's Working Man* (Chicago: University of Chicago Press, 1984), p. 34.
35. Junda Woo, "Workers Who Must be 'On Call' Go to Court Seeking Overtime Pay," *Wall Street Journal,* July 13, 1992.
36. Kirk Johnson, "Limits on the Work-at-Home Life," *New York Times,* November 3, 1997.
37. Quoted in Tom Dwortzky, "The Virtual Water Cooler," *Modern Maturity,* July/August 1997, p. 26.
38. Lawrence Shames, *The Hunger for More: Searching for Values in an Age of Greed* (New York: Times Books, 1989).
39. Sam Keen, *Fire in the Belly: On Being a Man* (New York: Bantam Books, 1991).

Chapter 11. Leisure and Consumption

1. Aristotle, *Nicomachean Ethics,* trans. W. D. Ross, ed. Jonathan Barnes, in *The Complete Works of Aristotle: The Revised Oxford Translation* (Princeton: Princeton University Press, 1984), vol. 2, p. 1861.
2. Josef Pieper, *Leisure, the Basis of Culture* (New York: Pantheon Books, 1952), p. 27.
3. G. K. Chesterton, "On Leisure," in *Generally Speaking* (London: 1928), p. 130.
4. Sebastian de Grazia, *Of Time, Work, and Leisure* (New York: Twentieth Century Fund, 1962), p. 7.
5. Ibid., p. 266.
6. Ibid., pp. 202–203.
7. *The Compact Oxford English Dictionary,* new ed. (Oxford: Clarendon Press, 1991).
8. Walli F. Leff and Marilyn G. Haft, *Time without Work* (Boston: South End Press, 1983), p. 30.
9. Kathy Peiss, *Cheap Amusements* (Philadelphia: Temple University Press, 1986), pp. 17–23.
10. Ibid., 32.
11. Christopher Lasch, *The Culture of Narcissism: American Life in an Age of Diminishing Expectations* (New York: W. W. Norton, 1978), p. 71.
12. Irving Howe, "Notes on Mass Culture," *Politics* (Spring 1988) pp. 120–123.
13. Witold Rybczynski, *Waiting for the Weekend* (New York: Viking Penguin, 1991), p. 193.
14. Karl Marx, "Economic and Philosophical Manuscripts," in *Karl Marx: Selected Writings,* ed. David McLellan (Oxford: Oxford University Press), 1977, pp. 80–81.
15. Stanley Parker, *Leisure and Work* (London: Allen Unwin , 1983), p. 17.
16. Ibid., p. 76.

17. Ibid., p. 84.

18. Ibid., p. 33.

19. See Rybczynski (1991), p. 219.

20. Juliet B. Schor, *The Overworked American: The Unexpected Decline of Leisure* (New York: Basic Books, 1991), p. 107.

21. Ellen Greenberger and Laurence Steinberg, *When Teenagers Work: The Psychological and Social Costs of Adolescent Employment* (New York: Basic Books, 1960), pp. 6–8.

22. Ibid., p. 173.

23. See Jeylan T. Mortimer and Michael D. Finch, "Work, Family, and Adolescent Development," in *Adolescents, Work, and Family: An Intergenerational Developmental Analysis,* ed. Jeylan T. Mortimer and Michael D. Finch (Thousand Oaks, Calif.: Sage Publications, 1996), pp. 9–10.

24. Fred Hirsch, *Social Limits to Growth* (Cambridge, Mass.: Harvard University Press, 1976), p. 2.

25. Juliet B. Schor, *The Overspent American: Upscaling, Downscaling and the New Consumer* (New York: Basic Books, 1998), p. 4.

26. Ibid., p. 112.

27. Barbara Ehrenreich, *Fear of Falling: The Inner Life of the Middle Class* (New York: Pantheon Books, 1989), p. 262.

28. Stanley Lebergott, *Pursuing Happiness: American Consumers in the Twentieth Century* (Princeton: Princeton University Press, 1993), p. 13.

29. Judith Williamson, *Consuming Passions: The Dynamics of Popular Culture* (New York: Marion Boyars, 1986), p. 11.

30. Mark R. Lepper and David Greene, "Undermining Children's Intrinsic Interest with Extrinsic Reward," *Journal of Personality and Social Psychology* 28, no. 1 (1973), pp. 129–137.

31. Edward L. Deci, "Intrinsic Motivation, Extrinsic Reinforcement, and Inequity," *Journal of Personality and Social Psychology* 22, no. 1 (1972), pp. 113–120.

32. Nathan Ausubel, ed., *A Treasury of Jewish Folklore* (1948; New York: Crown Publishers, 1976), p. 440.

Chapter 12. The Search for Something More

1. Hugh S. Moorhead, *The Meaning Of Life* (Chicago: Chicago Review Press, 1988), p. 122.

2. Ibid., p. 98.

3. Ibid., p. 155.

4. Ibid., p. 161.

5. Ibid., p. 125.

6. Ibid.

7. Milan Kundera, *The Book of Laughter and Forgetting,* trans. Michael Henry Heim (New York: Alfred A. Knopf, 1980), p. 91–92.

8. *Letters of Sigmund Freud,* trans. Tania Stern and James Stern, ed. Ernst L. Freud (New York: McGraw-Hill, 1964), p. 436.

9. Arthur Schopenhaur, *The World as Will and Idea,* 7th ed. (London: Kegan Paul, Trench, Trubner, 1909), vol. 3, p. 383.

10. Viktor E. Frankl, *Man's Search for Meaning: An Introduction to Logotherapy,* trans. Ilse Lasch, rev. and enlarged ed. (London: Hodder & Stoughton, 1964), pp. 110–113.

11. Robert N. Bellah et al., *Habits of the Heart: Individuality and Commitment in American Life* (Berkeley: University of California Press, 1985), pp. 122–127.

12. M. Scott Peck, *The Road Less Traveled* (New York: Simon & Schuster, 1985), p. 19.

13. Bellah et al. (1985), p. 124.

14. Leo Tolstoy, "My Confession," in *The Meaning of Life,* ed. E. D. Klemke (New York: Oxford University Press, 1981), p. 18.

15. David F. Swenson, *Kierkegaardian Philosophy in the Faith of a Scholar* (Philadelphia: Westminister Press, 1949).

16. Reinhold Niebuhr, *The Self and the Dramas of History* (New York: Scribner's, 1955).

17. Klemke (1981), pp. 4–5.

18. R. M. Hare, *Applications of Moral Philosophy* (London: Macmillan, 1972), p. 38.

19. R. W. Hepburn, "Questions about the Meaning of Life," in Klemke (1981), p. 224.

20. Ibid., pp. 212–213.

21. Robert Nozick, *Philosophical Explanations* (Oxford: Clarendon Press, 1981), p. 596.

22. L. J. Russell, "The Meaning of Life," *Philosophy* 28 (1953), pp. 30–40.

23. Aldous Huxley, *Do as You Will* (London: Chatto & Windus, 1949), pp. 128–132.

24. Kurt Baier, "The Meaning of Life," inaugural lecture delivered at Canberra University College, October 15, 1957, p. 28.

25. See Aristotle, *Eudemian Ethics,* in *The Complete Works of Aristotle: The Revised Oxford Translation,* trans. J. Solomon, ed. Johnathan Barnes (Princeton: Princeton University Press, 1984), vol. 2, pp. 1929–1930.

26. Aristotle, *Nicomachean Ethics,* trans. W. D. Ross, ed. Jonathan Barnes, in *The Complete Works of Aristotle: The Revised Oxford Translation* (Princeton: Princeton University Press, 1984), vol. 2, p. 1860.

27. Aristotle, *Eudemian Ethics,* p. 1981.

28. Hannah Arendt, *The Human Condition* (Chicago: University of Chicago Press, 1958), p. 134.

29. Mihaly Csikszentmihalyi, *Flow: The Psychology of Optimal Experience* (New York: Harper & Row, 1990), p. 158.

30. Michael Novak, *Business as a Calling: Work and the Examined Life* (New York: Free Press, 1996), p. 37.

31. "God Gets Down to Business," *Across the Board* 14, no. 5 (Conference Board, May 1988), pp. 11–12.

32. Novak (1996), pp. 44–45.

33. Charles B. Handy, *The Hungry Spirit* (New York: Broadway Books, 1998), p. xii.

34. Jay A. Conger and associates, *Spirit at Work* (San Francisco: Jossey-Bass, 1994), p. 205.

35. Ibid., p. 9.

36. David W. Chen, "Fitting the Lord into Work's Schedule," *New York Times,* November 29, 1997.

37. Richard Leider, *The Power of Purpose: Creating Meaning in your Life and Work* (San Francisco: Barrett-Koehler, 1997), p. 3.

38. Lee G. Bolman and Terrence E. Deal, *Leading with Soul: An Uncommon Journey of Spirit* (New York: Jossey-Bass, 1995), p. 12.

Epilogue: Honest Work

1. See James K. Galbraith, *Created Unequal: The Crisis in American Pay* (New York: Free Press, 1998).

2. Laura Koss-Feder, "Perks That Work," *Time,* November 9, 1998.

3. Richard Sennett, *The Corrosion of Character: The Personal Consequences of Work in the New Capitalism* (New York: W. W. Norton, 1998), p. 31.

4. Immanuel Kant, "On a Supposed Right to Lie from Alturistic Motives," in *Critique of Practical Reason and Other Writings in Moral Philosophy,* trans. Lewis White Beck (Chicago: University of Chicago Press, 1949).

5. See Robert J. Samuelson, *The Good Life and Its Discontents: The American Dream in the Age of Entitlements* (New York: Times Books, 1995).

Index

About the Author

JOANNE B. CIULLA is a professor and holds the Coston Family Chair in Leadership and Ethics at the Jepson School of Leadership Studies, which she helped design, at the University of Richmond. She also holds the UNESCO Chair in Leadership Studies at the United Nations Leadership Academy. She earned degrees from Temple University and the universities of Delaware and Maryland, and has taught at Boston University and La Salle University. Dr. Ciulla was a postdoctoral Fellow at the Harvard Business School, a visiting scholar at Oxford, and Senior Fellow at the Wharton School. In addition to her academic career, she once worked as a waitress, a cook, and at a number of odd jobs. Now she consults, lectures, reviews, and writes for a variety of corporations, organizations, and journals around the world. She lives in Richmond, Virginia, with her husband, René.